4389

D1631825

2

THE COMPLETE

OLD ENGLISH SHEEPDOG

CHRISTINA SMITH

RINGPRESS

RINGPRESS

Published by Ringpress Books Ltd,
Spirella House, Bridge Road,
Letchworth, Herts, SG6 4ET.

Discounts available for bulk orders
Contact the Special Sales Manager at
the above address. Telephone (0462) 674177

Distributed to the Book Trade in the United Kingdom by
Bookpoint Ltd.
39 Milton Park, Abingdon, Oxon OX14 4TD
Telephone 0235 835001

First Published 1993
© 1993 CHRISTINA SMITH

ISBN 0 948955 23 6

Printed and bound in Singapore
by Kyodo Printing Co

CONTENTS

This book is dedicated to the late Mrs H. F. M. E. Backx-Bennink and her lovely Reeuwijk Old English Sheepdogs, in particular for my lovely 'Krumel' – Ch. Reeuwijk's Filmstar in Silver.

ACKNOWLEDGEMENTS

My sincere gratitude goes to my friends and everyone else who has sent photographs and information: Lynn and Barry Espie (New Zealand), Billie Machell (Norway), Barbara Muller (Switzerland), Claude Ritter (France), Birgitte Schjoth (Denmark), Per and Ingela Wallstrom (Sweden) and Helen Harris and Carol Birdsall for allowing me to use their American publications.

Special thanks to Barrie Croft, who accompanied me on my journey into the past, and always found the time to help me, to Caj Haakannson, whose knowledge and readily-given advice I always appreciate. Last, but not least, to John, who became very domesticated and put up with my writing during the past few months.

Chapter One

HISTORY OF THE BREED

ORIGINS OF THE BREED

The Old English Sheepdog was first and foremost a working dog, emerging as an identifiable breed in the 1850s. However, the Bobtail was kept by shepherds and drovers whose main interest was in the breed's working ability, and so its type differs a great deal from the dog we know today. This can be seen in some of the earlier paintings, where it is a matter of trying to pick out sheepdogs which bear a resemblance to the OES.

In my opinion, the Russian Owizarka bears a striking resemblance to the Old English Sheepdog, although it is much heavier in body. The similarity with the Bearded Collie, although much lighter in body than the OES, is also undeniable. However, both these breeds carry tails. At the beginning of the 20th century, quite a number of breeders reported the birth of tail-less pups, which would imply that the Bobtail was a separate type. In a record book, kept by Miss E. M. Flint of the famous Newcote kennels, a number of pups are recorded with the note "born tail-less".

We know that docking was carried out in the 19th century. According to Henry Arthur Tilley (known as Arthur), a pioneer of the breed and owner of the world-famous Shepton kennels, there were two reasons for this: "It is the natural instinct of most dogs to chase rabbits, hares, cats or errant fowls by the wayside, and to do so with any chance of success they must be ready for every sudden and unexpected twist or turn of the "quarry", but the necessary counter movements would be severely handicapped if the tail or "rudder" had been removed. This tendency to chase small animals would be one of the least desirable habits of a dog which has to work for shepherds or cattle drovers." The second reason which Tilley gives is that tail-less dogs were recognised by the Inland Revenue officials as working dogs, and were exempt from taxation.

THE OES AS A SHOW DOG

The breed's first appearance at a show was in Birmingham in 1873. The first stud book entries were in 1875 – only two years after the foundation of the English Kennel Club.

One of the most famous dogs in these early days was Ch. Fairweather, born on May 8th, 1898 (Sir James – Birthday), owned by Helen Fare-Fosse. Fairweather won a total of nineteen CCs, which was a record at the time. Her body has been preserved, and she is on display at the Natural History Museum in Tring, Hertfordshire. Arthur Tilley managed to buy Ch. Fairweather's sire, but apparently Sir James failed to substantiate his hopes and did not produce any outstanding stock.

SHEPTON

Ch. Bouncing Lass (Young Watch – Peggy Primrose) made a name for herself at the turn of the

The great Ch. Fairweather (1898-1907): Winner of nineteen CCs.

century. She was bought by Arthur Tilley as a puppy for the incredible sum of £200. At the time, Arthur's elder brother, who was in partnership with him in the early days of the kennel, disagreed with the "extravagant" price, as the pup had not had distemper and her condition was said to be 'soft'. However, they both agreed that if luck was in their favour, the investment would have been worthwhile.

Bouncing Lass developed well, and history shows that she fulfilled all expectations as a show dog. Lass was one of the four OES Arthur took on his first journey to America when he attended the Westminster Show in 1904. He had hoped to win the Vanderbilt Cup with Bouncing Lass, but she went Reserve to his male, Merry Party. The judge was Mr J. Freeman Lloyd, the most respected all-round expert in the dog world, and considered by many to be one of the best judges ever. Arthur rated Lass as the better specimen out of the two, but he was quite happy with the result. On the voyage back to England, Bouncing Lass was mated to Ch. Stylish Boy, who had also been shown at Westminster. The resulting litter was described as "wonderful", and all but one pup were sold to America, together with the dam and the sire for a "record" sum.

WEATHER

There were a number of other British breeders who had major impact on the breed before the outbreak of the First World War. Helen Fare-Fosse, owner of the Weather kennel made up her first two Champions in 1899. They were Ch. Fairweather, and Ch. Thundercloud (same breeding as Fairweather). Fairweather whelped several litters but, to my knowledge, she produced only one Champion, Ch. Ragged Man (sired by Ch. Cupid's Dart), owned by A. Hopwood.

In 1904, at four years of age, Ch. Rough Weather (Sir James – Daphne) finished his title. He was bred and owned by Mrs Fare-Fosse. Despite the excellent quality of the Weather OES, it was ten

Frank Brocklesby Snr (centre) of the famous Danum kennel, pictured with his brother and his mother in 1923. This kennel was started in 1890 and is still active today.

years before the kennel had its next Champion. This was Ch. Tip Top Weather (Typical Weather – Clara), born on August 31st 1912; he gained his title at two years of age. He was bred by the well-known Miss McTurk and registered by Mrs Fare-Fosse. Miss McTurk was the owner of the famous Ch. Old Bill, and she also bred two of the most influential males ever to be exported to America. These were the above-mentioned Ch. Tip Top Weather, and Ch. Night Rider (Tiptoes – Lucy). Both were widely used at stud in the USA, and also shown there with excellent results. Tip Top Weather was to become the first OES to sire more than five Champions in the USA.

On April 1st 1912 Melbourne Daisy whelped a litter sired by a dog called Dennis. The litter was bred by W. Harris and registered by Mrs Fare-Fosse. One of the puppies became a Champion. Originally called Bethnal Green Daisy, Mrs Fare-Fosse changed the bitch's name to Ch. Midsummer Weather, and she gained her title in 1917 at five years of age. In 1922 Ch. Whimsical Weather, sired by Ch. Night Rider out of Juno, was shown to his title, and in 1923 Ch. Matchless Weather, formerly Storm Maid, (The Bearer of Hallaton – Kennington Floss) finished her Championship. As with a number of other Weather Champions, Matchless Weather was not bred by Mrs Fare-Fosse. The last Weather Champion was made up in 1925, and this was Ch. Glorious Weather (Shepton Moonshine – Peaceful Tramp).

HILLGARTH

In 1925 Mary Sheffield, owner of the Hillgarth affix, made up her famous homebred Champion, Ch. Blue Knight (Shepton Moonshine – Ch. Blue Lady). Ch. Blue Lady (Gerrards Hero – Gerrards Mary) and Ch. Blue Blossom (Snowstorm – Snowy Lass) were Mary's first two OES Champions, and, in fact, she bought both bitches unseen. Blue Blossom had been booked to go abroad, but the deal was cancelled at the last minute, and Blue Lady was the last pup left in her litter because of her head markings. It is interesting to speculate on the feelings of those who bought the white-headed puppies in that litter, as not one became a Champion. Mary Sheffield still recalls Blue Lady's first show, where she carried off four prizes, and the CC!

Both Blossom and Lady also excelled as brood bitches. Lady's litter to Shepton Moonshine produced Ch. Blue Knight and Ch. Blue Coat. Ch. Blue Blossom was mated to Ch. Blue Knight in 1925, resulting in Ch. Hillgarth Blue Princess (made up 1928). The same combination in 1927 produced Ch. Hillgarth Blue Boy, who finished his title at just two years of age. In 1930, at almost six years of age, Ch. Newcote Blossom was made up. She was bred by Mary from a litter out of Blossom, sired by Blue Knight's litter brother, Blue Coat, who was registered by Miss E. M. Flint, owner of the well-known Newcote affix.

PASTORALE

In 1930 one of the most famous dogs of this era gained his Championship title. Ch. Tommy Tittlemouse of Pastorale was bred by Miss A. Tireman, sired by Ch. Faithful Tramp out of River Girl. Like Blue Knight and Blue Coat, Faithful Tramp was sired by Shepton Moonshine. Both Moonshine and Tramp proved to be excellent sires, with ten Champions credited to Moonshine, and four to Tramp. Tramp's Champion son, Tommy Tittlemouse, was not his owner's first success. Four years earlier she made up a bitch called Ch. Mistress Sylvia, out of Waysgreen Peggy, bred by Miss H. Hickson, also by Faithful Tramp, and then in 1928 Ch. Pastorale Bo Peep (formerly Mountford Lucy) gained her title. She was sired by Careful Jim out of Lady Morna, and was bred by O. J. Stupple, but registered with the famous Pastorale affix. Several more Champions came out of this highly successful kennel. Tommy Tittlemouse became the sire of three Champions: Hammerwood Hurly Burly (out of Ch. Hammerwood Honeybee), and Mistress Flounce of Pastorale and Pastorale Mistress of Fullson, both out of Ch. Mistress Petticoats of Pastorale (Ch. Beara Leader – Biddy the Tramp). Tommy Tittlemouse's Champion son, Ch. Hammerwood Hurly Burly, became a great sire with five Champions to his credit, continuing the line of sires with Champion offspring, going back through his father, Tittlemouse, his grandfather, Faithful Tramp, and his great-grandfather, Shepton Moonshine (Ch. Tip Top Weather – Betsy Day). In fact, Shepton Moonshine's tally of ten Champions was a British record in England until 1982 when Ch. Pockethall New Shoes (Ch. Shaggyshire Bumblebarn Caesar – Ch. Cornelia of Trimtora) broke the record, ending up with a total of eighteen English Champions to his name. This amazing record is still unbeaten in the the breed in the UK.

PICKHURST

During the early thirties when the show scene was dominated by the excellent Pastorale and Hillgarth dogs, Mrs T. E. T. Shanks started breeding and showing Old English Sheepdogs, using her Pickhurst affix. She got off to a spectacular start, and from the two litters out of her bitch, Peggy Anne of Pickhurst, she got an incredible total of seven Champions. On both occasions, 1931 and 1933, she was mated to Wadhurst Bobby of Pastorale. The first litter included Lady Flirt, Pride, Rag Tag, Saucy Girl and Dolly Dimple; and Bobs Son and Bouncer were both out of the 1933 litter. Bouncer of Pickhurst finished his title in 1937, the same year as the famous Ch. Shepton Dolly Grey (Ch. Southridge Rodger – Pensford Blue Mist). Dolly Grey was sold to the Mobla kennels, owned by Mrs Schloss, in Baltimore, USA, and this bitch enjoyed a most illustrious career with her Group wins and placements.

MARKSMAN PASTELBLUE

In 1938 Miss J. Webster, owner of the beautiful Marksman Pastelblue OES, made up her first homebred Champion. Her kennel was established in 1928, and her dogs were well-known for their lovely type and quality. Ch. Sir John Marksman was born on February 26th 1935, sired by Tit Willow of Pastorale out of Blue Coquette. Marksman was a very substantial male with a lovely expression, a wealth of coat and a good neck.

He commenced his show career at seven months of age, winning first in puppy and first in junior class at Maidstone in 1935. He was unbeaten until he was eighteen months old. His first CC came from Miss A. Tiremann (Pastorale) at Crufts in 1938, his second CC at Kensington Ch. Show 1938, when Arthur Tilley was officiating, and his third qualifying CC was awarded by Mrs Gatehouse at Harrogate within the same year. Due to the outbreak of the Second World War his career was cut short, but he was intensively used for stud. When he died peacefully in his sleep on January 3rd 1947, at almost twelve years of age, he had left some top-class progeny to carry on his type.

HAMMERWOOD
This affix was owned by Miss C. Ashford, and her first homebred Champion was Hammerwood Honeybee (Hammerwood Jolly Roger – Hammerwood Honeysuckle). This bitch was mated to Ch. Tommy Tittlemouse of Pastorale, and in 1932 she produced Hammerwood Hurly Burly. Hurly Burly finished his Championship in 1935, and he became one of the most important stud dogs of the late thirties. His Champion progeny includes: Ch. Watchers Watermark (out of Beara Shepherdess), Ch. Hammerwood Halcyon, formerly Pastorale Grey Shadow (out of Mistress), Ch. Perfect Lady (out of Ch. Mistress Flash of Pastorale), Ch. Tom Noddy of Pastorale (out of Mistress Prudence of Pastorale), and Ch. Pastorale Dame of Fullson (out of Mistress Prudence of Pastorale).

THE POST-WAR ERA
No Champions were made up in the breed from 1940 to 1947. The first two certificates issued after the war were for Ch. Shepton Home Guard (Nosey Parker of Pickhurst– Snowhite of Pickhurst) and Ch. Bashurst Sally Ann of Pickhurst. Sally Ann was of the same breeding, but a later litter, bred by Mrs. Shanks of Pickhurst fame.

In 1948 five Champions gained their titles; two of them were the litter brothers Ch. Watchers Boulgehall Toby and Ch. Watchers Bobs Son (Watchers Warrant – Watchers Grey Dawn), bred by Miss M. Tucker of the Watchers kennels. Like his sire, Bobs Son subsequently sired Champion offspring. A year later, in 1949, the three-year-old Shepton Sonny Boy of Marlay (formerly Marlay Top Dog) became a Champion. He was sired by Beau Brigand of Marlay out of Comedy Starlight, bred by Mrs H. Booth, and owned by the Perrywood kennel. Sonny Boy amassed a total of seventeen CCs, only two CCs behind the record holder, Ch. Shepton Indomitable (Ch. Shepton Surf King – Ch. Shepton Perfect Picture), who was born in 1948.

Considering how difficult it must have been during the war years to keep dogs, not just finding enough food for them, but also finding the time to groom and look after a long-coated breed, I can only pay my greatest respects to these early breeders and lovers of the Old English Sheepdog. Despite the almost overwhelming difficulties, they managed to keep their dogs in good enough condition to be ready to compete in the show ring after the war, and to continue important bloodlines. Not every breeder was able to do this, and there are tragic stories of whole kennels being wiped out in the UK and in Europe. We are therefore even more grateful to those who helped to keep the breed alive – their efforts should never be forgotten.

Chapter Two

OWNING AN OES

TAKING ON A LONG-COATED BREED

Owning an Old English Sheepdog most certainly means having your work cut out, as far as grooming is concerned. Anyone who is not prepared to spend a minimum of three hours grooming per week should not even think about owning the breed. You can, of course, keep the coat clipped, but there are plenty of short-coated breeds that are equally nice in temperament.

Three hours grooming a week may be sufficient for an OES kept solely as a companion dog, but if you are showing your dog, the time needed for grooming increases dramatically to 6-8 hours a week, depending on coat quality. Both pet and show dog need to be 'cleaned up' after every meal and dried after every drink of water. The OES has a long beard, and a soaking wet beard rubbed against your clothes or furniture is no joke. In our house we have small dog towels deposited virtually everywhere.

A further consideration – and a less attractive side to owning a long-coated breed – is the consequence of an upset stomach and loose stools. With a short-coated breed you do not have to clean the bottom, but with a long-coated big dog you must be prepared to pay extra attention to the rear end, especially in summer.

During the bad weather period Bobtails still need to go out for their daily walks, and, inevitably, they will need to be cleaned afterwards. This can be quite a job when you have a wet, muddy OES on your hands. However, for me, there is no more pleasing sight than that of a well-groomed and well-cared for Old English Sheepdog having fun, playing outside. But be warned: keeping a fully-grown Bobtail in good condition takes a lot of time, and total dedication to the breed.

CHOOSING A BREEDER

In order to get a basic idea about your future companion you should talk to at least three different breeders. Go and see their dogs, get to know them, and see how the adult dogs are kept. Find out how the pups are reared. Are they inside during their first few weeks? How much socialising will they have had by the time they leave for their new homes? Will they be registered with the Kennel Club? Will they have had any vaccinations? You should also ask if the parents have been eye-tested, and if they have been X-rayed for hip dysplasia. All these questions should be answered to your satisfaction before you commit yourself to a particular breeder. You will also find that travelling around and talking to different breeders will give you a good idea as to whether the Old English Sheepdog is really the right dog for you. Responsible breeders will ask you many questions in return, and if you cannot provide a suitable home for an Old English Sheepdog, they will say so. Those I would classify as being unsuitable are:

OES puppies are irresistible, but you must be prepared for a lot of hard work if you are taking on a long-coated breed. Note the blue eye.

1. Anyone living in a flat – without an exercise area nearby.
2. People who do not like dogs jumping up.
3. People who like to be dressed in designer clothes – even when relaxing at home.
4. A home where everyone is out at work all day. An Old English Sheepdog who is lonely and bored will very soon find its own amusement, such as chewing wallpaper and furniture

I would consider the ideal home for an OES would be a house with a big garden, with a family which has children, who have grown out of the baby stage. Old English Sheepdogs living in that sort of environment are happy dogs and a pleasure for everyone around.

MALE OR FEMALE

If you are not planning to breed, the decision as to whether you buy a male or a female should, in my opinion, be made on the basis of which pup appeals to you the most. Both male and female need an equal amount of attention. The male needs his belly-coat washed regularly, and special care has to be taken of a bitch in season. They are both loving and sensitive, but also boisterous at times. The adult male Old English Sheepdog must have his belly and hind leg coat washed regularly. As soon as a dog starts cocking his leg, he will mess his coat. If this is not attended to, you will find that your dog starts to smell unpleasant. As long as you use warm water and a little mild shampoo, your dog will not object. Females usually keep themselves clean, although a bitch in season will need to have her backside washed. However, some bitches take care of themselves and if the season is not too heavy, you might not have to do anything.

If you have not got a particular preference as to whether to have a male or a female, just go and look at a litter (when you have found the breeder of your choice). Sit down with the puppies and play with them. You will soon feel attracted to one more than all the others. There is a saying that a puppy chooses his owner and not the other way round – and I feel there is a lot of truth in that.

When you have finally chosen your puppy, I always suggest that the new owners leave a blanket, which will be left with the pups. When the puppy is ready to be collected, the blanket will go home as well. This will help the new baby to settle down in new surroundings as the blanket will smell of all the brothers and sisters, and so the move will not be quite as traumatic.

THE FIRST NIGHT
My experience has taught me that the older the puppy, the easier it is for the owner to achieve a quick and easy transition to the new home. Unless you have an older dog who will keep the new puppy company during the night, I prefer the puppy to be kept within human contact, so you can give reassurance. Every new experience can be frightening for a young puppy, and you should do everything possible to create a warm and secure environment so that the puppy stays calm and learns that all is well.

FEEDING
Under no circumstances should you change over to a different food the day you get your puppy home. The upset of leaving the litter is enough for the puppy to deal with, without the added stress of an unfamiliar diet. Ask your breeder for a diet sheet, or to give you detailed instructions on the diet fed to date, and keep to this, at least to begin with. Once your pup is happily settled in your house, you can slowly change over to whatever diet suits your puppy best. The following diet, which I use, should therefore be followed as a general guide.

FROM TEN WEEKS
Puppies of this age should be fed three or four times daily. It is difficult to state exact amounts, but the meal should be eaten up within ten or fifteen minutes. Do not leave food lying around. Throw away any leftovers, and start with fresh food at the next meal.

The first meal in the morning can be milk with cereal (I use cornflakes or weetabix), and I add some natural yoghurt. For the other meals, feed a complete puppy food, which has been soaked in warm water, or you can feed meat with biscuits. The complete food does not need any additives, whereas the meat and biscuit meal needs to be supplemented with some calcium, and a vitamin and mineral product. To avoid the risk of over-supplementing, I prefer to feed a perfectly balanced complete diet. Whichever type of food you decide to give, the given amount per meal has to be increased slowly, according to the pup's appetite.

THE GROWING PUPPY
When a puppy is twelve weeks old I cut down to three meals, and from about five months of age, I feed two meals a day. In fact, all my adult dogs are fed twice every day. The morning meal is milk with water, and a heaped tablespoon of yoghurt. In the evening I feed the main meal, which is a complete diet, and the type and the quantity vary according to age and individual requirements.

BAD EATERS
One of the most frustrating dogs to own is a poor feeder, who is reluctant to eat up – no matter what sort of food you offer. In most cases this applies to younger males, or to bitches just after being in season. Not all bad eaters lose weight, and if a dog seems to be maintaining condition, I try not to make too much of a fuss. I find out which food the dog seems to like – a complete diet,

fish, chicken, or beef – and I feed this every day at the same time. If it is not eaten after about fifteen minutes, I pick it up and the dog has to wait until the next mealtime. I do not attempt to coax the dog to eat, and I do not hand-feed. This is so that the dog does not become affected by my anxiety.

The situation is obviously exacerbated if the dog is losing weight. If this is so, and a vet has established that the thyroid gland is not malfunctioning and there are no other physical problems which can be treated, you will have to tempt the dog's appetite, trying out different foods, such as rice pudding, eggs, cottage cheese, milk, pasta, cooked or raw meat. Even when you are trying to get a dog to eat, do not leave the food standing in the bowl for longer than fifteen minutes. Dogs are very intelligent and the poor feeder will soon realise that this is a way of getting more attention. Be careful that you do not get into a vicious circle, which will only make matters worse.

TRAINING YOUR PUPPY
Old English Sheepdog puppies are irresistible, and it can be hard to correct the antics of a playful, loving 'clown'. However, the OES grows up to be a dog of considerable size and weight, and it is important that you train your puppy from an early age, establishing that you are the 'boss' before any serious problems arise.

WHY DO DOGS MISBEHAVE?
All puppies, and indeed, all adult dogs instinctively want to please the boss – the pack leader. You must assume this role and demand that your is dog obedient – and in nearly all cases, a dog *wants* to be obedient. Why, you may well ask, is it that so many dogs are disobedient and refuse to do as they are told? The answer is that it is often the owner's fault if a dog wilfully misbehaves. Puppies are like children. They learn by playing, and they also try and find out who is the boss. Many people are much-loved by their dogs, but they are not respected. These people never demand obedience from their dogs – they rarely ask for it – and so a dog in this situation does not have a figure in authority to obey instinctively. Many owners make the mistake of not being consistent in their commands. Do not allow your puppy to do something on one occasion (because it is amusing or endearing), and then forbid it on a subsequent occasion – the puppy will be completely bewildered. If you do not want your OES to beg at the table, you must correct your pup on the first occasion, and on all subsequent occasions, until the puppy gets the message.

Jumping up at people, or jumping on to the furniture is amusing in a twelve-week-old puppy – but it is far from amusing when a fully-gown OES tries to knock you over, or takes up all the room on the sofa. Again, consistency is the key word, and a firm "No", every time your puppy attempts to jump up, will soon be understood. However, this reprimand may have to be repeated on many occasions, as with children, but in the end, firmness and consistency will win the day.

WHEN TO START TRAINING
I believe in teaching a puppy the 'house rules' from Day One. Obviously, you cannot expect miracles from a small puppy, but at about ten to twelve weeks, a puppy is old enough to learn "No" and "Sit". If you say "No" in a stern voice when the puppy is doing something, and at the same time redirect the puppy's interest on to something that is allowed, you will find that it soon learns that "No" means "No"!

HOUSE TRAINING
This is another area where the older puppy learns more quickly and more easily than a very young

pup. A young puppy can be compared with a baby; both will forget themselves when playing, and it is up to you, the owner, to be on the alert. A pup should be put outside after every meal and after every sleep. The puppy will always need to relieve itself on these occasions, and this gives you the opportunity to reward with plenty of praise. Do not make the mistake of rewarding success other than with kind words. Years ago I rewarded a young puppy with a tidbit every time he did his business outside. After a few days he woke me up in the middle of the night. When I took him outside he just looked at me, waiting for his biscuit. He had no need to relieve himself – he just fancied a biscuit and felt he had to go outside for it!

Like all things that you demand from a dog, house training needs time and patience. Puppies are not stupid, and most will soon understand what you want from them. Obviously if it is cold, wet and windy outside, they might feel happier to stay inside and relieve themselves on the carpet. A firm "No", and a walk outside should soon teach them.

TRAINING CLASSES
Dog training classes are an excellent way of giving your dog a good grounding in basic obedience. I find these classes are beneficial to pet and show dog alike. It is also useful for the owner, as it is important to train your dog in a structured and consistent manner in order to get the best results.

In recent years there has been an increase in puppy socialisation classes, for puppies to attend as soon as the inoculation programme has been completed. These are a very useful way of puppies getting used to meeting each other under controlled circumstances – a great deal can be learnt before the more formal education is started.

INTELLIGENCE OF THE OES
There is no doubt that OES puppies are intelligent, so much so, that I do not have to 'train' my puppies, because they copy the adults. When I say "Down" to the adults, the puppies go down as well. If I call "Come", the puppies copy the adults and come rushing up to me. This ability to copy means that many habits and reactions come naturally to a pup who lives in a 'pack'.

BASIC OBEDIENCE
A single pup has to be taught everything from scratch, and the owner must be prepared to spend a little time every day teaching a puppy the basic commands. These sessions should be kept short, and you should reward with plenty of praise (and tidbits, if desired) in order to create a happy 'learning' atmosphere.

I prefer to teach a puppy to come before I start with lead training. Many unfortunate accidents can be avoided if a pup comes back to the owner every time the command is given. This lesson can be taught in the garden or in a park, where it is safe for the puppy to run around. Some puppies might need to be encouraged with tidbits, others will be happy to come just for a fuss.

When you are teaching this command, avoid moving about, and wait for the pup to come to you – even if it does take a long time. Do not chase the pup who has suddenly become 'deaf'; wait patiently until your puppy stops playing and eventually responds to your voice. Then reward with plenty of praise. I cannot stress how important it is to be patient and considerate when training your OES puppy. This breed is intelligent – and all the dogs I have owned have long memories!

LEAD TRAINING
I prefer not to start lead training until a puppy is five or even six months old. However, some owners may wish to start earlier, depending on different circumstances. With OES I like to use

nylon leads, with the collar and lead all-in-one. They are very light and do not damage the coat.

A slightly older puppy will not object to this, especially if you allow the puppy to decide where to walk, in the first few days. As soon as the puppy has got used to the feel of the collar, I gradually teach the pup to go where I want to go. Some stubborn or head-strong puppies may take a few days to accept the loss of total freedom, but in my experience, a puppy will learn to accept restriction if it is practised in a calm and firm manner. In no time at all, the puppy will accept the collar and lead as a way of life.

GROOMING THE PET OES

While a puppy is young it is best to groom every day. A few minutes at a time is sufficient, so long as the pup gets used to the routine. Teach your OES to stand or lie still, either on the floor or a suitable non-slippery table. It is much easier to teach a puppy to keep still, rather than expecting an adult dog to suddenly put up with the procedure of grooming. If you start when the puppy is young

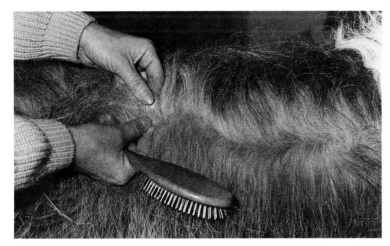

When grooming an OES all the knots must be taken out carefully. A good-quality brush (such as a Mason Pearson) is an essential item of grooming equipment.

Pearce.

this also helps you to gradually get used to coping with more and more coat.

When your dog is about four to eight months of age, the coat will begin to change from the black puppy coat to the new grey junior coat. If the coat is brushed regularly it will not tangle up, but it will come out with the brush, giving room for the junior coat. This is usually very dense with a lot of soft undercoat, which needs regular attention. If it is left untended for too long, you could end up with a solid matted coat, and you will need scissors to get through it.

The third and last coat change normally happens between sixteen months and two-and-a-half years of age. The worst time for knotting is usually around twenty months of age, and this can be a very trying time for dog and owner. When the adult coat comes through, it still needs regular attention, but it does not mat as easily as the junior coat.

I like my dogs to lie on one side for grooming, and there are two methods to choose from. You can start at the feet and work your way up, layer by layer, always making sure you get right down to the skin. Or, if you prefer, you can start at the back, and, layer by layer, work your way downwards. Try not to use a comb too often. It is worth investing in a high-quality brush, such as a Mason Pearson bristle and nylon brush. If this is used gently, plucking apart any knots with your fingers, you will not upset or hurt your OES. If you have started grooming from a very early age, your dog will be used to lying still and will enjoy the attention.

Grooming is time-consuming but very rewarding. Note the contrast between the groomed and ungroomed front legs.
Pearce.

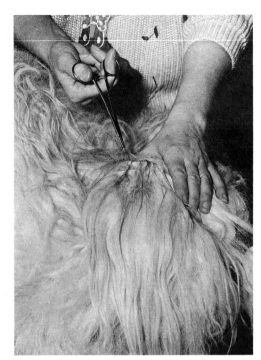

Ears must be checked regularly, and any excess hair needs to be removed.
Pearce.

EARS
Every time your dog is groomed, check the ears for excess hair growth and wax. If the hair has grown too long or is growing too thickly, you will need to remove the hair using a pair of tweezers, making sure you do not intrude too deep into the ear-hole. If wax is present, this must be cleaned from the ear, using some damp cotton wool (cotton). Again, make sure you do not probe too deeply.

TEETH
Teeth need to be cleaned about every two weeks, depending on the dog and the diet. Some dogs' teeth stay very clean without major attention from the owner, others seem to collect tartar and this needs to be removed. I use a tooth-scaler and gently scrape the plaque downwards. Make sure you do not scratch the gum.

FEET
About every four weeks, you should check your dog's feet. The hair between the pads has to be cut to prevent it growing too long. Grit and mud can get caught in the hair unless it is kept short.

EXERCISE
Pet and show dogs alike need regular daily exercise. I prefer free runs to lead-walking, because I

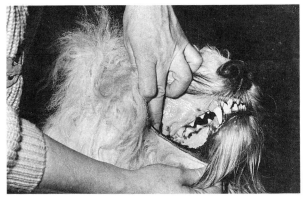

Teeth should be kept clean, as this is important to the well-being of the dog and ensures sweet-smelling breath. Pearce.

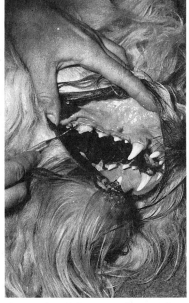

A tooth-scaler can be used to remove any tartar that collects on the teeth. Pearce.

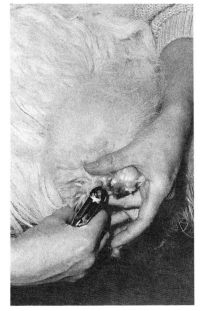

Nails need to be kept as short as possible to prevent the foot from spreading. Pearce.

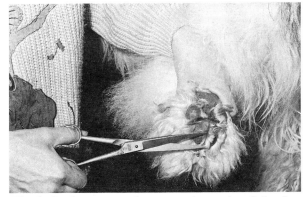

The hair that grows between the pads of the feet must be trimmed regularly. Pearce.

feel it is more natural to a sheepdog. I consider a bare minimum for an adult dog (from seven to eight months) to be two runs a day, both lasting half-an-hour – anything more than that can only be to the advantage of your dog.

No one would take a baby on a long walk, and in the same way you should not over-exercise your puppy. While the dog is growing, the bones are still soft, and too much exercise can cause serious damage.

Chapter Three

THE BREED STANDARD

Like all other recognised breeds, the Old English Sheepdog is judged on points, which are described in the Breed Standard. This Standard is meant as a guideline for breeders and judges alike. It was originally drawn up by several fanciers of the breed, plus Mr J. Freeman Lloyd. Freeman Lloyd was born and raised in Wales. He was a 'doggy' person through and through, and he made his living out of buying and exporting pure-bred dogs around 1880. He was also a well-respected writer. Due to his contacts with OES breeders, from whom he had bought dogs which he had exported to America, he was asked to write the Standard for the Old English Sheepdog in the early 1880s. After the original draft was polished up by the well-known breeder, Dr G. C. Edwards-Ker, from Suffolk, it was finally adopted by the Kennel Club in 1885.

The following is the original Standard, which was changed in 1986 to the Standard in use in Britain at the present time.

ORIGINAL BREED STANDARD (1885)

APPEARANCE: Body short, muscular, compact; great symmetry; elastic gallop; ambling or pacing characteristic of trot or walk.
EARS: Medium-sized; carried flat to head; moderately arched.
NECK: Fairly long; arched gracefully; well-coated with hair.
LOIN: Stout; gently arched.
TAIL: Preferably none; should never exceed 1 1/2-2in. in adults; puppies' tails docked at first joint if born with tails.
SKULL: Capacious, squarely formed; well-covered with hair; well-arched parts over eyes.
EYES: Vary with colour; very dark preferred.
NOSE: Black; large; capacious.
TEETH: Strong, large; evenly placed; level.
JAW: Fairly long; strong; square; cut off.
STOP: Well-defined.
SHOULDERS: Sloping, narrow at points; lower at shoulder than at loin.
FORELEGS: Straight; good bone; length medium; not leggy; well-coated.
FEET: Small, round; toes well-arched; pads thick, hard.
HINDQUARTERS: Round, muscular; hams densely coated.
HOCKS: Well let-down.
RIBS: Well-sprung; brisket deep; capacious.
COAT: Profuse; good hard texture, not straight; shaggy, free from curl; undercoat waterproof.

Ch. Beckington Lady of Welbyhouse. This great OES was a multi Best in Show winner, and bitch breed record holder for almost thirty years with a tally of twenty-nine CCs. She was used to illustrate the first Breed Standard, which was in use for nearly one hundred years.

COLOUR: Grey, grizzle, blue or blue-merled with or without white markings or in reverse. Shades of brown or fawn objectionable.

SIZE: Height, males 22in and up; females slightly less; measurement from shoulder to stern practically same as height. Type, soundness, balance, character more important than size.

BRITISH BREED STANDARD (1986)

GENERAL APPEARANCE: Strong, square-looking dog with great symmetry and overall soundness. Absolutely free from legginess, profusely coated all over. A thick-set, muscular, able-bodied dog with a most intelligent expression. The natural outline should not be artificially changed by scissoring or clipping.

CHARACTERISTICS: Of great stamina, exhibiting a gently rising topline, and a pear-shaped body when viewed from above. The gait has a typical roll when ambling or walking. Bark has a distinctive toned quality.

TEMPERAMENT: A biddable dog of even disposition. Bold, faithful and trustworthy, with no suggestion of nervousness or unprovoked aggression.

HEAD AND SKULL: In proportion to the size of the body. Skull capacious, rather square. Well arched above eyes, stop well defined. Muzzle strong, square and truncated, measuring approximately half of the total head length. Nose large and black. Nostrils wide.

EYES: Set well apart. Dark or wall eyes. Two blue eyes acceptable. Light eyes undesirable. Pigmentation on the eye rim is preferred.

EARS: Small and carried flat to side of head.

MOUTH: Teeth strong, large, and evenly placed. Scissor bite – jaws strong with a perfect, regular and complete scissor bite, i.e. upper teeth closely overlapping lower teeth and set square to the jaws. Pincer tolerated but undesirable.

NECK: Fairly long, strong, arched gracefully.

FOREQUARTERS: Forelegs perfectly straight, with plenty of bone, holding body well from ground. Elbows fitting close to brisket. Shoulders should be well laid back, being narrower at the point of withers than at the point of shoulder. Loaded shoulders undesirable. Dog standing lower at withers than loin.

BODY: Rather short, and compact, with well sprung ribs, and deep capacious brisket.

HINDQUARTERS: Loin very sturdy, broad and gently arched, quarters well covered, round and muscular, the second thigh is long and well developed, the stifle well turned, and the hocks set low. From the rear the hocks should be quite straight, with the feet turning neither in nor out.

FEET: Small, round and tight, toes well arched, pads thick and hard. Dew claws should be removed.

TAIL: Customarily completely docked.

GAIT/MOVEMENT: When walking, exhibits a bear-like roll from the rear. When trotting, shows effortless extension and strong driving rear action, with legs moving straight along line of travel. Very elastic at the gallop. At slow speeds, some dogs may tend to pace. When moving, the head carriage may adopt a naturally lower position.

COAT: Profuse, of good harsh texture, not straight, but shaggy and free from curl. Undercoat of waterproof pile. Head and skull well covered with hair, ears moderately coated, neck well coated, forelegs well coated all round, hindquarters more heavily coated than rest of body. Quality, texture, and profusion to be considered above mere length.

COLOUR: Any shade of grey, grizzle or blue. Body and hindquarters of solid colour with or without white socks. White patches in the solid area to be discouraged. Head, neck, forequarters and underbelly to be white with or without markings. Any shade of brown undesirable.

SIZE: Height: dogs: 61 cms (24 inches) and upwards; bitches 56 cms (22 inches) and upwards. Type and symmetry of greatest importance, and on no account to be sacrificed to size alone.

FAULTS: Any departure from the foregoing points should be considered a fault and the seriousness with which the fault should be regarded should be in exact proportion to its degree.

NOTE: Male animals should have two apparently normal testicles fully descended into the scrotum.

Reproduced by kind permission of the English Kennel Club.

The Old English Sheepdog is originally a British breed, and therefore the FCI has adopted the British Breed Standard, as it is their custom to take the Standard from the breed's country of origin. The American Breed Standard follows roughly similar lines, with two main exceptions, in relation to gait and coat markings.

AMERICAN BREED STANDARD (1990)

GENERAL APPEARANCE – A strong, compact, square, balanced dog. Taking him all around he is profusely, *but not excessively coated,* thickset, muscular and able-bodied. These qualities, combined with his agility, fit him for the demanding tasks required of a shepherd's or drover's dog. Therefore, *soundness is of the greatest importance.* His bark is loud with a distinctive "pot-casse" ring in it.

SIZE, PROPORTION, SUBSTANCE – Type, character and balance are of greater importance and are on no account to be sacrificed to size alone. *Size* – Height (measured from top of withers to the ground), Dogs: 22 inches (55.8 cm) and upward. Bitches: 21 inches (53.3 cm) and upward. *Proportion* – Length (measured from point of shoulder to point of ischium [tuberosity]) practically the same as the height. Absolutely free from legginess or weaselness. *Substance* – Well muscled with plenty of bone.

HEAD – A most intelligent expression. *Eyes* – Brown, blue or one of each. If brown, very dark is preferred. If blue, a pearl, china or wall-eye is considered typical. An amber or yellow eye is most objectionable. *Ears* – Medium sized and carried flat to the side of the head. *Skull* – Capacious and rather squarely formed giving plenty of room for brain power. The parts over the eyes (super-orbital ridges) are well arched. The whole, well covered with hair. *Stop* – Well defined. *Jaw* – Fairly long, strong, square and truncated. *Attention is particularly called to the above properties, as a long, narrow head or snipy muzzle is a deformity.* *Nose* – Always black, large and capacious. *Teeth* – Strong, large and evenly placed. The bite is level or tight scissors.

NECK, TOPLINE, BODY – *Neck* – Fairly long and arched gracefully. *Topline* – Stands lower at the withers than at the loin with no indication of softness or weakness. *Attention is particularly called to this topline as it is a distinguishing characteristic of the breed* *Body* – Rather short and very compact, broader at the rump than at the shoulders, ribs well sprung and brisket deep and capacious. Neither slab-sided nor barrel-chested. The loin is very stout and gently arched. *Tail* – Docked close to the body, when not naturally bobtailed.

FOREQUARTERS – Shoulders well laid back and narrow at the points. The forelegs dead straight with plenty of bone. The measurements from the withers to the elbow and from the elbow to the ground are practically the same.

HINDQUARTERS – Round and muscular with well let down hocks. When standing, the metatarsi are perpendicular to the ground when viewed from any angle.

FEET – Small and round, toes well arched, pads thick and hard, feet pointing straight ahead.

COAT – Profuse, but not so excessive as to give the impression of the dog being overly fat, and of a good hard texture; not straight, but shaggy and free from curl. *Quality and texture of coat to be considered above mere profuseness.* Softness or flatness of coat to be considered a fault. The undercoat is a waterproof pile when not removed by grooming or season. Ears coated moderately. The whole skull well covered with hair. The neck well coated with hair. The forelegs well coated all around. The hams densely coated with a thick, long jacket in excess of any other part. Neither the natural outline nor the natural texture of the coat may be changed by any artificial means except that the feet and rear may be trimmed for cleanliness.

COLOR – Any shade of gray, grizzle, blue or blue merle with or without white markings or in reverse. *Any shade of brown or fawn to be considered distinctly objectionable and not to be encouraged.*

GAIT – When trotting, movement is free and powerful, seemingly effortless, with good reach and drive, and covering maximum ground with minimum steps. Very elastic at a gallop. May amble or pace at slower speeds.

TEMPERAMENT – An adaptable, intelligent dog of even disposition, with no sign of aggression, shyness or nervousness.

Reproduced by kind permission of the American Kennel Club. Approved February 10th 1990.

INTERPRETATION AND ANALYSIS
GENERAL APPEARANCE AND CHARACTERISTICS

To explain what is meant by a strong and square-looking dog, it is important to try to visualise the original purpose of the OES. The breed's job was to look after sheep or cattle, and to take them to market. This required an able-bodied dog, that was absolutely sound all over – not just in body, but also in mind. The OES was a hardy and strong-built dog, without being coarse. If the legs were either too long or too short, the dog would be unable to carry out its work, as the physical effort of running would be too much to sustain throughout the day.

The profuse coat was necessary to protect the dog from extreme weather, either excessive heat or freezing cold. Bearing this in mind, it is easy to understand why the quality of the coat was so important. The working dog needed to have a harsh topcoat so that the rain would not soak

Am. Ch. Rholenwood Enjoli (clipped). I rate this as one of the most beautifully constructed OES I have seen. The clipped coat gives a rare opportunity to see the correct proportions and angulations of the OES, without actually 'going over' the dog.

through to the skin, and a soft undercoat was needed for protection against cold weather and wind.

It was essential that the OES's temperament was absolutely free of unprovoked aggression. The shepherds had to trust the OES with their herds – and sometimes with their own lives – and so the courageous, faithful, even disposition became a hallmark of the breed.

THE HEAD

The required big and square head gives enough space for the brain, and it should be in proportion to the whole outline of the dog. The ears should be small and flat, rather than big or folded. Ears that are big and folded prevent sufficient air circulating, which makes the ear prone to infections.

The eyes should be set well apart. There have always been dogs with either wall eyes (one blue and one brown) or china eyes (two blue eyes). The US Champion, Robbery in Broad Daylight, a most successful dog in his time and behind many present-day OES, had wall eyes with the most beautiful dark marking around the blue eye. Amber, yellow or hazel coloured eyes, which are commonly known as 'light' eyes, are undesirable. They are hereditary and should therefore not be encouraged when judging or breeding.

The jaw should be strong and in proportion to the skull. It should give the impression of being cut off abruptly, instead of pointing towards the nose. This, in turn, will give a wide and square jaw with the front teeth set in a straight line, rather than slightly rounded.

THE NECK

I see the neck as being a very important point in the Breed Standard at the present time, because there are too many exhibits in the ring with a U-shaped neck, rather than a neck that is gracefully arched. This gives the appearance of total disharmony, apart from being incorrect according to the Standard. In his book *The Old English Sheepdog*, Arthur Tilley gives an excellent explanation for the required well-arched neck. He writes:

"It is particularly essential for an OES to have a well-arched neck because when ordered 'down!', even if it be in long grass, they can still observe hand signals from their master."

The neck is also required to be "fairly long" and "strong". I find that necks that have been

Ch Lamedazottel Flamboyant: Top winning Dog All Breeds 1991 and 1992. 51 CCs, 25 BIS Ch. shows, 5 Reserve CCs. *Trafford.*

It is always difficult to write about dogs that you have bred and exhibited. 'Boysy' is obviously a very special dog, and is highly valued as a family companion as well as a show dog. In 1991 we entered him at the Crufts Centenary Show under judge Norman Harrison of the famous Fernville prefix. He wrote the following critique of Flamboyant:

"What a remarkable, polished, striking young dog this is. It is many years since I saw a male of this calibre, and this young man had everything that I was looking for, including a little flamboyancy, yes, he is flamboyant and that's why you don't miss him, but he has all the essentials of a working dog, so beautifully proportioned and perfectly balanced, superb head, well balanced muzzle, lovely dark eyes, correct bite, gorgeous reach of neck, gracefully arched, lovely shoulder placement with good straight A1 bone, deep brisket, short back, glorious topline, splendid hindquarters, well angulated with well set low hocks, lots of light grey coat, which excels in texture and has the desired break, a rare thing these days. Movement is of the highest order, a thrill to see such reach and drive. Presentation and handling absolute perfection, could find nothing to displease."

excessively stripped-out, to make them look thin and therefore longer, look equally wrong. An OES with a good shoulder placement, and a good angle to the shoulder, usually has a good neck.

It is also important to point out that even though a moving OES, carrying his head held up high looks more impressive in the ring, the working sheepdog would slightly lower his head. This is stated in the British Standard quite clearly. The OES should therefore not be penalised if he has not got a high head carriage when on the move.

THE BODY
Being a square-built dog, the OES needs to have a rising topline to give the extra length when moving fast. Otherwise the dog would be be forced to overreach, which is obviously an incorrect form of movement. It is therefore very important that the gentle rise goes to the loin, and not to the hips. If you look at the clipped OES from the side, the highest point of the back should be the loin, and not the part over the hips. The typical pear-shaped body gives enough strength from the backend and enables a free movement in the front.

Good shoulder placement is important with regard to front movement, as incorrect shoulders do not allow the dog to have the required reach. Wrong shoulder placement quite often goes along with loose elbows, which would also disadvantage a working dog.

Contrary to the opinion of some, I would like to point out that the Standard only asks for the point of withers to be narrower than the point of shoulder. I take this to means that, in relation to the width of brisket and shoulder, the point of withers should be narrower. It must be seen as totally wrong if judges just feel how narrow the point of withers is, and then credit or fault the exhibit on that, without feeling the point of shoulder.

Looking at the dogs in the show ring during the last five years, it is impossible to overlook the tendency of a great number of exhibits to be rather short in leg, sometimes in combination with a longer body. Both must be considered as highly undesirable, as the Bobtail is supposed to be a compact and square-built dog with "forelegs holding the body well from ground". This is not to be confused with legginess, as there has to be the correct proportion between leg length and depth of brisket. The brisket should not be flat or slab-sided, but deep and capacious with well-sprung but not rounded ribs.

The short and compact body gives the desired impression of sturdiness. Compactness is also necessary for the "elastic" movement which is asked for. Well developed hind legs with a good bend of stifle, a long second thigh, and low set hocks in combination with the compact body, and, most important, the rise over the loin, are the key factors for the typical OES gaits.

MOVEMENT
One of the main differences between the English Standard (and the FCI) and the American Standard is that the American Standard does not mention the typical "roll". The US Standard describes trotting – "free and powerful, seemingly effortless, with good reach and drive." A "very elastic" gallop is encouraged, and it is stipulated that the OES may amble or pace at slower speeds.

The best definition of the two OES gaits, which are different to other dogs' gaits, was given by my dear friend Caj Haakansson. With his kind permission, I will therefore give you his excellent, easy-to-understand explanation.

"The swaying of body and coat in the pacing OES is not the 'roll' I call the typical bear-like gait and roll. This roll comes from shifting his entire side, from loin to toe, in an easy elastic, shuffling stride, and in long definite steps. There are a number of key characteristics that produce this unique gait and roll. The combinations of correct arch over the loin (making the OES standing

Ch. Vigilats Different Yip: The OES is customarily docked according to the American and British Breed Standards. However, docking is now banned in some European countries.

higher at the loin than at the withers, not the too-often-seen sway in the back, and subsequently higher at the hipbones). The long second thigh, and uniquely short hock that is also well let down. The croup is neither steep nor level croup, but rather a well-filled-out and rounded croup of moderate and short slant. A dead level and too short a croup may be found in Bobtails with straight hindquarters i.e. lack of angulation, and not enough length in thighs, especially the second thigh. Too steep a croup is often seen, and found in OES that are underslung.

"The amble is by definition a smooth and leisurely gait, not a full pace or traditional trot, but a walk or trot in that easy in-between style, absolutely free from any high stepping or kick-out rear action. An amble is not a fast gait, whereas pacing can be very fast. The Bobtail that is correctly built and moves correctly for his breed never loses his roll in walk or in trot. In his elastic gallop, it is just not shown at all. In addition to structure, I also believe that these gaits are a matter of inherited mood factors."

Unfortunately, it has to be said that there are hardly any OES to be seen who have the typical roll. It is therefore a characteristic which should be highly encouraged when judging.

COAT AND COLOUR
Judges should also encourage the correct harsh coat without curl, but with a good break to it. I would agree with anyone who admires a heavily- and long-coated OES, but, so far, I have not seen many Bobtails with extreme coat length who also had the required harsh texture. This is because the harsher the coat, the easier it breaks – thus making it very difficult to produce length of coat.

The required coat colours are all shades of grey, grizzle or blue. This definitely excludes an all-black coat as well as the highly undesirable brown coat. In the American Standard it states that the coat can be with or without white markings, or in reverse. This implies white 'flashes', which are frowned upon in the UK and in Europe.

SIZE

With regard to height, I would again like to quote the late Arthur Tilley, who felt that the question of size should be determined by the type of work required of the dogs:

"For example, a farmer may need one for cattle and sheep for which a fairly big dog with strength would be preferable to a smaller one with speedier movement, and particularly so if the sheep were of the heavier breeds which are common in the southern counties in England. It would be obvious that a too active dog would be both unnecessary and inadvisable immediately before and after the lambing season. On the other hand, the lighter type should be selected for work on hills or high moorlands."

Considering these comments from one of the most respected early breeders, it is easy to understand why the given height in the Standard is only a recommendation, with the addition: "Type and symmetry of greatest importance, and on no account to be sacrificed to size alone."

Chapter Four

THE SHOW DOG

If you decide to take on the responsibility of owning a dog, you will be caring for it to the best of your ability – whether you have plans to compete in the show ring, or not. The advice given in Chapter Two, with regard to the pet dog is therefore equally applicable when you are caring for a show puppy.

CHOOSING A SHOW PUPPY
Unless you are an experienced breeder and familiar with the parents' lines, you should always rely on the breeder to make the pick. It is in his interest to send the best possible pups into show homes, and he will have noticed differences in the pups which are not apparent to the outsider.

GROOMING THE SHOW DOG
Grooming a show dog is rather rather more work-intensive than grooming a pet. With the puppy coat, I believe in regular daily grooming sessions. The sooner you lose all the black puppy coat, the sooner the junior coat will come through. The same applies to the junior coat once it starts changing. This transformation seems to happen almost overnight, and it is inadvisable to try and preserve any changing coat, as it will not last, whatever you do. All you will do is make it more difficult for the new coat to grow.

The method of grooming is the same as with the pet. You work your way slowly through the coat, only brushing one layer at a time. Once all the coat changes have taken place – usually between two-and-a-half and three years of age, you can start using a soft-padded pin-brush, instead of the Mason Pearson brush, previously recommended. If this is used gently, gradually working through layer by layer, you will take out less undercoat, which is needed in order to give the harsh guard hair its body.

If your dog's coat is very harsh, you can always spray a little water on the part you want to groom. The hair is less likely to break off when it has been dampened. Extra care has to be taken with the beard. Never ever leave food in it. You could lose an inch of length by just taking dried food out of the hair. With male show dogs, I frequently put conditioner on the belly and hind legs coat to prevent the hair from breaking off. Regular washing, even with a mild baby shampoo, will take out the natural oil and make the coat brittle, and the hair will eventually break. After you have groomed your dog through completely, stand him and brush all his back coat up, with the neck coat coming down. This emphasises the required rising topline and the squareness of the OES. The head coat should also be brushed up, making the head look big and impressive, and the coat on the front and back legs should be brushed up as well.

When you start to prepare your OES for the show ring, it is essential to start off with a clean dog, completely groomed through.

Pearce.

Clean the beard and dry it with a towel, also using baby powder or corn starch.

Pearce.

The powder then has to be brushed out to achieve maximum effect.

Pearce.

The coat should be brushed down the back, close to the body. *Pearce.*

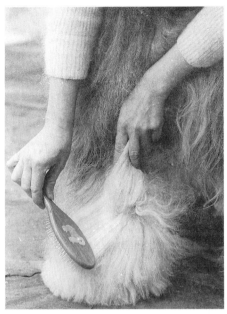

The hock-coat needs brushing through and fluffing up. *Pearce.*

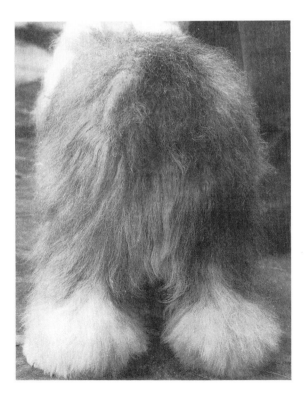

The finished effect, viewed from the rear.

Pearce.

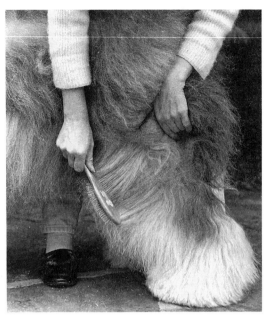

The coat on the thighs has to be brushed forward to show off the angulation. Pearce.

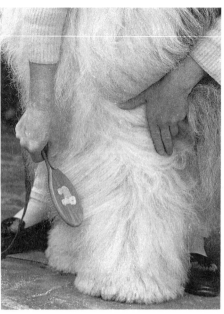

Fluff up the front leg coat, making it look as thick as possible. Pearce.

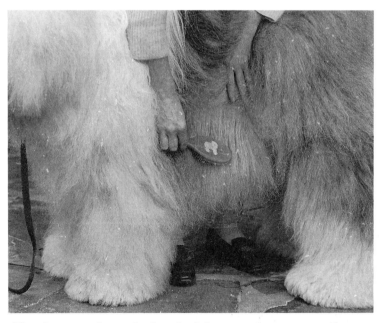

The chest coat has to be brushed downwards. Pearce.

 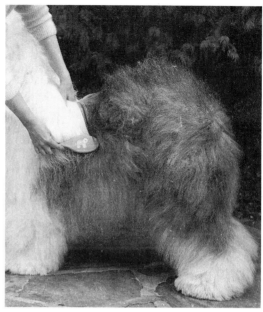

Start brushing up the back coat from 21/2 to 3in. behind the shoulder points.

Pearce.

The rest of the back coat has to be brushed flat, depending on the length, down either side of the dog.

Pearce.

Finally, concentrate on the head, fluffing up all the coat to make it look as big as possible.

Pearce.

Ready to go in the ring and win!					*Pearce.*

TRIMMING

The only trimming that is required for an Old English Sheepdog is the tidying up of the coat around the feet. The front legs should look like big straight columns, and at the rear, the feet should appear small with plenty of hock-coat. When you cut the coat around the feet, lift the top layer up all the way round and then let the top layer fall down naturally. You can then trim to neaten the appearance. Some dogs do not like any scissoring to be done on their feet. The easiest way to keep your dog from jumping off the table at a crucial moment is to have a second person holding the opposite leg to the one you are about to trim.

If you are uncertain about how much to trim, most exhibitors at shows will be quite happy to show you the tricks of the trade, once they have finished showing their exhibits. Do not ask for a favour like this before all the judging has been done. Most people are nervous at shows and need to prepare their own dogs first.

There are currently many exhibitors who favour trimming their Sheepdogs, even though this is not, strictly speaking, in accordance with the Breed Standard. However, I personally feel if a dog is trimmed with the greatest care, in a way that enhances the *natural* outline of the dog, without making it look overtrimmed, I would not penalise it while judging. But it is also important to remember that we are dealing with Sheepdogs, and not Poodles.

If your dog has a very thick and dense coat, you might have to thin out excessive coat round the neck to avoid the appearance of heavy shoulders. Use a very fine comb and gently go, layer by layer, through the coat and take out the undercoat. The novice should always start on the off-show side when trimming or shaping. Take only a little bit off at a time, stand the dog up and have a good look, and then carry on. This will hopefully save you the trauma of taking off too much hair. If you do your thinning-out or trimming at least a week before a show, the coat gets the chance to settle down properly, which will give a more natural impression.

BATH TIME
Bathing an Old English Sheepdog sounds worse than it is; you imagine that you will never be able to cope with all that wet hair. However, the most important aspect of bathing an OES is *not* to wash the grey body-coat. The legs and face of a Bobtail have to be washed frequently, sometimes every day depending on the weather, but you should avoid washing the dark body coat. If you attempted to do this, the natural oil would be destroyed, and this would make grooming almost impossible. The coat would also become soft and limp, just the opposite of the required harsh texture. Regular grooming will keep the body-coat sufficiently clean.

However, the legs and the face are a completely different matter. I wash my dogs' faces, or rather their beards, every day, and often their legs have to be rinsed after walks, particularly if the weather is bad. There are plenty of good dog shampoos on the market to choose from. I prefer to use a shampoo without any artificial brighteners, with natural oils only. I know many people who use washing-up liquid to clean their dogs' beards, and they are perfectly happy with the results. I personally prefer to use cleaners which are less aggravating to the skin.

The day before a show I try to bath the dog's legs early, so they can dry naturally, rather than having to use a hair-dryer on them. A useful tip is to sprinkle some corn starch or cornflour in the damp coat and brush it out. This helps to dry the coat, and it can also be used for cleaning a slightly grubby, dry coat. The corn starch or cornflour has to be groomed out thoroughly. It is particularly good for head coats where you might not want to use water and shampoo, as the coat can get too soft.

SHOW PRACTICE
The younger your dog is when you start training, the better it is. You can start with show pose practice as early as six weeks. I stand up all my show puppies for about half a minute at a time, every day. I hold the pup, with one hand under the chin and with the other under the backend, with the hand going in between the back legs, telling them gently to "stay".

Twelve weeks is a reasonable age to start lead training. I prefer to use nylon leads, where collar and lead are all in one. Nylon is also light in weight and therefore easier for a puppy to get used to. Some pups find it very difficult to accept wearing a collar; they need to be handled with care so they do not get frightened. When you start lead training, it is less of an ordeal if the pup wears the lead in the house first. Hold the lead gently and allow the pup to go where he wants to. Then take it off after a few minutes, and do the same again for the next few days. The pup will soon know what you want, and it should ensure that you do not end up in a tangle when you attempt the first proper walk outside.

From about four months of age, puppies can go to training classes, which specialise in ring craft or ring training. The pup will learn how to stand in show pose, walk on the lead, and, most of all, the puppy will get used to other dogs and an atmosphere which is similar to the hustle and bustle of a show.

As long as all this practice is done in a playful way, I feel it is enjoyable for a puppy. However, I know many people who take their puppy to every possible training class, sometimes three or four times a week, and expect it to perform like an adult. I do not think this is necessary, and I do not think it is fair to a puppy. Before long, your OES will be grown-up and will be expected to behave well at all times – so let your youngster enjoy its puppyhood.

THE FIRST SHOW

Six months is the minimum age for a puppy to enter a regular dog show. You can apply for entry forms from the show secretaries. Names and telephone numbers are advertised in the canine Press, and sometimes you can find entry schedules at the training classes.

To fill in the form you need all the details about the dog – pedigree, name, breed, sex, date of birth, breeder's name, sire, dam – and the number of the class to be entered, which are defined under every breed section.

THE ENGLISH SHOW SYSTEM

The following classes are available:

MINOR PUPPY: For dogs of six and not exceeding nine calendar months of age on the first day of the show.

PUPPY: For dogs of six and not exceeding twelve calendar months of age on the first day of the show.

JUNIOR: For dogs of six and not exceeding eighteen calendar months of age on the first day of the show.

MAIDEN: For dogs which have not won a Challenge Certificate or a First Prize at an Open or Championship Show (Minor Puppy, Special Minor, Puppy, Puppy and Special Puppy classes excepted, whether restricted or not).

NOVICE: For dogs which have not won a Challenge Certificate or three or more First Prizes at Open and Championship Shows (Minor Puppy, Special Minor Puppy, Puppy and Special Puppy classes excepted, whether restricted or not).

UNDERGRADUATE: For dogs which have not won a Challenge Certificate or three or more First Prizes at Championship Shows (Minor Puppy, Special Minor Puppy, Puppy and Special Puppy classes excepted, whether restricted or not).

GRADUATE: For dogs which have not won a Challenge Certificate or four or more First Prizes at Championship Shows in Graduate, Post Graduate, Mid Limit, Minor Limit, Limit and Open classes, whether restricted or not.

POST GRADUATE: For dogs which have not won a Challenge Certificate or five or more First Prizes at Championship Shows in Post Graduate, Minor Limit, Mid Limit, Limit and Open classes, whether restricted or not.

MID LIMIT: For dogs which have not won three Challenge Certificates or five or more First Prizes in all at Championship Shows in Mid Limit, Limit and Open classes, confined to the breed, whether restricted or not, at Shows where Challenge Certificates were offered for the breed.

LIMIT: For dogs which have not won three Challenge Certificates under three different judges or seven or more First Prizes in all at Championship Shows in Limit and Open classes, confined to the breed, whether restricted or not, at shows where Challenge Certificates were offered for the breed.

OPEN: For all dogs of the breed for which the class is provided and eligible for entry at the show.
VETERAN: For dogs of not less than seven years of age on the day of the show.
ANY VARIETY NOT SEPARATELY CLASSIFIED: For breeds of dog for which no separate breed classes are scheduled.
SPECIAL BEGINNERS: For dogs shown by an exhibitor who has never won a Challenge Certificate in the breed. Note: It is the exhibitor who has to qualify, not the dog.

THE AMERICAN SHOW SYSTEM
The following classes are available:
PUPPY: For puppies that are six months of age and over, but under twelve months, that are not Champions.
TWELVE TO EIGHTEEN MONTHS: For dogs that are twelve months of age and over, but under eighteen months, that are not Champions.
NOVICE: For dogs six months of age and over, whelped in the USA, Canada or Mexico, which have not won three First Prizes in the Novice class, a First Prize in the Bred by Exhibitor, American-bred or Open classes, nor one or more points towards their Championships.
BRED-BY-EXHIBITOR: For dogs whelped in the USA, or if individually registered in the AKC Stud Book, for dogs whelped in Canada or Mexico, that are six months of age or over, that are not Champions, and that are owned wholly or in part by by the breeder (or spouse). The dogs should also be handled by the breeder or a member of the immediate family.
AMERICAN-BRED: For all dogs (except Champions) six months of age and over, whelped in the USA.
OPEN: For any dog six months of age or over.
WINNERS: This is divided by sex, and each division is only for undefeated dogs of the same sex which have won First Prizes in either the Puppy, Twelve to Eighteen Month, Novice, Bred-by-Exhibitor, American-bred or Open classes. At each show, after the Winners prize has been awarded in one of the sex divisions, the second prize-winning dog, if undefeated except by the dog awarded Winners, shall compete with other eligible dogs for Reserve Winners.

PREPARING FOR A SHOW
During the week before a show, allow yourself plenty of time to groom your dog as well as cleaning the ears and the teeth. The day before, wash the legs (all of the front legs and the back feet). The beard and the foreface might also need washing.

Usually the first few shows are a bit nerve-racking. You should therefore make sure you have plenty of time in the morning to get to the show. There might be traffic delays on the way and also at the entrance to the car park of the showground. With a young dog you should aim to be at the showground at least one and a half hours before the judging is scheduled to start. This will give you enough time to find your way around, get a catalogue, find the ring, and also give you the time to give the dog another groom through before you go to the ring. The classes will be called for by the ring steward, but it is still your responsibility to be there on time.

RING PROCEDURE
While you are in the ring, watch the judge carefully and do exactly as you are asked. You will have learned at the training class how to stand your dog, not to crowd the judge, or your exhibit. You should also have learned to move your dog, if asked, in a triangle or straight up and down in a line. Some judges like their exhibits to stand in numerical order in the ring. It helps to find out

before you are due to go in the ring what is required of you. Also make sure that you have got your ring number clip ready for when the steward hands out the numbers.

If you are showing in a big class, I do not think a young dog should be expected to stand and show off all the time. While the judge is going over the other exhibits, I allow my dogs to relax – unless I notice the judge glancing along the line while he is judging. If that is the case, I try to keep my dog brushed up properly but still try to give the opportunity to relax as well. I believe the show should be enjoyable for the dogs as well, and constant pressure on the dog to stand still, hold up his head and perform non-stop, cannot contribute to an enjoyable day for an animal.

Once the judge has seen all but the last two dogs, get your OES brushed up again. Stand the dog up and stop brushing while the judge is looking at the whole class. Constant use of the brush gives the impression of nerves, and it may appear as if the dog has faults which you might want to hide. A calm and collected exhibitor, on the other hand, gives an impression of confidence. Never forget that confidence or nerves travel down the lead. This can make a dog look absolutely spectacular or a shambles, irrespective of the breed characteristics.

Preferably, the OES should be shown on a short but loose lead, not moving too fast but at a steady pace. In Old English Sheepdogs there are, thankfully, still some older judges who like to see the dogs going in different paces, such as trot, pace and gallop. Make sure that you and your dog know these different paces. No dog or handler is perfect, but the better the performance in the ring, the better your chance of winning.

When I am judging I like to see good handling, although I do not like to see a dog strung up like a puppet. The aim is to find a medium between a happy dog showing himself off to his best advantage, and an expert handler. Bringing out the best in your dog, yet making it all look easy, requires time and practice. There is no sudden success for anyone; but with a good dog, plenty of dedication and preparation, anyone can make it and get right to the top.

SPORTSMANSHIP

Even with the best possible dog and the best possible preparation, combined with good handling, there will be shows where you do not do as well as you hoped. At these shows you will learn to show true sportsmanship. Be gracious to the winner by congratulating him. The dogs placed in front of yours also deserve a "Well done!" Remember it is only one judge's opinion, and you do not have to enter under that particular judge again.

There are always people at the ringside watching, and bad behaviour has never done anyone any good. By accepting your placing gracefully, you show that you can win and lose in style. There is also a saying: 'There is always another show'. Unfortunately there are some exhibitors, who, despite some great success, have still not learned to lose. They are even known to tear up prize cards at times. Never take these people as an example. Not only do they spoil their own day, but everyone else's as well. The atmosphere at a show stands or falls with the exhibitors; these include winners but most of all losers, as there are always more losers than winners. So it is up to us all to make a dog show a super day out.

Chapter Five

THE OES IN BRITAIN

THE FIFTIES TO THE SEVENTIES
SHEPTON
After the struggles of keeping the breed alive during the Second World War, the fifties was a time for rebuilding. In fact, the decade was still very much dominated by the kennel which had started before the turn of the century – Arthur Tilley's Shepton kennel. He was now joined in his work by his daughter, Florence, who was universally liked and respected. Like her father, she was passed for judging on CC level, and their knowledge of the breed was unrivalled. In fact, most of the kennels before and after the war went back to dogs connected, in one way or another, with the Shepton OES. Both Florence and her father served on the committee of the parent OES Club for many years. Arthur Tilley was the president 1926-1927, 1937-1939, and from 1945 to 1947, and in his last term he served from 1949 to 1955. Florence served on the same committee as president from 1967 until her tragically early death in 1985.

Nine more Champions with the Shepton prefix were registered during the fifties. Three of these nine Champions were sired by Ch. Shepton Surf King. They were Ch. Shepton Indomitable, Ch. Shepton Lovely Memory, and Ch. Shepton Prince Charles, all out of Ch. Shepton Perfect Picture. The litter was whelped on August 5th 1948, and the puppies inherited the fine qualities of both sire and dam. Perfect Picture (Nosey Parker of Pickhurst – Snowhite of Pickhurst) was bred by Mrs Shanks (Pickhurst). Surf King was bred by Mrs Grillett, who had used Boldwood Bombardier on Boldwood Bustle. Looking closer at Perfect Picture's breeding, the records show that this litter also produced another Champion sire, Ch. Shepton Home Guard, and, out of a later litter, Ch. Bashurst Sally Ann.

PERRYWOOD
Mrs Jones and her Perrywood OES was another kennel which made an impact during the fifties. Most of this breeding was sired by the great Ch. Shepton Sonny Boy of Marlay (Beau Brigand of Marlay – Comedy Starlight), bred by Mrs H. Booth and registered originally as Marlay Top Dog by the breeder. He was then sold to Florence Tilley, and the registered name changed into Shepton Sonny Boy of Marlay, which was to become a household name. He went Best in Show at several variety shows and was the CC winner at Crufts 1948.

Five of the Perrywood's title holders were sired by Sonny Boy. They were: Ch. Perrywood Blue Carm (out of Perrywood Linda of Yasabel), Ch. Perrywood Shepherd Boy (out of Lady Diamond Warridge), Ch. Perrywood Maid Marion (out of Daybreak of Shirehall), Ch. Perrywood Old Faithful and Ch. Perrywood Bonny Boy (both out of Perrywood Lady Merry).

Bonny Boy and Shepherd Boy both looked very much like their sire – masculine and thick-set, with big strong heads. Like their father they also gave their owners a lot of pleasure in the ring. Shepherd Boy was retired from showing when five years of age, having won ten CCs, seven Reserve CCs, and sixteen Best in Show all Breeds. Bonny Boy was handled to CCs at Bath in May 1957 (under J. S. Burgess) and at Blackpool June 1958 (under Captain S. E. Bower), and the CC and Best of Breed was awarded to him at the Birmingham City Show in 1959 (under Mabel Gibson). He also won the Champion of Champions award in October 1959 at the OES Club Show.

In the late fifties the Jones family, together with their lovely Perrywood OES – including Sonny Boy, the great sire – emigrated to California, USA and were greatly missed by the OES fraternity in England.

In 1952 Sylvia Talbot, who was to become another important figure in the OES world, made up her first Champion. He was the homebred Ch. Kentish Man bred out of an early Pastelblue bitch, Pastelblue Showlady sired by Gay Lad of Pickhurst. Gay Lad was also the sire of Sylvia's second Champion, Ch. Watchers Butterfly. She was bred by the famous Miss M. Tucker out of Watcher Sweetbriar.

RECULVER
In 1954 Mr and Mrs A. G. Wilkinson of the Reculver kennels made up their first Champion. Ch. Pastelblue Carol Ann was bred by Miss J. Webster and was sired by Pastelblue Sir John (who was by the great Ch. Sir John Marksman) out of Cobbydale Perriwinkle. The first homebred Champion was made up in 1955 and this was Ch. Reculver Sally Ann (Pastelblue Sir John – Fridays Beautiful Dream), the dam being one of the Wilkinson's brood bitches.

It was not long before the kennels had a third Champion, and this was Ch. Reculver Sugar Bush (Julian of Bewkes – Ch. Pastelblue Sally Ann), who went on to have a brilliant show career. She was of excellent feminine type, with good topline and beautiful low-set hocks. Her litter to Nicefella of Danehurst in 1961 produced two quite outstanding Champions: Ch. Reculver Christopher Robin, owned by his breeder, and Ch. Reculver Little Rascal. Rascal was originally sold to Mr P. Gardner, who showed her with some success, gaining one CC. However her career took off with a change of ownership, and her new owner, Ann Davis of the Loakespark affix, campaigned her extensively. She ended her show career with thirteen CCs, several Best in Shows, Group 1st, and Group placements. Little Rascal ('Cuddles') might have been the last famous Reculver OES to finish her title, but she certainly did it in style.

BECKINGTON
The Beckington affix was owned by Mabel Gibson, who was regarded as the best in the art of presenting. OES in the show ring. All her dogs were kept in absolutely immaculate condition. The place where she groomed her dogs before the show was usually covered with chalk (permitted in those days), but when she was ready to take her exhibits in the ring, they looked splendid.

In 1952 she bred Shepton Charming to Shepton Celebrity. The litter was whelped on July 13th, and one of the pups was to become the most successful Ch. Beckington Tom Tod. With the help of Mabel's excellent handling he amassed a total of fifteen CCs and many Reserve CCs. He went Best in Show at the OES Club Show in 1955, BIS All Breeds Leeds Championship Show, May 1955, and BIS on the second day at Welks Championship Show 1955, with Reserve BIS for both days. The entry at Welks was 7,250 dogs.

In 1958 Mabel made up her three-year-old Ch. Beckington Lady of Welbyhouse (Shepton Bridewell Brave Brigadier – Shepton Butterfly), bred by H. and R. Houghton. When Lady was

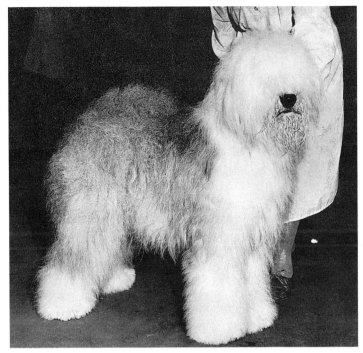

Ch. Beckington Fernville Flamingo: A great winner for Mabel Gibson and the sire of many winning Bobtails around the world.

retired from the show ring she had become the most successful Old English ever in England, taking the breed CC record. Her wins included: twenty-nine CCs, Best in Show at Blackpool Ch. Show in 1959, Best Non-sporting bitch at Birmingham City Ch. Show 1959, Best in Show at the Ladies Kennel Association Ch. Show 1959, Best Non-sporting bitch at Birmingham National Ch. 1960, plus many more awards. She was also 4th top dog all breeds in 1959 in the Dog of the Year contest.

Lady was to keep her bitch CC record for almost thirty years until 1987 when at the Lancastrian OES Club Show Mrs P. Jones of Wenallt fame awarded the thirtieth CC to Ch. Zottel's Miss Marple of Lameda, which broke the female record. The overall record had already been broken in 1971 by Mr and Mrs C. Riddiough's homebred Ch. Pendlefold Prince Hal (Ch. Oakhill Peter Pan – Smokey Jane of Nelson), whelped August 1st 1967, and winner of thirty-four CCs.

DANUM

Finding the right place in this book for the Danum kennel was rather difficult. It was started in 1890 by the present owner, Dorothy Brocklesby-Evans', great-grandfather, who then passed the kennel on to his son Frank, whose son (also named Frank) eventually left the kennel to his daughter Dorothy, bringing it up to four generations, spanning 103 years.

During the first two generations OES were bred for working purposes only, as the first Frank lived on a farm and needed the dogs to take his sheep to the market. One generation later, the Brocklesbys' profession had changed from working a farm to owning a butcher's shop, but they carried on with breeding Old English Sheepdogs. In 1903 Frank Brocklesby (the third owner) was born. He was the present owner's father. Encouraged by his parents, and with the help of his brothers and sisters, Frank changed the original breeding for workers only, to breeding for show dogs as well. Despite this change, Frank was determined that, even though he was producing show

Frank Brocklesby (the second) pictured with Danum Squire and Danum Monarch.

stock, the dogs should not lose their working ability. Frank had tremendous knowledge of the breed, and he was a highly respected figure. He became the president of the North Western OES Club and awarded CCs at Crufts in 1961 and 1972. Dorothy was twenty-one years old when her father made up his first Champion. This was the legendary Ch. Perrywood Sonny Boy (Prince Willow of Lyneal – Perrywood Sun Bonnet), bred by Mrs L. M. Jones (Perrywood). Sonny Boy was almost five years old when he gained his title. His pedigree shows a lot of the early Pastorale dogs, and he was line-bred to the great Ch. Sir John Marksman.

Frank and Dorothy started showing their dogs together, and in 1962 they made up another male, Ch. Blue Brigand of Tansley (Daphne's Fearless Blue Brigand – Silver Bell of Tansley). Blue Brigand was the most successful show dog of the Danum kennel. In 1962 he went Best in Show at the Blackpool Championship Show. He was also the sire of the well-known Ch. Prospect Shaggy Boy, bred and owned originally by the Prospectblue kennel and later exported to America to Caj Haakansson (Bahlambs).

Other Champions owned by the Brocklesbys were Ch. Mosscarr River Girl (Ch. Boss of Duroya – Sheba of Mosscarr), whelped December 21st 1967, and Ch. Hillgarth Blue Commander (Saffwalden Eskgrove Bushy – Pastelblue Top Notcher). The last Danum litter was whelped in 1991 out of Dican Blue Amanda Jane of Danum and sired by Ch. Lameda Zottel Best Seller, producing Danum Blue Tyson, Danum Blue Lady Madonna and Danum Blue Dolly Girl.

Like her father, Dorothy is also passed to judge on CC level, having officiated in many countries. The highlight of her judging career was awarding CCs at Crufts in 1989. She gave the Bitch CC to Ch. Drover's Jekiaterina of Krisina and the Dog CC and Best of Breed was handed to Ch. Starjanda Love on the Rocks at Timadunk.

SQUAREFOUR

Four Champions were bred by Mrs J. C. Nicol from Scotland, who owned some of the best-coated dogs of her time. Her dogs carried the desired blue coat with excellent texture to it. Mrs Nicol was also a very smart lady, who would completely change her clothes before showing her dogs. The flamboyant Norman Harrison once said, full of admiration: "Mrs Nicol was always a real lady."

She had her first Champion before the war years in 1939. This was Ch. Dinah of Woodburn (Ch. Southridge Roder – Lady Pamela), whelped on November 24th 1934. 'Woodburn' was the affix she applied to register with the English Kennel Club, as it was the name of her home in Greenock. But the Kennel Club picked the name 'Squarefour' out of the selection she had sent to them.

Squarefour was the name of her son's motorbike. In 1948 she mated her bitch Prudence of Squarefour to Shepton Brave Boy and from the resulting litter, whelped on November 9th 1948, she kept a male, 'Paul', and a female, 'Priscilla'. Ch. Paul of Squarefour became one of the most well-known and successful males bred and owned in Scotland. Priscilla of Squarefour won her first CC from the great Mrs Tireman (Pastorale) at Blackpool Championship Show, but she missed out on gaining her title. However, she proved to be an excellent brood bitch. Her record litter in 1952 of three Champions, sired by Gordale Grey Guardsman, was only surpassed by the famous Pickhurst litter which produced five Champions; Priscilla kept the Scottish record.

One of the three Champions-to-be was sold to Arthur Tilley and became Ch. Shepton Rowena of Squarefour. The other two were kept and campaigned by Mrs Nicol to become Ch. Roderick of Squarefour and Ch. Rosalinda of Squarefour. It seems astounding that Rosalinda did not finish her title until she was almost eight years old, in comparison to her litter brother who was made up just before his third birthday. Three Champions were sired by Roderick, but he became even more famous through his grandchildren and great-grandchildren, especially the 'Fernvilles'. In the meantime, Ch. Paul of Squarefour had made his mark in his new home in America, where he became a Champion, adding this to his English title.

ROLLINGSEA

The world-famous Rollingsea OES are owned by Jean Gould, who has loved the breed from childhood. She rescued a very muddy and dirty OES called Lassie, who, at two years of age, suddenly refused to bark when rounding up sheep. The owners could not afford to keep a dog who was not working, and wanted to shoot the bitch. Jean intervened, and despite the initial apprehension of her parents, once the bitch was bathed and fed and the worst 'mats' were cut from her coat, she was allowed to keep her. From then on, Lassie was a loved and well-cared for family companion, and was responsible for starting Jean's great devotion to Bobtails.

Jean's first Champion was made up in 1956. This was Ch. Linifold Mischief (Ch. Watchers Bobs Son – Shepton Lovely Souvenir), bred by Mr and Mrs J. S. Mason. Ch. Rollingsea Starlight was the first Champion who carried the affix that was to become world-famous. Starlight, who gained her title at five years of age, was sired by Greystoke Gem out of Broadwell Rosy Dawn, and bred by J. Wasley. Jean's first homebred Champion was called Ch. Rollingsea Ringleader out of Starlight, sired by Rollingsea Surfrider. Ringleader was owned by Stan and Margaret Fisher of the Wrightway affix, and he became the sire of their first homebred Champion, Ch. Wrightway Glorious Day, out of Amberford Cwoen.

A repeat mating of Ch. Rollingsea Starlight and Rollingsea Surfrider produced probably the most successful Rollingsea ever, Ch. Rollingsea Snowboots, who was whelped on May 15th 1965. Snowboots finished his career with fourteen CCs to his name. Jean lives in Cornwall, and that makes the achievement even more remarkable when the time and effort needed to campaign the dog are taken into consideration. Snowboots eventually became the sire of three important Champions: Ch. Bumblebarn Paddy's Pride (out of the famous Ch. Bumblebarn Holloways Homespun) bred by Corinne Pearce, and the two litter sisters Ch. Prospectblue Twotrees Arabella and Ch. Rollingsea Twotrees Aurora (out of Prospectblue Louise), bred by Grace Little of the Twotrees affix.

Arabella went to the Prospectblue kennel owned by Isobel Lawson, and Aurora went to live with her sire in Cornwall. In 1969 Jean mated Aurora to Rollingsea Hawthorn Pride, which resulted in, amongst others, the well-known Ch. Rollingsea Viceroy. Viceroy was almost four years old when he became a Champion. After much persuasion Jean agreed to let him go to the Bahlambs kennel

Ch. Rollingsea Katie Bay: A representative of the Rollingsea kennel.

in America. He went when he was nearly seven years of age, leaving behind his litter sister Ch. Rollingsea Venus, and his daughter, Ch. Rollingsea Christobelle, who was out of Ch. Rollingsea Venus. This full brother/sister mating produced in Christobelle an extremely typey OES bitch, with the most gorgeous coat. Over the years many kennels in the UK and abroad started their breeding programmes with Rollingsea dogs. The Loyalblue kennel in America imported many Rollingseas, my Zottel OES in Germany were originally based on Rollingsea lines, the Peekaboo kennel also in Germany, and many more in Norway, Sweden and other parts of the world have benefitted from Jean's breeding. Jean awarded CCs at Crufts 1982. Her Dog CC and BOB was Ch. Jemsue the Judge, and the Bitch CC went to Liverbobs Snow Shoes.

PROSPECTBLUE

The Prospectblue kennel, owned by Isobel Lawson, were known for their heavy-boned and thick-set Bobtails. In fact, Isobel had not been involved in dogs before she married Ernest. It was his family who had always bred OES to work on the farm. In their early days, the Lawsons had a 200-acre mixed farm, with a Friesian dairy herd, black-faced sheep and Tamworth pigs. While Ernest bred his large farm animals, Isobel reared poultry, hens, ducks, geese and turkeys.

When the time came that they needed a replacement for their working sheepdog, Shep, Isobel and Ernest contacted Miss J. Webster of the Pastelblue kennel. Not long after the first enquiry, a young bitch puppy arrived in a large hamper at the station. Her name was Pastelblue Briar Bud. Bud was a most intelligent female, with great working abilities, and she was a much-loved pet. In time she was mated to Boldwood Bardolph, and she produced ten beautiful puppies. Ernest and Isobel enjoyed rearing these pups so much that it started their passion for breeding OES. Apart from the enjoyment they both got out of it, Ernest, who was a dedicated farmer, knew that if he put his knowledge of breeding good stock into force, he could create a successful business.

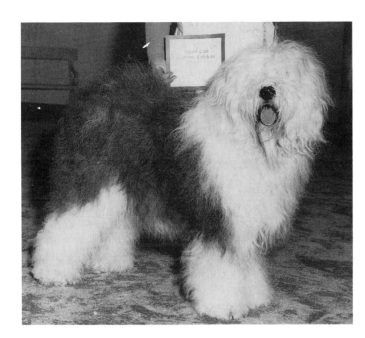

Ch. Blue Glamour Girl:
The first winning OES
for the Prospectblue
kennel.

Out of this first litter they retained a bitch called Prospect Miss Jill. Sally Blue Mist followed, and then her daughter, Blue Glamour Girl, sired by Newcote William. Glamour Girl's first show was Crufts 1963, and this was also Isobel's first show. However, both were well received, and Glamour Girl came away with a first prize card. From that moment Isobel was hooked, and an application for the registration of the affix was immediately sent to the Kennel Club. They refused her first choice 'Prospect', but suggested 'Prospectblue'. In 1964 Blue Glamour Girl gained her Champion title, and this was the real beginning of the kennel which was to become world-famous.

Glamour Girl's dam, Sally Blue Mist, was mated to Reculver Son of Carol in 1959, producing Bette Tidley's famous Ch. Bess of Coldharbour. Isobel's other brood bitch, Farleydene Peggotty (Farleydene Reculver King Pin – Burford Bunty) was mated to Prospect Shaggy Boy, and this resulted in Ch. Prospectblue Bulk, whelped in 1963. Shaggy Boy (Ch. Blue Brigand of Tansley – Glamour Girl) was whelped on May 10th 1961, and at five years old he gained his title.

A repeat mating of Prospectblue Bulk's litter produced Ch. Prospectblue Cindy and Ch. Prospectblue Rodger. Rodger and Shaggy Boy eventually went to America. Rodger lived with the famous Mona Berkowitz, who handled him to his American title, picking up Groups and Best in Shows on the way. Shaggy Boy was bought by Caj Haakansson of Bahlambs fame. He finished his Scandinavian title and the American title, and also became one of Caj's most treasured stud dogs. For Caj, who is regarded as one of the most knowledgeable OES breeders, Shaggy Boy was, as near as possible, bred to the Standard.

Fortunately both males had been used for stud before they left for America. Stan and Margaret Fisher (Wrightway) selected Rodger for Ch. Wrightways Glorious Day, and she produced Ch. Wrightway Blue Mantle, later owned by Mr Jan Morrison (Bobbingay), and Ch. Wrightway Charmaine, who was kept by the Fishers. Rodger was mated to Rollingsea Sunbeam, who produced Ch. Twotrees Break O'Day, whelped in 1967.

The Bumblebarn OES: (pictured left to right) Ch. Bumblebarn Bluejeans, Ch. Bumblebarn Holloways Homespun and Ch. Bumbelbarn Ragamuffin.

BUMBLEBARN

Corinne Pearce's first Champion was Ch. Bumblebarn Holloways Homespun (Farleydene Reculver King Pin – Holloways Penny Dreadful Homespun) bred by Mrs J. Innocent of the Holloways OES. Corinne had owned Old English Sheepdogs prior to this, but they were not made up. Merry Maid of Daleroy, President Perry, Bumblebarn's Beau Brummel, and Bumblebarn's White Bryony, all shared their home with Corinne.

The next Bumblebarn Champion was bred by Mrs A. Maidment. Ch. Bumblebarn Bluejeans (Shepton Holloways Benjamin – Faithful Tramp) was born in 1964, and she finished her Championship in 1967. Homespun, the first Champion, later became the dam of a number of well-producing offspring, including the three Champions: Ch. Bumblebarn Paddy's Pride (sired by Ch. Rollingsea Snowboots), and the litter brother and sister Ch. Bumblebarn Ragamuffin and Ch. Shaggyshire Bumblebarn Caesar (sired by Somerstreet Chieftain). To my knowledge, Caesar sired only one Champion, but this one, Ch. Pockethall New Shoes (out of Ch. Cornelia of Trimtora) was to become the new record-holder for Champion offspring – finally breaking Shepton Moonshine's record of siring ten Champion children.

Ch. Bumblebarn Bluejeans was mated to Ch. Lameda Perfect Pal, and in 1971 this resulted in the next Bumblebarn Champion, Ch. Bumblebarn New Penny. Perfect Pal shared the same breeding as Caesar (Somerstreet Chieftain – Bobbycroft Majestic Moonbeam). Ch. Bumblebarn New Penny was owned by Phil and Margaret Cooper of the Beowulf prefix.

The first Champion for one other great kennel was also the last Champion of the Bumblebarns. Ch. Bumblebarn Scramble of Pelajilo was sired by the former breed record-holder, Ch. Aberfells Georgey Porgy, out of Ch. Bumblebarn Ragamuffin.

HYAL

The Hyal Old English Sheepdog kennel were established in 1959. Betty Ince based her breeding originally on the Rollingsea bloodlines through her foundation bitch, Roycroft Penny. Penny was sired by Rollingsea Lone Ranger out of Blue Chiffon. Ch. Hyal Penny's Pride (Beaucott Blues Boy – Shepton My Fair Lady, who was sired by Shepton High and Mighty) was whelped on November 20th 1965, and she finished her title in 1969. Her five CCs came from George Leatt at Richmond 1968, Arthur Sharp, Crufts 1969, Bill Siggers, Manchester, Percy Whitaker, SKC, and George Gooch, Manchester Championship Show.

In 1970 Betty's homebred Hyal Pennys Pastime (Ch. Bevere Stalwart – Roycroft Penny) whelped a litter sired by Ch. Oakhill Peter Pan, which produced Ch. Hyal Pastime Panspal. Panspal gained her first CC at Richmond 1971 under Percy Whitaker, her second at Welks under Norman Harrison, and her qualifying third at Blackpool under Mrs A. Woodiwiss; No. 4 came from Jean Gould at Leeds, and CC No. 5 was awarded by W. E. Foster at Richmond.

BEAUCOTT BLUE
The Beaucott Blue kennel was originally owned by Mrs J. M. Woodford and her daughter, Gwen Mogford. After her mother's death, Gwen carried on with the kennel on her own. There had always been dogs of various breeds in Gwen's life, but it was not until after the war that the first OES took residence in the Beaucott kennel. This first OES came from the Shepton kennel and was called Shepton My Fair Lady.

My Fair Lady became a good show girl, but she proved to be an even better brood bitch. Mated to Shepton High and Mighty, she produced the legendary Beaucott Blue Boy. Blue Boy did not gain his title, but there are not many present-day pedigrees which do not include his name. His name is in the pedigrees of my two joint breed record-holders, Ch. Zottel's Miss Marple of Lameda, and Ch. Lameda Zottel's Flamboyant in the sixth and seventh generations.

Blue Boy was a stallion type male, with a lovely head and neck – a truly beautiful dog. His picture is on the front cover of Gwen Mogford's most interesting OES book *My Inheritance*, showing the ten-month-old Blue Boy. Gwen now concentrates on judging OES and many other breeds in the Working Group. 1985 saw her judge OES at Crufts, where she awarded CC and BOB to Ch. Simberdale Henry Higgins, and the bitch CC (which was a first) to Trushayp Effervescence at Greyfell, later to become a Champion.

TYNYCOED
Joan Real first got involved with OES through her friendship with Arthur Baker of the Bluemark affix. One of his bitches, Pastelblue Lady Tops, bred by Mrs J. Webster, was greatly admired by Joan, and when she had her first litter, Joan and her husband Walter purchased a male puppy, hoping to show him. Unfortunately, he did not like other dogs, and he did not turn out to be show quality. However, he was a much-loved pet and lived to the good age of eleven and a half years.

After he had gone, Joan decided that her next dogs must come from the Beckington and the Wenallt kennels. Beckington Blue Rhapsody (Shepton Pal – Beckington Lady Luck) and Wenallt Masked Man (Beaucott Blues Boy – Wenallt Sit Down Mary) eventually became the parents of the first Tynycoed litter. Meanwhile, a bitch from the Welsh Beaucott Blue kennel called Beaucott Busy Lizzie (Prospectblue Herdsman – Shepton My Fair Lady) had also taken residence in the Tynycoed home.

Out of the first Tynycoed litter, whelped on January 1st 1970, Joan and Walter kept Tynycoed Ty Gwyn, a dog puppy, who was made up in 1972, becoming the Top OES the same year. Ty Gwyn was later sold to America, finishing his US title and the Canadian title for good measure. While Ty Gwyn was enjoying his career in the show ring, his sister, Merch Dda, became an important brood bitch for the Tynycoed kennel. She was mated to Ch. Pendlefold Prince Hal (the former breed

Eng. Can. Am. Ch. Tynycoed Caradog ap Tegwch: A Best in Show winner and sire of six Champions before being exported to America.

Pearce.

record-holder) and produced Ch. Tynycoed Pen-y-Bryn of Southview for Roy and Maureen Cowie (Southview). When Busy Lizzie was old enough to have puppies, she was mated to Ch. Dorian Blue Shepherd Boy (Gwelelog Bess's Nos-Dda – Blue Rapture), bred by Mrs Barbara Cousins. Having bred one Top OES in 1972, this litter now produced the Top OES for 1976, Ch. Tynycoed Merch Lisi Fisi. At almost five years of age, Lisi Tisi was mated to a Pen-y-Bryn brother, Tynycoed Coedwig Dean. This litter included the famous Tynycoed Un Prydferch, whelped on November 23rd 1978, who became a Champion in 1981. Un Prydferh (Beauty) was not shown as widely as the other Tynycoed OES, due to Walter's death. Joan decided to have a litter from her, and she felt that there was only one male she wanted to use. This was the well-known Ch. Jedforest Don Carlos (Ch. Bartines Most Happy Fella of Jenards – Shaggyshire Little Mo).

Unfortunately, Beauty whelped only two pups. One of them was born dead, and the other one, a male puppy was to become the last Tynycoed Champion. However, Ch. Tynycoed Caradog ap Tegwch ('Benny', as he was lovingly called) did Joan proud. In 1986 he became Top OES, Top in the Working Group, and to top all that, he made Joan Top Breeder of that year. As a puppy he had been given to Joan's dear friend, Christine Cherrington, who eventually let Benny go to America. Thankfully, he had already been widely used at stud and produced six Champions.

They were: Ch. Greyfell Storm Warning (out of Ch. Trushayp Effervescence at Greyfell), bred by Mr and Mrs Sculthorp and owned by Mr and Mrs J. Simmonds – he was Top OES male in 1990; Ch. Southview Celebrity Guest (out of Ch. Southview Celebrity Miss), bred and owned by the Southview kennel – 'Wilma' achieved the Top OES for 1990 award; Ch. Soundwell Lisi Fisi (out of Tynycoed Cadi) bred and owned by Mrs D. Walker of the Soundwell affix; Ch. Achardia Benny's Junior (out of Tarth Y Wawr of Soundwell), bred and owned by Mrs Haynes; Ch. Southview Juliet Bravo (litter sister to Celebrity Guest), owned by Mrs C. Guest; and Ch. Wenallt What's Wanted (out of Wenallt Bens Girl), bred and owned by Mrs P. Jones of the Wenallt affix.

The first litter of Wenallt Old English Sheepdogs, whelped in 1966.

WENALLT

Leading the life of a farmer's wife, 'Topsy' Jones has been involved with OES since the mid-forties. She bred her first litter in 1966. Three years later Arabella of the Embages (Ch. Reculver Christopher Robin – Bess of the Embages) whelped a litter sired by Wenallt Farmers Boy. This litter included Mrs Jones's most successful show dog, Ch. Wenallt Trooper. Trooper's sire, Farmers Boy, was sired by Prospectblue Herdsman out of Somerstreet Snowy, combining most of the early influential dogs in his pedigree.

Looking back, Topsy considers Trooper to have been the most influential OES for her breeding, as he passed on his large head and excellent temperament. Bred back to his dam, he produced Wenallt Magnolia, who when mated to Copenacre Billy the Kid of Sallowood (Brackens Brumus out of Copenacre Grand Attraction – mostly Shepton and Rollingsea lines) whelped a litter of pups on August 21st 1979, which included Ch. Wenallt Western Star. Western Star was later, as a seven-year-old, sent to Australia, where he produced good stock for his new owners, Mr and Mrs Moore. Ch. Wenallt Trooper was mated to Twotrees Esmeralda (Twotrees Brandy Snap – Prospectblue Louise), bred by Grace Little of the Twotrees affix, and she produced Ch. Wenallt Emerald, owned and shown by Mr and Mrs Underwood of the Krisina affix.

Other Wenallt Champions were: Ch. Wenallt Andrew (Ch. Oakhill Peter Pan – Wenallt Wensday), Ch. Wenallt Wiley Star, whelped on June 21st 1984 and made up in 1988, Wiley Star was sired by Western Star out of Wenallt Ben's Girl, and her pedigree includes all the former Wenallt Champions. Ben's Girl mated to the Top OES of 1986, Ch. Tynycoed Caradog ap Tegwch, produced the latest Wenallt Champion, Ch. Wenallt What's Wanted, who was made up in 1989. His three CCs come from David Bloomfield (Snowserf), Pat Guest (Lamacres), and Carol Sinclair-Day (Boundalong), at the National Working Breeds, the East of England, and the Leicester Championship Shows respectively. At the National Working Breeds he also went on to Reserve BIS.

WRIGHTWAY
The Wrightway kennel, owned by Stan and Margaret Fisher, was the home of three Champions, two of them homebred. Ch. Rollingsea Ringleader was born on February 9th 1960 (Rollingsea Surfrider – Rollingsea Starlight). Ch. Wrightway Glorious Day was sired by Ch. Rollingsea Ringleader out Amberford Cwoen. Cwoen was by Amberford Rough & Ready (Watchers lines) out of Beanville Miss Bo Peep (by Ch. Roderick of Squarefour). Ch. Wrightway Blue Mantle was bred out of Glorious Day, sired by Eng. & Am. Ch. Prospectblue Rodger. Blue Mantle's litter sister, Ch. Wrightway Charmaine stayed with the Fishers and her Champion sire and dam.
The Fishers have always shared their interest in Bobtails, although it is only Stan who is interested in judging the breed. Apart from several Championship Shows, Stan has officiated in Australia and at Crufts 1981, where he gave the bitch CC to Ch. Pelajilo Mistletoe and the dog CC and BOB to Ch. Branduin Cotton Picker.

TWOTREES
Grace Little's Twotrees Old English Sheepdogs were based on Prospectblue and Rollingsea lines. The first homebred Champions were born on November 23rd 1966 out of Prospectblue Louise, who was a daughter of the great Eng. Am. Scan. Ch. Prospect Shaggy Boy and Pastelblue Lady Jane. The litter was sired by Jean Gould's Ch. Rollingsea Snowboots (Rollingsea Surfrider – Ch. Rollingsea Starlight). The litter produced two Champion bitches, Ch. Prospectblue Twotrees Arabella and Ch. Rollingsea Twotrees Aurora. Arabella went to Isobel Lawson (Prospectblue), Aurora went to her sire's home in Cornwall.
Am. Eng. Ch. Prospectblue Rodger (Int. Ch. Prospect Shaggy Boy – Farleydene Peggotty) and Rollingsea Sunbeam (Rollingsea Surfrider – Rollingsea Starlight) were the parents of a litter whelped on May 14th 1967. This litter included Ch. Twotrees Break O'Day, owned by James Lynn. Grace Little's next Champion was bred by Ann Davis (Loakespark) and sired by Somerstreet Chieftain out of out of Fernville Debutante. Twotrees Loakespark Tosca was whelped on August 19th 1968 and gained her crown in 1973.
Other well-known dogs in the Twotrees household include: Bumblebarn Jolly Waggoner (Nicefella of Danehurst – Merry Maid of Dalcroy), Twotrees Euripides (Twotrees Brandy Snap – Prospectblue Louise), Twotrees Iphigenia (Twotrees Euripides – Twotrees Aphrodite), and in the more recent past Longdorhams Melisande of Twotrees (Ch. Dorianblue Shepherd Boy – Wenallt Wood Nymph of Longdorham), bred by Mrs and Miss Duffin.

THE GOLDEN YEARS
The late sixties to the late seventies was undoubtedly the prime time for our lovely breed in the UK. There were so many excellent breeders producing one excellent specimen after another, and watching Open dog and Open bitch classes at shows made you feel proud to be able to witness great dogs in the ring. In fact, judges had to split hairs in order to place them in order of merit. In both sexes there were usually at least a handful of dogs worthy of the CC, and a judge had to go on preference, and not solely on merit. It would be virtually impossible to mention all the excellent

dogs that graced this wonderful era. However, I will attempt to highlight those who have had a major impact on the breed in general, and those who are still important in the breed today.

BARNOLBY

The Barnolby affix, owned by Ronnie and Rita Ashcroft, is probably one of the most influential kennels at the present time. Rita was brought up with Old English Sheepdogs, as her father liked to have them on the farm. Some litters were bred, but mostly for working purposes.

After Rita and Ronnie got married they purchased their first bitch, named Shepton Tessa, from the famous Shepton kennel. She whelped the first Barnolby litter in August 1966, sired by a dog whose pedigree carried a lot of the Reculver breeding. His name was Crawford Shepherd. Their first show bitch was Miss Bruin of Halsall, bought in from the famous Halsall kennel, which was owned by Mrs Sharman.

Even though Rita recognised the show potential in this young pup, she was not convinced until she went to buy pig food from someone who happened to be a terrier judge. He managed to get Ronnie enthusiastic about showing the six-month-old Miss Bruin. She was a beautiful, feminine and compact bitch with an excellent coat, but her show career was overshadowed by a later addition to the Barnolby kennel.

The famous Ch. Oakhill Peter Pan arrived in the house at four months of age. Rita and Ronnie had seen him as a puppy when they went to see a litter sired by Ch. Bevere Proud Monarch (another great dog of his time) out of Beth of Oakhill. Beth was similar in type to Miss Bruin, which explains the interest in this litter. According to Rita, Peter Pan looked awful as a pup. Everything was in the right place, but the overall picture was such that only a breed expert could spot the excellent type. Miss Bruin was eventually mated to Proud Monarch's brother, Bevere Stalwart. Their daughter, Barnolby Eastertide, was later put to Peter Pan, starting off the successful line breeding of this kennel. The result of this mating was Ch. Barnolby Mr Barrymore.

Miss Bruin certainly made her mark on the breed. In litters sired by Peter Pan she produced Barnolby Cinderella (the dam of Ch. Cinderwood by Jupiter of Craigsea) and Ch. Snowserf Lancer of Barnolby. In their third litter, these two outstanding animals produced one of my most favourite bitches, Ch. Barnolby Wendy Bruin. Unfortunately, I was not lucky enough to see her in the flesh, but if she was only half as nice as her photographs – and her reputation – she must have been gorgeous. Like her mother, she proved to be a dominant brood bitch. In her litter with Ch. Aberfells Georgey Porgy (the former breed record-holder), she produced Ch. Barnolby White Bear, who is behind all the present Barnolbys. After this litter, Wendy Bruin was very ill, and so she was not mated again as Rita and Ronnie did not want to risk losing her.

The years 1971 and 1972 saw the addition of Barnolby Midwinter and Ginnsdale Stargazer Blue of Barnolby (later to become a Champion). Midwinter was bought to line-breed to Proud Monarch's stock (he was a grandson), but Stargazer was an outcross – both Rita and Ronnie felt that new blood was needed. Looking at his pedigree, you can see Peter Pan's dam's brother, only a few generations back, tying up with the Barnolby stock, but he was of the same type as all Barnolbys and therefore the right choice for outcross breeding.

These two new dogs proved to be excellent choices for the kennel. Midwinter, put to a daughter of Peter Pan and Miss Bruin, produced Ch. Sincerity of Barnolby, who, together with Stargazer, produced Ch. Barnolby Presentation of Gojolega and several other winners. In 1981 Weatherproof of Barnolby was born. He was out of Janmay of Kenstaff by Barnolby Lord Shavley (Stargazer – Sincerity of Barnolby). Weatherproof was bred by Mrs Clare of the Janclares affix, who kindly allowed the Ashcrofts to register the pup themselves. He was bought to maintain type but reduce

Ronnie and Rita Ashcroft pictured with five of their Champions. Back row (left to right): Ch. Oakhill Peter Pan and his son Ch. Barnolby Mr Barrymore. Front row (left to right): Ch. Sincerity of Barnolby, Ch. Barnolby Wendy Bruin and Ch. Ginnsdale Stargazer Blue of Barnolby.

size a little. The size was coming from Sincerity, who herself was slightly bigger than Rita's ideal.

Weatherproof was mated to Ch. Barnolby Wedding Bells (Stargazer – White Bear) in 1982 and produced the famous Ch. Barnolby Troubleshooter at Oldoak (a Group and BIS winner). This dog, one of the best type males you could want, is behind many Champions in the UK and overseas. The Barnolby story could go on and on, but limited space leaves just two more important facts to mention. Two former CC breed record holders were sired by the Ashcrofts' dogs. Peter Pan was the father of the great Ch. Pendlefold Prince Hal, and Barnolby Midwinter sired the glamorous Ch. Aberfells Georgey Porgy.

FERNVILLE

When Norman Harrison the owner/breeder of the world-famous Fernville OES started showing Bobtails, he was no newcomer to dogs or dog shows. He had started by owning a Chow Chow as a child, and then in his teens he exhibited West Highland White Terriers. Neither of these two breeds are similar to Old English Sheepdogs, but the experience trained Norman in the art of knowing a good dog. It was at the Leeds Championship Show, 1957, that he first exhibited an OES. The breed specialist, Mary Sheffield (Hillgarth OES), was officiating, and Norman was pipped at the post by the famous Mabel Gibson with her homebred bitch, Ch. Beckington Aristocrat. The older and established breeders all encouraged Norman to carry on with the "good work".

Norman's first OES, Fernville Fascination, was the pick of litter, with all the other puppies going to Florence Tilley of the Shepton OES. Fascination was born in 1956, carrying famous bloodlines such as Shepton, Pastelblue and Pickhurst in her pedigree. By the time Norman went to his next show, Aristocrat had been sold to the USA, and the career of one of the most successful breeder/exhibitors of our time had started. In 1958 Fascination produced her first litter of twelve puppies (eleven reared), sired by the famous Ch. Roderick of Squarefour. The decision to use this most beautiful male proved to be correct, as the puppies combined the type and quality of the

Ch. Fernville Special Style of Trushayp: Best in Show winner.

Pastelblues with the bone and substance of the Sheptons, and the rare beautiful jackets, both in colour and texture, of the Squarefours. From this first Fernville OES litter, Norman kept Fernville Fiona, who later became the dam of the famous Ch. Beckington Fernville Flamingo and Fernville Flora. Flora later produced the top OES in 1963, the history-making Ch. Fernville Fantasy. Fantasy won the triple at Crufts, taking the CC in 1963, 1964, and 1965. Other well-known Fernvilles of that period were Ch. Fernville Flanagan, Swedish Ch. Fernville Fair Friday, Int. Ch. Fernville Fine Future, Am. Ch. Fernville Felicity, Am. Ch. Fernville Florence and Am. Ch. Fernville Juliet. By 1964 Norman's affix was known worldwide and many important kennels in England and abroad decided to add Fernville blood into their breeding programmes.

However, the greatest star was still to come. This was Ch. Fernville Lord Digby (a grandson of Ch. Fernville Fernando), who won his first CC at eleven months of age and gained his title in nine shows. In October 1971, at the age of twelve months, Digby won the JCJ Dulux competition beating an entry of 450 Old English Sheepdogs. Digby the Dulux dog became a household name, and the breed reached unprecedented heights of popularity. He also proved his quality as an outstanding sire, producing top winners such as: Ch. Fernville Special Style of Trushayp, Ch. Bartines Most Happy Fella of Jenards, Aust. Ch. Fernville Gay Future and Int. Ch. Fernville Forever Free. These males are also behind many of the top-winning dogs today, ensuring that even though Norman Harrison himself does not breed any more, the Fernville affix is not forgotten.

POCKETHALL

Pockethall is the name of a field in Norwich belonging to Ray and Ruth Wilkinson, and it is also the affix for their world-famous Old English Sheepdogs. Ruth's mother, who showed and bred Sheepdogs when Ruth was a child, started Ruth's lifelong passion for our lovely breed. When Ray and Ruth were married, their first Bobtail was Roncote Blue Cloud. He was shown for quite a while, winning one CC and three Reserve CCs. When he was ten months old, Cornelia of Trimtora was acquired. She was to become a Champion, and also the foundation bitch of one of the most

Ch. Cornelia of Trimtora: The foundation bitch for the famous Pockethall kennel.

Pearce.

successful kennel in the last twenty years. 'Lyn' was sired by Fairacres Rollalong out of Tina of Trimtora. During her show career she not only amassed nine CCs and five Reserve CCs, but also proved to be an excellent brood bitch. For her first litter she was mated to the well-known Ch. Bumblebarn Caesar of Shaggyshire producing Ray and Ruth's first homebred Champion, the famous Ch. Pockethall New Shoes. 'Billy', a superb show dog with nine CCs and ten Reserve CCs, was even more successful as a producer. Siring almost sixty litters, he became Top Stud Dog for all breeds in 1982 and the father of eighteen UK Champions, plus several Champions abroad.

For Lyn's next litters she was mated to Ch. Pendlefold Prince Hal, and produced three more Pockethall Champions: Ch. Pockethall Shoeshine of Southview, Ch. Pockethall Silver Shoes, and Ch. Pockethall Blue Cloud. Blue Cloud, a top-winning male of his time, and one of Ruth's all-time favourites, ended his show career with eighteen CCs and nineteen Reserve CCs.

Later on, Ch. Pockethall Silver Shoes was mated to her half-brother, Ch. Pockethall New Shoes, and she produced Ch. Pockethall Ballet Shoes of Brinkley, Ch. Pockethall Shoemaker of Oakfarm, Ch. Pockethall Silver Lady of Kildon, and Ch. Pockethall Silver Charm. Ballet Shoes proved to be a valuable brood bitch for the Brinkley kennel, Shoemaker was a useful sire for the Oakfarm affix, and Silver Charm became the mother of Ch. Pockethall I'Mashootoo, sired by Ch. Trushayp Eckythump of Jenards. I'Mashootoo was only shown for a very short time due to the Wilkinsons' other personal commitments, but he won six CCs, and in his short life he sired two top winning Bobtails: Ch. Shimorill This Is It (out of Ch. Zottel's Moonlight Serenade of Lameda), top-winning OES bitch in 1992, and Ch. Lamedazottel Flamboyant (out of Ch. Zottel's Miss Marple of Lameda), the Top Dog of All Breeds in 1991 and 1992, and the joint breed record holder together with his mother. Many kennels in the UK and abroad owe a lot of their success to the Pockethall stock – so much so that wherever you go the 'Pockethall coat' is an expression that everyone knows, and something that everyone aims for.

SOUTHVIEW

The story of one of the most successful kennels in England during the past twenty years started rather unexpectedly. Roy and Maureen Cowie were just married and were farming cattle, and their

Ch. Southview Celebrity Guest: Top CC winning OES in 1990.

Alan V. Walker.

local vet recommended they should have an OES to work on the farm. As the vet was also a friend, Roy and Maureen trusted his advice and Maureen had a look in the farm magazine, *Farmers Weekly.* Under Pets For Sales she found an advert from a couple from Plumstead, whose son had died in a plane crash, and they were now looking for a new home for his boisterous six-month-old OES bitch.

Roy agreed to meet them at Euston railway station, with the proviso that if he liked the bitch, he would take her home. Myfanwyts Charm, known as 'Beth' (later changed to 'Snoopy') proved to be an excellent choice for a working farm dog, as she instinctively knew how to work cattle.

Later, Roy and Maureen decided to breed from her, and Maureen happened to see in the *Dog World Annual* that Ch. Pendlefold Prince Hal had just gained his Champion title. This outstanding male appealed so much to Roy and Maureen that they phoned Mr and Mrs Riddiough and asked if they could bring their bitch for a mating. The result of this mating was eight dogs and one bitch – the first Southview litter. From this first meeting the two couples became very close friends. Brenda Riddiough got her new friends interested in showing, and the real Southview story started.

The next step was to acquire a show puppy, and Joan Real of the well-known Tynycoed affix was recommended. This resulted in a new addition to the farm – Tynycoed Pen-y-Bryn of Southview. Pen-y-Bryn was a Prince Hal son out of Tynycoed Mercha Dda. Not many people are lucky enough to pick their show dog and then make it to the top, but with the Riddioughs' help and encouragement, Tynycoed Pen-y-Bryn of Southview became a Champion, along with Ch. Arlil's Cilla of Southview, a bitch that Roy was showing at the same time.

Cilla had been acquired for Roy to show, after their friend the vet had seen the litter at Dorothy White's Arlils kennel. Cilla was really the kennel's foundation bitch, as she started the impressive line of twenty-four Southview Champions. She is the dam of the well-known dogs: Ch. Southview Artful Dodger, Ch. Southview Eliza Doolittle, Irish Ch. Southview Aristocrat (a BIS winning OES in Ireland), and Ch. Southview Saracen of Nytimber. Two years after acquiring Cilla and Pen-y-Bryn, the Cowies were well and truly hooked on the show-going game. Their bitch, Ch. Pockethall

Shoeshine Southview became the mother of four more Champions carrying the Southview affix: Ch. Southview Crackerjack, Ch. Southview Canterbury Belle of Macopa, Spanish Ch. Southview Colonel Boogey, and Ch. Southview Snowshoes.

Many more Southview Champions have followed – too many to mention them all, but there are some significant dogs who carried on the line. When Ch. Southview Society Miss was bred to Ch. Southview Fly By Night, the result was Ch. Southview Celebrity Miss. When she was later mated to Am. Eng. Ch. Tynycoed Caradog ap Tegwch, she produced the top CC winning OES for 1990, Ch. Southview Celebrity Guest. Knowing Roy and Maureen's dedication, the Southview story will not stop here, and we can expect many more important dogs to come from this kennel.

LAMEDA

At the Lameda kennel, owned by Stuart Mallard and John Smith, many attempts had been made to own a good show dog. Stuart had been promised the pick of the litter out of a bitch called Shepton Gay Lady (Rusherman – Gittis Minx). 'Folly' was the litter sister to John Featherstone's Ch. Shepton Pick of the Bunch. Then Stuart received a phone call informing him that the bitch was not in whelp, but if he was interested he could purchase the bitch. Stuart agreed, and, together with a friend, went to pick up Shepton Gay Lady. She was in such a state that neither Stuart nor his friend Barry dared to let John see her before she had a bath and a good groom. In the process of doing this, Stuart and Barry discovered that Folly *was* in whelp, and soon the first eight OES puppies were born in the Lameda kennel. However, neither John nor Stuart felt that they were good enough to show, because of their brown coats.

Several other OES came to the kennel with various faults, which excluded them from being show quality dogs. However, perseverance eventually paid off, and John and Stuart were able to buy a bitch bred by Keith Rallison out of Amanda Faithful Lady, sired by Bruce Faithful Master. She was born on October 18th 1967 and registered by Stuart and John with the illustrious name Lameda Pandora Blossom. Pandy was the show girl John and Stuart always wanted, and she finished her Champion title in 1972 with several CCs to her name, and she was the top-winning bitch in the same year. Having been lucky with Pandy, Stuart now trusted his judgment when he decided to buy another puppy. This time the pup was bred by Mr T. Petitt, sired by the well-known Ch. Wrightway Blue Mantle out of Lena of Lingar. The bitch puppy, who was named Lameda Lucy Locket, was later to become a top-winning Champion, and one of John's favourite pets. The highlight in Lucy's career was Crufts in 1973 when she won the Bitch CC and BOB under Mabel Gibson (Beckington).

At the same show Lucy's older kennel-mate, Lameda Perfect Pal (Somerstreet Chieftain – Bobbycroft Majestic Moonbeam) won the Reserve Dog CC. Perfect Pal ('Guy') had been very successful as a youngster, but due to a serious kidney infection he had lost all his coat. When he was ready to come back, he took the show ring by storm. He confirmed his quality by winning his third CC and BOB under the famous Catherine Sutton at LKA in 1974, while his young daughter, Ch. Bumblebarn New Penny (out of Ch. Bumblebarn Blue Jeans) took the bitch CC. Guy was in absolute top form, impressing the Working Group judge Mrs H.N. Warner Hill and the Best in Show judge Mrs A. Riggs (USA) alike. By the end of the show he had beaten several thousand dogs, taking home some of the most beautiful perpetual BIS trophies in the country.

Guy's litter brother, Lameda Mr Kipp, did not have the same show personality as Guy. However, he proved himself by siring a litter in 1972 to Andrews Delight (by Ch. Wrightway Blue Mantle) which produced Ch. Lameda Midnight Rebel. While Guy had been at home re-growing his coat, Stuart had been able to concentrate on the homebred Pearly Princess. 'Julie' was sired by the

Ch. Lameda Pandora Blossom: A top quality showgirl.

famous Ch. Pendlefold Prince Hal out of Lameda Pearly Queen. Like her sire, she was very showy, and she gained her title in 1973. At Crufts 1974, under Mary Bloor (Fairacres), she took the Bitch CC, topped by the Dog CC winner, Ch. Lomax of Lingar, for BOB.

Due to personal circumstances, it took seven years for another OES from the Lameda kennels to be made up. Ch. Lameda Pollyanna was almost four years old when she gained her title. She had been sold as a puppy, but bought back after John and his new partner, Gary Carter, recognised her show potential. 'Rosie' was bred by John and Gary out of Rosie Lee of Lameda, sired by their own Brinkley's Ring Lord of Lameda.

John was passed for CCs in OES in 1975, and since then he has been judging regularly including Crufts 1992, where he gave the Dog CC to Ch. Pick of the Pack of the Viewpoint (Ch. Oldoak Crackshot at Malcro – Dervance Dinky Doo) and the Bitch CC and BOB to Ch. Bellablue Nikita (Ch. Bellablue Prince Charming – Raggletaggle Rag Doll).

While John Smith carried on breeding in England under the Lameda affix, Stuart Mallard moved to Holland, where he bred several successful OES and dogs of various other breeds under the Tuckles affix. Stuart has been passed for CCs in OES in 1974 and, over the years, for several other breeds in the Working, Utility and Toy Group. He judged Old English Sheepdogs at Crufts in 1993, giving a first CC to Hollyhams Little Rascal (Ch. Kalaju Resident Rascal – Hollyham Millie Molly Mandy) and a fifty-first CC and BOB to Ch. Lamedazottel Flamboyant (Ch. Pockethall I'Mashootoo – Ch. Zottel's Miss Marple of Lameda).

LAMACRES
Pat and Vic Guest purchased their first OES, Fairacres Bobbin, in 1955, who was followed later by Fairacres Blue Belle (Ch. Bevere Proud Monarch – Fairacres Shepherdess), who became Vic and Pat's foundation bitch. The first litter, which also produced the first Lamacres Champion, was bred in 1972. Lamacres Leading Lady was exported to Norway where she gained her Champion title. Then in 1976 Blue Belle whelped a litter, sired by Ch. Pockethall New Shoes. One of the puppies

*Ch. Lamacres
Melans Boy Blue:
Top-winning male
OES in 1987 and
1988, winner of
twenty-two CCs.*

Pearce.

went to Mary Bloor (Blue Belle's breeder) and was registered with the Fairacres affix. Melody of
Fairacres gained her title in 1978.

The next Lamacres Champion, Ch. Lady Milly of Lamacres (Ch. Snowserf Lancer of Barnolby –
Venator Elixir), was bred by Mrs P. Birkett, and she finished her title with a bang in 1979 by
winning the Working Group at the Welsh Kennel Club Show, as well as her crowning third CC.
Champion number four was Ch. Lamacres Super Girl. She was sired by Ch. Pockethall New Shoes
out of Kelly Winter Wonder (Fernville Playboy – Eleventowns Azure). Whelped on February 11th
1976, Super Girl was four years old when she was made up. She did not just excel in the show
ring, but also as a brood bitch. In her litter to Ch. Tumbletop Trademark of Denimblue, whelped
on March 15th 1981, she produced the litter brother and sister Champions, Ch. Lamacres Laura
and Ch. Lamacres Lancelot. Laura's and Lancelot's pedigree was closely line-bred back to Ch.
Bumblebarn Holloway's Homespun, who is behind Super Girl's sire, New Shoes, and also several
times behind Tumbletop Trademark.

They took the double for their first CCs at Paignton Championship Show in 1983, under Sally
Penney Duffin (Londorhams). Laura went on to take seven more CCs in 1983, and she ended her
career with a total of thirteen CCs and top-winning female in 1984. Ch. Pockethall New Shoes is
also the sire of another brother/sister Champion team, Ch. Lamacres Ben and Ch. Lamacres
Melody Shoes (out of Fairacres Midsummer Melody).

In 1983 Super Girl whelped another litter, this time to the Cowies' Ch. Southview Crackerjack,
who was sired by Ch. Cinderwood Great Gatsby of Bartine (who was out of Prince Hal's litter
sister, Ch. Pendlefold Sweet Charity of Cinderwood) out of Ch. Pockethall Shoe Shine of
Southview (a Prince Hal daughter). This very well thought-out litter produced Ch. Lamacres
Lucinda. However, the most successful Lamacres Champion was still to come. This was Ch.
Lamacres Melans Boy Blue (Ch. Lamacres Lancelot – Ch. Lamacres Melody Shoes). 'Digby'
amassed a total of twenty-two CCs, he was top-winning male in 1987 and 1988, and took the CC
under Jean Borland (Jeabor) at Crufts in 1988. Digby was handled to most of his wins by Sue
Goddard (Oakfarm).

A more recently campaigned Lamacres bitch is Ch. Lamacres Golly Miss Molly (Bowson of
Lamacres – Pockethall Shady Lady).

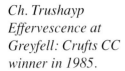

*Ch. Trushayp
Effervescence at
Greyfell: Crufts CC
winner in 1985.*

Pearce.

TRUSHAYP

Owned by Martin and Lynette Lewis, the Trushayp kennel was based on Fernville lines and was one of the most successful kennels during the mid-seventies to the mid-eighties. Lynette and Martin's first Champion was bred by Norman Harrison sired by the famous Dulux dog Ch. Fernville Lord Digby out of Fernville Gypsy Madonna. Ch. Fernville Special Style of Trushayp was a dog to be proud of. A multi-Group and Supreme Best in Show winner, 'Dooley' had the charisma a good dog needs to make him special. He was only two years old when he went Best in Show at Windsor 1975 (under the late Lilly Turner), and LKA 1975 (under judge L.C. James). Stuart Mallard (Tuckles), the breed judge of the day, wrote about him: "a splendid specimen and a credit to our breed, grand head, super reach of neck which is correctly arched, best lay of shoulders here today, very sound in front, good bone, enough brisket, excellent top line, beautiful broad back and with correct bend of stifle and well let down hocks, very best of coats, both in colour and texture, never gave up showing, full of sparkle. At two years of age must have a fantastic future as will mature even further."

Dooley went on to prove himself at stud. His litters to three different bitches, Lady Amber, Trushayp Premonition of Payleblue, and Snowfax Abby Amber, produced the following Champions: Ch. Trushayp Special Edition (out of Lady Amber), winner of 7 CCs, 8 Reserve CCs, 1 Working Group, bred by Lynette and Martin, Ch. Something Special of Trushayp (out of Trushayp Premonition of Payleblue), winner of 4 CCs, 13 Reserve CCs, bred by Mr and Mrs Pinder, and Ch. Abbyfax Jungle Rock at Trushayp, bred by Mr R. Kirby. Jungle Rock was jointly owned by Lynette and her mother, Gwen Hayes, who handled him to his Working Group win at the SKC Show in 1981. The breed judge was Jean Borland (Jeabor). What a splendid day that must have been, as he had also received his third CC on the day! His first CC had come from Stuart Mallard (Tuckles) and the second was awarded at the Border Union Show in 1981, under Reginald Gadsden.

In a later litter, the homebred Special Edition sired Sweet Charlotte of Trushayp. She was out of Fernville Tudor Rose (Ch. Fernville Lord Digby out of Fernville Gypsy Madonna – the same breeding as Special Style). Sweet Charlotte never finished her Championship, as she did not like showing and therefore lacked that little extra sparkle. However, she was a beautifully made bitch and produced a lovely litter to Ch. Bartimes Most Happy Fella of Jenards (Ch. Fernville Lord Digby – Bartimes Precious Holly). Two dogs and one bitch finished their Champion titles: Ch. Trushayp Eckythump of Jenards, Ch. Trushayp El Cid and Ch. Trushayp Effervescence at Greyfell. At Crufts in 1985, under Gwen Mogford, Effervescence took the bitch CC, while Ch. Simberdale Henry Higgins gained the dog CC and BOB. When eventually bred to Ch. Tynycoed Caradog ap Tegwch, she produced the top-winning male, Ch. Greyfell Storm Warning. Eckythump was mated to Ch. Pockethall Silver Charm, which resulted, in 1987, in Ch. Pockethall I'Mashootoo.

Due to personal reasons, the affix does not exist anymore, and Lynette breeds now under the Nushayp affix with equally good results. Her bitch, Jenards Gaze Atmee for Nushayp (Eckythump – Searwell What Am I Gonna Do of Jenards), winner of two CCs and three Reserve CCs, was bred to Ch. Greyfell Storm Warning, and this resulted in Ch. Nushayp Stormy Weather of Paintaway, owned by Mavis Chapman.

OLDOAK

The successful Oldoak kennel is owned by Della Oakes. Della's first Champion, Ch. Winstonholme Memory's of Oldoak, was whelped on August 17th 1974, sired by the great Ch. Lomax of Lingar (Ch. Barnolby Mr. Barrymore – Blue Mist of Ramnee) out of Drakeshead Redscare Lady Jayne. 'Sarah' was bred by Norma Fielding-Dower, the owner of Lomax. She was Lomax's last daughter, and therefore of extra-special brood potential. When bred to her half-brother, Alan and Elaine Horner's Ch. Cinderwood By Jupiter of Craigsea (a Lomax son out of Barnolby Cinderella), she produced Oldoak Enchanting Memories.

In 1982 'Sarah' and 'Emily' were joined by Barnolby Troubleshooter at Oldoak. 'Trent' was to become Della's most successful show dog and one of the most prepotent sires in England and abroad. He was Best in Show at Paignton Championship Show in 1985, under Catherine Sutton (Craigsea). Trent was bred by Ron and Rita Ashcroft. He was sired by Weatherproof of Barnolby out of Ch. Barnolby Wedding Bells, which made his pedigree closely line-bred back to the Ashcrofts' Ch. Ginnsdale Stargazer Blue of Barnolby, and also back to their Ch. Oakhill Peter Pan. Looking at Emily's (Enchanting Memories) pedigree, Peter Pan figures once in her third generation back, and three times in the fifth generation. Inevitably, the combination of both Emily and Trent had to be extra special, and so it turned out to be. Emily's litter by Trent in 1983 produced Della's dual CC-winning Oldoak Tempting Memory, and Barrie Croft's Ch. Oldoak Crackshot at Malcro. Crackshot ('Patrick') swept the board, winning five CCs in 1986, and the Working Group at SKC, under Harry Jordan.

A repeat mating in 1984 produced the litter brother/sister team which put the Oldoak kennel on the map in New Zealand – Grand Ch. Oldoak Troublemaker and NZ Ch. Oldoak Enchanting Trouble. More recent Champions bred in the Oldoak kennel are the two litter-sisters, Ch. Oldoak Krisco Kisses and Ch. Oldoak Power of Love (Frenick Goes To Hollywood – Oldoak Tempting Memory).

OAKFARM

Sue and Roger Goddard's first OES was purchased under quite unusual circumstances. Roger had always promised Sue an OES as soon as they had their own place, as she had been unable to take her German Shepherd Dogs with her when they got married. One day Roger went out to buy a car, and came back with a Bobtail – Wisebeck Leading Lady. Leading Lady was to become the dam of the first Oakfarm Champion, Ch. Strawberry Fair, whelped on April 3rd 1976, sired by Dustville

Ch. Oakfarm Strawberry Fair: The first Champion for the Oakfarm kennel.

Mr Universe. The next Oakfarm Champion came to the house almost like a rescue dog. Pockethall Shoemaker of Oakfarm was only eight months old; he had already been clipped down, and was very thin, and was about to be rehomed when Sue and Roger took him home. They liked him and his breeding (Ch. Pockethall New Shoes – Ch. Pockethall Silver Shoes) so much that they put their own affix at the end of his registered name and started showing him. He was made up in 1983 at almost five years of age.

When bred to Dustville Spinning Jenny (Ch. Barkaway Tattie Bogal – Dustville Playful Poppet) in 1980, he sired Ch. Oakfarm Wild Basil of Roustabout. When Shoemaker was mated to Barnolby Shaggyshires of Brackenhome, the litter produced Brackenhome Shadow of Oakfarm, who later became the sire of Miss Angie Burrows' Ch. Allmark Olympic Gold. One other Champion, sired by Shoemaker, was Miss Burrows' second Champion. This was Ch. Allmark New Addition. Swanbobs Super Hallmark (out of Misty Springtime Swanbobs), who was the dam of both Allmark Champions.

Oakfarm Oleanna was the last puppy left of a litter out of Woodnymph Sweet Charity (Wildahar Forester – Wildahar Sofia), sired by Shoemaker, so Sue and Roger decided to keep her. This was a wise decision as Oleanna became the kennel's top-producing brood bitch. Her litter, in 1984, to Ch. Barnolby Troubleshooter at Oldoak produced the Group winning Ch. Oakfarm Lively Lad. A repeat mating in 1985 produced Ch. Oakfarm Oberon, Ch. Oakfarm Ms Behavin at Mirene and Ch. Oakfarm Beth of Bobbington. Another repeat litter in 1987 resulted in a Champion bitch, Ch. Oakfarm Pure Genius at Allmark.

BRINKLEY
The well-known Brinkley affix is owned by Pam Tomes. Pam's first Champion, Ch. Morgans Lady of Amethyst (Bobbingay Plainsman of Amblegait – Mosscars Silver Lace) was whelped on October 3rd 1973, and was bred by Mrs P. Kelsey. This bitch finished her Champion title in 1977, a year she had started with a bang by winning the bitch CC at Crufts under Norman Harrison (Fernville). She was beaten for the BOB by Bartines Most Happy Fella of Jenards, who later

Ch. Brinkley Ballet Dancer of Heathop: A beautifully made bitch.

became a Champion. However, winning the strong open class of fifteen bitches (only four absentees) was an achievement in itself, topped later by winning the CC.

Pam's next Champion was born in 1978. Ch. Pockethall Ballet Shoes of Brinkley was bred by Ruth Wilkinson out of Ch. Pockethall Silver Shoes sired by Ch. Pockethall New Shoes. Ballet Shoes' first CC came from Betty Tidley at the Birmingham National in 1982; Ann McGill, at SCCA, gave her the second CC; and in the same year Sally Penney-Duffin, at Three Counties, gave the third crowning CC and Best of Breed. In 1983 Ballet Shoes gained the CC at Crufts, under Mrs M. Murray, which she repeated in 1984 at Crufts, under Audrey Woodiwiss.

While Pam was showing Ballet Shoes, a bitch from her own breeding picked up two CCs and four Reserve CCs. This was Brinkley Bubbly Blue of Watchglen (Ch. Pockethall New Shoes – Ch. Morgan's Lady of Amethyst), who was born in 1979 and owned by Mr and Mrs M. Ramsay. Her first two CCs came from Percy Whitaker at Paignton Championship Show, and from Sylvia Talbot at the South Eastern Club Championship Show. Her third CC came from Reg Gadsden at the North Eastern OES Club Show, and CC number four was awarded at the North Western OES Club Show by Isobel Lawson.

In 1981 Ballet Shoes was mated to Pockethall Playboy of Brinkley (Ch. Fernville Lord Digby – Ch. Cornelia of Trimtora) which produced John Dervance's Ch. Brinkley Beautiful Dreamer of Derwanz. Beautiful Dreamer's seven CCs came from the late Bobby James, Ruth Wilkinson (Pockethall), the late Catherine Sutton, Joe Braddon, Violet Yates, Reg Gadsden and Ferelith Hamilton. A repeat mating of Ballet Shoes and Playboy produced, in 1982, Suzette Rogers' Ch. Brinkley Ballet Dancer of Heathtop, a beautifully made feminine bitch. Her three CCs came from Sally Penney-Duffin (Longdorhams), Betty Ince (Hyal) and Vic Guest (Lamacres). Her litter sister, Brinkley Blue Stocking at Jemsue, owned by Jem and Sue Swatkins, was made up in 1987. She gained three CCs and five Reserve CCs.

Pam Tomes has also bred several Champions who have gained their titles abroad. She is passed to award CCs in Old English Sheepdogs, and is currently showing two young bitches, Brinkley Ballerina (Brinkley Boy George – Brinkley Pearl Drops) and Brinkley Uptown Girl (Brinkley Boy George – Brinkley Special Lady).

*Ch. Pelajilo Dan
Dare and his
daughter, Ch. Pelajilo
Nifty Nancy, just
before she left for
Australia where she
became an Australian
Champion.*

Pearce.

PELAJILO

Jilly Bennett (former Layton), the owner of the well-known Pelajilo Bobtails, first got interested in the breed in 1969. Like most people, she started off with a pet but soon found that one OES needs company, and so a second Bobtail was purchased. This time the puppy came from a proper breeder, the well-known chairman of Bath Championship Show, Colonel Bury Perkins. Diamond Blue Duchess of Pelajilo was sired by Lamyatt Harvester out of Lamyatt Betsy. The pedigree went back to the Shepton lines, and to Ch. Bevere Stalwart. It did not take Jilly long to get interested in the show scene. Being involved in the acting world at the time, she was won over by the special atmosphere of the show ring, the challenge of handling well-groomed and well-presented exhibits, the applause for winning dogs and the compliments paid to their owners, and she vowed to own a top-winning OES one day. Jilly most certainly fulfilled this dream. Her first show OES, Pelajilo Lady Peggotty (Ch. Shaggyshire Bumblebarn Caesar – Diamond Blue Duchess of Pelajilo) did not finish her title, but she produced three Pelajilo Champions. They were Ch. Pelajilo Pud'n and Pie of Bedivere and Ch. Pelajilo Simply Sensational of Viento (sired by Ch. Aberfells Georgey Porgy), and Int. Ch. Pelajilo Pincushion (by Flockmaster John Barleycorn). In 1981 the Pelajilo kennel was the top-winning OES kennel, starting with Ch. Pelajilo Milly Mistletoe winning the bitch CC at Crufts under Stan Fisher (Wrightway). Mistletoe was out of Cobbicot Polly Flinders of Flockmaster, sired by Flockmaster John Barleycorn. Beautifully-coated and well-constructed, she was probably the most successful Pelajilo OES in England. A repeat mating of Mistletoe's litter produced, in 1980, Ch. Pelajilo Myrtle Milkshake of Monoval, who was made up by her owners, Mrs R. and Miss J. Rampton in 1981, before she was two years of age.

In 1983 Jilly's Bumblebarn Champion, Ch. Bumblebarn Scramble of Pelajilo (Ch. Aberfells Georgey Porgy – Ch. Bumblebarn Ragamuffin) was bred to the Best in Show winner of Scottish Working Breeds in 1984, Ch. Pelajilo Dan Dare (Flockmaster John Barleycorn – Cobbicot Molly Mandy of Pelajilo), which resulted in a litter whelped on April 2nd 1983. This litter included the first dual UK and Aust. Champion, Pelajilo Nifty Nancy. There have been Pelajilo Champions all over Europe, Scandinavia, Australia and New Zealand – too many to mention them all. It has to be seen as a great loss that the kennel does not breed OES any more.

Ch. Zottel's Miss Marple of Lameda: Winner of fifty-one CCs, joint breed record holder with her son, Ch. Lamedazottel Flamboyant.

LAMEDAZOTTEL

The Lamedazottel affix is the result of the merger of two kennels – the English Lameda kennel and the German Zottel OES kennel. It is owned by myself and my husband, John Smith. It all started in 1985 when I came to England with five of my OES: Int. Germ. Swiss VDH Ch. Reeuwijk's Filmstar in Silver, and her offspring, Int. Germ. Lux. Monaco Ch. Zottel's Eagle Has Landed, Int. Germ. Swiss, Dutch, VDH, Ch. Zottel's Estee Lauder, and two bitch puppies out of Filmstar's last litter sired by Int. Danish Germ. VDH Ch. Lohengrin a. d. Elbe Urstromtal, Zottel's Moonlight Serenade and Zottel's Miss Marple. The time spent in quarantine was most distressing for the dogs and for myself. Filmstar ('Krumel') kept eating all the time, ending her six months in prison weighing eight stone, and Estee Lauder lost her first litter of eleven pups. All five dogs were most unhappy as they had never lived in a kennel before.

The first Lamedazottel litter was born in 1986. It was sired by another German import of mine, Ufo-Star a. d. Elbe Urstromtal (Int. Ch. Chris a. d. Elbe Urstromtal – Ch. Hot Dog a. d. Elbe Urstromtal) out of Ch. Zottel's Estee Lauder. This litter was closely line-bred back to the American-bred Int. Ch. Ellenglaze Ladies Choice (Fezziwig lines). The result was three Champions: Eng. Ch. Lameda Zottel A New Jonathan at Craigsea, Swed. Ch. Lamedazottel A Star is Born, and Int. Italian Ch. Lamedazottel His Nibs. A repeat mating in 1987 produced Norwegian Ch. Lamedazottel Diorissimo.

Meanwhile a litter had been whelped in quarantine out of Int. French Swiss Ch. Zottel's Get Up and Boogie (Int. Ch. Ellenglaze Ladies Choice – Int. Ch. Reeuwijk's Filmstar in Silver), sired by Int. Ch. Lohengrin a. d. Elbe Urstromtal (a Ladies Choice grandson). Boogie's six weeks in quarantine (she went back to her owners in France) did not affect her. The owners of the kennels did a great job, and the puppies had an excellent start to their lives. This litter included Eng. Ch. Lamedazottel Bestseller, Irish Ch. Lamedazottel Best of Times, Lamedazottel Bright Future, a CC-winning male in Italy, Int. Swiss Ch. Zottel's Ebony and Ivory, and Lamedazottel Brandy Soda, who won two CCs in England, plus Lamedazottel Petite Fleur with Malcro, who was very successfully shown as a youngster.

Meanwhile both puppies which had come over with me, Zottel's Moonlight Serenade of Lameda and Zottel's Miss Marple of Lameda, had developed into beautiful bitches. Moonlight ('Jilly') went to live with Bill and Shirley Moore, who showed her to her title. She also became a Group winner. Miss Marple ('Missy') went on to become the most successful show OES female in history. She was made up by the age of eighteen months with her first CC coming from Jilly Bennett (Pelajilo), the second from Jean Borland (Jeabor) and the crowning third at Leeds Championship Show, in 1986, from Betty Ince (Hyal). Missy ended the year 1986 with eleven CCs to her name, and was the top-winning OES bitch. In 1987 she won twenty-one CCs – taking over the bitch breed record – three Working Groups and one Best in Show all breeds. She was also top OES in 1987 and top-winning female all breeds. Despite maternal duties, in the following years she added nineteen more CCs, three Groups, and several Best in Shows at Breed Club Shows, especially the OES Club Centenary Show in 1988 (with a record entry of 235 OES), under Ferelith Somerfield, which also gave her the new breed record.

Over the years she produced five litters. Her first litter in 1989 was to Ch. Pockethall I'Mashootoo (Ch. Trushayp Eckythump of Jenards – Ch. Pockethall Silver Charm). This litter included Int. Swiss Ch. Zottel's Freemason, Int. French Ch. Zottel's Fatal Beauty, Int. Germ. VDH and World Ch. Lamedazottel Fond of Me, and Lamedazottel Fancy Free, top dog all breeds in 1990 in Yugoslavia, who unfortunately died young before he could finish his title. The fourth Champion out of this litter is our own Ch. Lamedazottel Flamboyant, who is currently holding the joint breed record with his dam. He was also the top-winning dog all breeds in 1991 and 1992 in England, with a total of fifty-one CCs, sixteen Groups and ten Best in Shows all Breeds. He has already sired CC and Reserve CC winning stock in England, plus Portuguese Ch. Lamedazottel Honeymoon, Swed. Ch. Lamedazottel Heatwave, and the Group and BIS winning Lamedazottel High 'N Mighty in Yugoslavia.

In 1990 the litter out of Miss Marple to Ch. Greyfell Storm Warning included the following Champions: Eng. Ch. Lamedazottel Garbo (owned by myself), Eng. Ch. Lamedazottel Givenchy, Int. Lux. Dutch Ch. Lamedazottel Good Gossip, Int. Ch. Lamedazottel Gershwin, Int. Ch. Lamedazottel Graffiti, a Group and Best in Show winner, NZ Aust. Ch. Lamedazottel Good Timing, also a Group and BIS winner, and Int. Danish Ch. Lamedazottel Go Miss Sophie (another BIS winner).

OTHER TOP-CLASS KENNELS
Several other OES kennels have been active during the last forty years. They might not have bred many litters or Champions due to different circumstances, but their dogs were by no means less deserving.

GWEHELOG: Owned by Betty Tidley, this kennel was the home of the beautiful Ch. Bess of Cold Harbour. Bess was bred by Isobel Lawson (Prospectblue) out of Sally Blue Miss, sired by Reculver Son of Carol. She was born on October 25th 1959 and finished her Championship at almost six years of age in 1965. Gwehelog Welsh Melody and Gwehelog Welsh Tammie were the parents of Betty's homebred Champion, Ch. Gwehelog Welsh Maid, made up in 1970.

Betty awarded CCs at Crufts in 1979. Her dog CC and Best of Breed was Ch. Pockethall Blue Cloud, the Bitch CC went to Ch. Tagalong Overshadowin.

ROMNEYDENGE: Clarice Masterson's family has been associated with OES for many years. The most successful and well-known show girl was the beautifully-coated Ch. Farleydene Fezziwig (Farleydene Dombey – Fernville Francesca), bred by George Gooch. Fezziwig was born on December 23rd 1966 and finished her title in 1969. Other Bobtails in the family were

Romneydenge Cobnest (Lameda Mr Kip – Farleydene Carol), Farleydene Carol, sister to Fezziwig Cobnest's daughter, Romneydenge Poppy (by Britannias Prince of Boventor), and one other Cobnest daughter, Romneydenge Trixie (by Fernville Royal Hope of Longdorham).

Clarice Masterson officiated at Crufts in 1987 awarding the Dog CC to Ch. Tynycoed Caradog ap Tegwch and the Bitch CC and BOB to Ch. Zottel's Miss Marple of Lameda.

JEABOR: Owned by Jean Borland and Charles Anderson: Jean and Charlie have been involved with Old English Sheepdogs since the early sixties. Bobtails with the Jeabor affix include Jeabor Bleu Bonnet of Glinabbey (Bluecrest Masterpiece – Jeabor Bonnie Lass), Tycehurst Valhalla of Jeabor (Ch. Rollingsea Snowboots – Cherrywood Pride & Joy), Jeabor Honey Bunch (Eng. Am. Ch. Prospectblue Rodger – Jeabor Kudle Bunch), Aust. Ch. Jeabor Sugar Bush, who was the sire of Craigsea Sweet Serenity of Jeabor (out of Jeabor Bleu Seaspray). Serenity later produced Jeabor Lady Grey, who was sired by Barnolby Beethoven at Jeabor (Ch. Aberfells Georgey Porgy – Ch. Barnolby Wendy Bruin). On December 27th 1982 Lady Grey whelped a litter sired by Ch. Pockethall Shoemaker of Oakfarm (Ch. Pockethall New Shoes – Ch. Pockethall Silver Shoes). This litter produced, amongst others, Eng. Ch. Jeabor Shugga Puff. Shugga Puff gained her qualifying CCs at the North Eastern OES Club Show in 1986 under Mr F. Selva, and at the Lancastrian OES Club Show 1986 under Jem Swatkins, and her crowning third CC came from John Smith at the Birmingham National Championship Show in 1987.

A lifelong dream was fulfilled for Jean when she had the honour of officiating at Crufts in 1988. Her Bitch CC and Best of Breed went to Ch. Zottel's Miss Marple of Lameda, and the Dog CC was awarded to Ch. Lamacres Melans Boy Blue. Charlie Anderson has also been passed to judge at Championship Show level. Champion stock has been exported to America, Australia and Germany.

KRISINA: Chris and Nina Underwood's prefix, Krisina, was established twenty-two years ago in 1971. The first Champion in the Krisina household was Ch. Wenallt Emerald (Ch. Wenallt Trooper – Twotrees Esmeralda), bred by Mrs T. Jones (Wenallt). Emerald ('Mandy') gained five CCs, the most exciting CC coming from the great Mona Birkowitz in 1976 at Windsor Championship Show. The Dog CC that day went to Wenallt Andrew. Only one year later Jean Collins made up Ch. Krisina Magic Moments of Jedfcrest (Ch. Barkaway Tattie Bogal – Krisina Miss Jessie), bred by the Underwoods. Magic ended the year 1977 as top-winning OES Bitch and winning the Working Group at the Welsh Kennel Club Championship Show.

Krisina Sunday Splendour (Krisina Patrolling Tramp – Ch. Wenallt Emerald), born in August 1977, is considered by Chris and Nina to have been one of their best homebred OES. Currently shown are the offspring of their Finish import, Ch. Drover's Katerina at Krisina (Int. Ch. Alexander Nikita – Proper Havis Amanda), bred by Mrs S. Tanner.

JEMSUE: Jem and Sue Swakins' interest in showing OES started in 1972 with their bitch, Arjems Lady Molly, who was sired by Ch. Bevere Stalwart. She was quite successful at Open Shows taking several BOBs and even Best in Show awards. When she was old enough to have a litter, Jem and Sue decided on Ch. Pockethall New Shoes as the sire, because they felt he would give the texture and the length of coat which she was lacking. This decision proved to be right, as the litter resulted in the beautiful Jemsue Just Jessica. Jessica was very successful gaining four CCs in 1979, and two more CCs in 1980. The highlight of her career was Crufts 1980, under breed specialist Ann Arch, when she won the CC and BOB, while her younger full brother, Jemsue the Judge, won

Ch. Jemsue Just Jessica: BOB Crufts 1980.

his two classes. Unfortunately, Jessica never produced any puppies, so Jem and Sue concentrated on the younger Jemsue the Judge ('Sam').

Sam was a very handsome masculine boy, and I can still see Sue's proud face when he won the big open class and the CC, under Jean Gould (Rollingsea), at Crufts in 1982. This was his third crowning CC. His fourth CC and BOB came from the late Sylvia Talbot at the South Eastern OES Club Show, also in 1982. Both Sam and Jessica lived to almost thirteen years of age, and according to Sue, they were always a joy to live with.

In 1982, when it was certain that Jessica would not produce, Jem and Sue decided to buy a puppy in. They went to Pam Tomes (Brinkley) and picked Brinkley Blue Stocking at Jemsue. 'Sophie's' pedigree carried all their favourite lines, in particular the Pockethall line. She was bred out of Ch. Pockethall Ballet Shoes sired by Pockethall Playboy. Like her ancestors, Sophie had a fantastic amount of coat. Her three CCs came from Mr Ian Morrison (Bobbingay), Mr S. Fisher (Wrightway) and Mr S. Hall (Shenedene). She also gained five Reserve CCs.

LONGDORHAMS: Mr and Mrs Duffin's first significant OES was bred by Topsey Jones (Wenallt) out of Arabella of the Embages sired by Wonder Boy of Shepton. The puppy, Follyfoot of Shepton and Longdorham, was whelped on December 4th 1972. She gained her title in 1975, but was even more successful as a brood bitch. Her litters to Ch. Dorianblue Shepherd Boy and Ch. Pockethall New Shoes produced three English Champions and one International Champion. They were: Ch. Longdorhams Sheps Folly, Ch. Longdorhams Clowns Folly and Int. Ch. Longdorhams Folly by George (by Ch. Dorianblue Shepherd Boy), and Ch. Longdorhams Folly-Footsteps (by Ch. Pockethall New Shoes). In 1982 Ch. Longdorhams Clowns Folly whelped a litter sired by her half-brother, Ch. Longdorhams Folly Footsteps. One of the dog puppies went to live with Mr Ivor Thick (Hamwih), who showed him to his title. Ch. Longdorhams Lord of the Ring at Hamwih received his three CCs from John Smith (Lameda), Pat Guest (Lamacres) and Maureen Cowie (Southview). He also gained four Reserve CCs.

LOAKESPARK: This kennel is owned by one of our most well-known judges, Mrs Ann Arch (former Davis) and her daughter, Alexandra Davis. Ann has not bred many litters as she concentrated on an extremely successful judging career very soon after her first involvement with OES. She is now passed to judge all breeds in the Working Group at Championship Show level. Ann's most well-known OES was Ch. Reculver Little Rascal (Nicefella of Danehurst – Ch. Reculver Sugar Bush). Cuddles enjoyed a tremendous success, winning thirteen CCs, seven Reserve CCs and several Best in Shows, Group first and Group placements at Open and Championship Show level. In 1968 Ann mated her Fernville Debutante to Somerstreet Chieftain, and this resulted in Grace Little's Champion, Ch. Twotrees Loakespark Tosca.

AMBLEGAIT: Ch. Amblegait Artistic Addition (Waterglen Wizard – Barnolby Artistic of Amblegait) was the first Champion owned by Ray and Glenda Owen. He was whelped on September 20th 1978 and gained his title at the Three Counties Championship Show in 1981 when Rita Ashcroft (Barnolby) gave him his third CC and BOB over the bitch CC, Ch. Jedforest Queen of the Night. Bred to Amblegait Auld Acquaintance (King Hotspur of Amblegait – Amblegait Aedi), he sired Amblegait Adams Addition, who later sired Ch. Amblegait Amboyna of Stourvale. 'Ross' was whelped on October 16th 1981 out of Barnolby Artistic of Amblegait (Ch. Ginnsdale Stargazer Blue of Barnolby – Ch. Sincerity of Barnolby). A repeat mating in May 1982 produced Ch. Amblegait Atlantic Conveyor. She gained her three CCs in 1985 from Rita Ashcroft (Barnolby), John Smith (Lameda) and Jenny Griffiths (Monoval).

EMBAGES: Owned by Dorothy Malins, this kennel has bred a number of Scandinavian Champions. In 1976 Mr Bluedan of the Embages (Foxtwist Mr Jumbo – Blueberry of the Embages) gained his English title. One other English Champion was Ch. Nan of the Embages (Ch. Reculver Christopher Robin – Bess of the Embages), owned by the late George Gooch. This kennel bred the famous Ch. Farleydene Bartholomew (Farleydene Rudolph – Shepton Misty Light). 'Barty' was the foundation sire of the world famous American Fezziwig kennel. His son, Am. Ch. Fezziwig Ceiling Zero (out of Am. Ch. Patchwork Gillian of Van R.) became the top sire in America of all time, with sixty-four Champions to his credit.

George Gooch was also the breeder of Mesdames Tingle and Masterson's Ch. Farleydene Fezziwig, who was a top-winning OES bitch in England during the late sixties. She was out of Fernville Francesca sired by Farleydene Dombey.

DUROYA: Owned by the late Audrey Woodiwiss, this kennel's most influential OES was Am. Ch. Baroness of Duroya (Ch. Fernville Fernando – Azure Queen of Duroya). Baroness produced the famous Rivermist litter, sired by Ch. Fezziwig Ceiling Zero, which resulted in nine Champions out of a litter of eleven pups. An English Champion, bred by Miss Woodiwiss, was Ch. Boss of Duroya (Holloways Royalist of Duroya – Azure Queen of Duroya).

DALCROY: Two English Champions have been bred by Ann McGill, the owner of the Dalcroy affix. Ch. Thor of Dalcroy (Fairacres Commander – Weirwood Shepherds Joy) was whelped on September 6th 1956. Thor was made up in 1961. The second Champion, Ch. Summer Grace of Dalcroy, whelped on July 29th 1970, out of Pandora of Dalcroy sired by Raydor Bundle. She finished her title in 1973.

JEDFOREST: Owned by Jean Collins, this small kennel was responsible for breeding one of the most successful OES of this century. In 1979 her bitch, Shaggyshire Little Mo of Jedforest produced a litter, sired by Ch. Bartines Most Happy Fella of Jenards, which included Ch. Jedforest Don Carlos, born on April 25th 1979. When he retired from the show ring he had beaten the former breed record holder, Ch. Aberfells Georgey Porgy, and had amassed a total of thirty-nine CCs, nine Group wins, a Supreme Best in Show in 1983 at SKC, and three Reserve Best in Shows. Little Mo was also the dam of Suzette Roger's Ch. Jedforest Queen of the Night, sired by Ch. Ginnsdale Stargazer Blue of Barnolby. Jean's Champion, Ch. Krisina Magic Moments in Jedforest was out of Krisina Miss Jessie, sired by Ch. Barkaway Tattie Bogal. The Jedforest OES now share their home with Jedforest Hungarian Pulis. Jean is passed to award CCs for both her favourite breeds.

WOOLWOOD: This kennel is based on Pockethall and Tumbletop lines. Mr and Mrs Mott have bred two Champions, Ch. Woolwood Mr Magoo and Ch. Woolwood Isn't She Lovely, both out of Tumbletop Talk About Me, sired by Pockethall Playboy.

BREED RECORD HOLDERS AND LEADING DOGS
CH. PENDLEFOLD PRINCE HAL
The former breed record holder Ch. Pendlefold Prince Hal was sired by the great Ch. Oakhill Peter Pan out of Smokey Jane of Nelson, bred and owned by Mr and Mrs Riddiough. Smokey Jane (Crawford Shepherd – Honeymoon of Marlay) whelped her first litter by Peter Pan on August 1st 1967. The Riddioughs kept the most promising dog puppy, called Prince Hal, who was to become the new breed record holder with a staggering thirty-four CCs. He was the top-winning OES in 1970 and 1971, winner of multiple Groups and two Supreme Best in Shows and several Reserve Best in Shows.

Ch. Pendlefold Prince Hal: Winner of thirty-four CCs, a Champion sire and grandsire.

Stepping into his father's shoes, he also became a Champion sire and grandsire with five Champions to his credit. They were: Ch. Lameda Pearly Princess (out of Lameda Pearly Queen), Ch. Tynycoed Pen-y-Bryn of Southview (out of Tynycoed Merch Ida), Ch. Pockethall Shoeshine of Southview (out of Ch. Cornelia of Trimtora), and Ch. Pockethall Silver Shoes, litter sister and brother to Shoeshine. A repeat mating produced in 1969 Ch. Pendlefold Sweet Charity of Cinderwood. Sweet Charity was owned by Messrs. Banks and Bentley and campaigned to her title in 1971.

CH. ABERFELLS GEORGEY PORGY
Georgey Porgy (Barnolby Midwinter – out of Aberfells Cindy Lou), line-bred back to the great Ch. Bevere Proud Monarch was whelped on May 3rd 1972. He was owned by Jeff and Sheelagh Curd, and he was their first Old English Sheepdog. Jeff and Sheelagh are the best proof that 'novice' owners, with the right determination in combination with a good dog, can make it to the top. Jeff and Sheelagh are schoolteachers and like many in the profession they are both

Ch. Aberfells Georgey Porgy: Top OES in 1975, 1977 and 1978, Top Working dog in 1977 and 1978, and No. 3 All Breeds 1978.

perfectionists. This was always reflected in the immaculate presentation of Georgey Porgy ('Jake'). Watching Sheelagh and her dog in the ring, I always had the impression that both of them had come to win. The records prove that this attitude paid off. Georgey Porgy was Top OES in 1975, 1977 and 1978, Top Working Dog in 1977 and 1978, and No. 3 All Breeds in 1978. He gained thirty-six Challenge Certificates, nine Working Groups, and three Best in Shows at All Breed Championship Shows. Apart from all these accolades, Georgey Porgy was probably one of the most glamorous OES ever. When Georgey Porgy died on April 25th 1983 he left a great many promising youngsters and ten Champions who were out of so many different bitches and lines that his qualities as a great sire are unquestionable. His Champion progeny included:

1. Ch. Barnolby White Bear (out of the lovely Ch. Barnolby Wendy Bruin), bred and owned by Mr and Mrs Ashcroft (Barnolby).
2. Ch. Branduin Cotton Picker (out of Sireva Blue Beauty of Branduin), bred and owned by Mr and Mrs Hodgson (Branduin).
3. Ch. Snowfall Gentle Ben of Marleigh (out of Waterhead Lady Sarah), bred by Mrs Freeman and owned by Marion Fraser (Marleigh).
4. Ch. Bumblebarn Scramble of Pelajilo (out of Ch. Bumblebarn Ragamuffin), bred by Mrs C. Pearce (Bumblebarn), owned by Jilly Bennett (Pelajilo).
5. Ch. Pelajilo Simply Sensational of Viento (out of Pelajilo Lady Peggotty), bred by Jilly Bennett (Pelajilo), owned by Mr and Mrs T. Wallis (Viento).
6. Ch. Bellablue Prince Charming (out of Ir. Ch. Bon Accord), bred and owned by Mr & Mrs S. Keane.
7. Ch. Southview Saracen of Nytimber (out of Ch. Arlils Cilla of Southview), bred by Mr and Mrs R. Cowie (Southview), owned by Mr and Mrs Jeff Curd (Nytimber).
8. Ch. Meadowsweet Anastasia (out of Meadowsweet Katie Sue), bred by Mr and Mrs P. Herratt, owned by Mr & Mrs M. Robins.
9. Ch. Pelajilo Pud'n and Pie of Bedivere (out of Pelajilo Lady Peggotty), bred by Jilly Bennett

(Pelajilo), owned by Mrs Inwood and Mr Price (Bedivere).

10. Ch. Cinderwood Great Gatsby of Bartines (out of Ch. Pendlefold Sweet Charity of Cinderwood), bred by Messrs. Banks and Bentley, owned by Christine Siddall (Bartines).

CH. CINDERWOOD GREAT GATSBY OF BARTINE

A son of Georgey Porgy and Prince Hal's sister, Sweet Charity Gatsby, was all set to make his owner Christine Siddall and breeders Messrs. Banks and Bentley proud. He was whelped on August 16th 1974 and finished his Championship in 1977. He was shown until July 1981 and retired with fourteen CCs, five Working Groups, and one Best in Show All Breeds.

His Champion offspring included: Ch. Bradyll Ice Poppett (out of Ilckmaster Bo-Peep of Bradyll), bred and owned by Mr and Mrs K. Nelson, Ch. Southview Canterbury Belle of Macopa (out of Ch. Pockethall Shoeshine of Southview), bred by Mr & Mrs R. Cowie (Southview), owned by Mr and Mrs C. Barnes (Macopa), and Ch. Southview Crackerjack, litter sister to Canterbury Belle, owned by the breeder.

CHAMPION LOMAX OF LINGAR

Lomax (Ch. Barnolby Mr. Barrymore – Blue Mist of Ramnee) was born on November 17th 1969, bred by Mr G. D. Mitchell. He was in the show ring at the same time as Pendlefold Prince Hall, which must have led to fierce competition at times. Lomax was owner-handled by Norma Fielding, and despite Prince Hal, he won a total of fifteen Challenge Certificates and the top-winning OES spot for the year 1973.

In 1973 Lomax sired the well-known Cinderwood by Jupiter of Craigsea out of Barnolby Cinderella, bred by Messrs Banks and Bentley. 'Odin' was owned by Elaine Horner and handled by her husband, Alan. Ch. Winstonholme Memories of Oldoak (out of Drakeshead Redscare Lady Jayne) was the foundation bitch of Mrs D. Oakes' Oldoak kennel. She was bred by Lomax's owner Miss N. Fielding, and added one more Champion to his credit. Unfortunately, Lomax died very prematurely at four and a half years of age.

Ch. Lomax of Lingar: Top OES in 1973 and winner of fifteen CCs.

CH. JEDFOREST DON CARLOS

On April 25th 1979 Mrs J. Collin's Shaggyshire Little Mo of Jedforest whelped a litter by Ch. Bartines Most Happy Fella of Jenards which produced a new record-breaker. Ch. Jedforest Don Carlos was awarded his first CC in 1980 at the Welsh Kennel Club under Joan Real. Due to his age he was entered in the Junior class at this show. He finished his title at twenty-six months, and he went on to break Georgey Porgy's breed record in 1984 at Leeds Championship Show under Barrie Croft (Malcro).

His last CC (No. 40) came from the late Bobby James at the Southern Counties Championship

Ch. Jedforest Don Carlos: Winner of forty CCs.

Show in 1985. Out of his forty CCs, twenty-nine were with Best of Breed. He topped the Working Group nine times and took the Best in Show rostrum once at the Scottish Kennel Club Championship Show in 1983, and was Reserve Best in Show on three occasions. Carlos is the sire of the top-winning Ch. Tynycoed Caradog ap Tegwch (out of Ch. Tynycoed Un Prydferth) and Ch. Ragglebarn Summer Symphony of Jachelle (out of Bartines Summer Serenade), bred and owned by Dr Ann Hodgson (Ragglebarn).

Chapter Six

THE OES IN NORTH AMERICA

EARLY HISTORY

THE PIONEERS

The first OES to be registered with the American Kennel Club was called Bob, with an unknown date of birth and unknown breeder. This was 1886. He belonged to a Collie breeder with the affix Glencho. In 1887 the same kennel registered the first female, Judith, who was by Bob out of a bitch called Gipsey (by UK Ch. Sir Guy out of Dame Dorothy). Judith was to become the dam of the first American-bred and registered Bobtail litter. This first litter was sired by Bob (a father-daughter mating). Unfortunately at the time it was not common practice to register all dogs, or even all litters with the AKC, and this explains why there were dogs shown and imported without any registrations being recorded in the early register books.

One of the very early OES admirers was William Wade, who was wealthy enough to be able to import a number different breeds, which he thought should be introduced to America. The imported dogs were given to suitable friends, together with instructions for feeding and general care. In 1889 Wade hired Mr J. Freeman Lloyd to write a monograph in an issue of *Turf, Field and Farm,* with the title 'The Old English Sheepdog'.

Freeman Lloyd was described by the late Arthur Tilley (of Shepton fame) as "an early enthusiast and International judge. He did much by writing to arouse interest in the breed in the USA. Probably our greatest authority on this type of dog." This monograph had a big influence on the future press coverage, although at the Westminster Show in 1890 – the first show where separate classes for Old English Sheepdogs were scheduled – only two entries were reported. Both the dog, called Orson, and a female, Queen Vick, belonged to S. M. Cleaver from the Glencho Collie kennel.

Around the turn of the century many wealthy Americans took a fancy to the breed. The Vanderbilts, the Guggenheims and other families, owned, showed and bred Old English Sheepdogs. In 1903 Arthur Tilley crossed the Atlantic for the first time to show several of his best English-bred OES at Westminster. Freeman Lloyd was the breed judge, and he gave Best of Breed to Merry Party, and Winners Bitch to Bouncing Lass, both owned by Tilley. Four of the exhibited dogs were sold after the show to Charles Frohmann and Charles B. Dillingham, who were both involved in the theatre world and knew many well-connected people, who eventually became interested in the breed.

Frohmann and Dillingham also owned one of the first large kennels mainly dedicated to OES. It is not known how much they paid for Stylish Boy, Bouncing Lass, and the other two bitches they bought from Tilley – but it was reputed to be a considerable sum. Tilley writes in his book *The Old*

English Sheepdog that he would expect the price to remain a "record" for a very long time – and he would have been in a position to know! Stylish Boy was sired by Big Young Watch, who was by Watch Boy. His dam was Larkfield Watch Lass, who was also by Watch Boy, showing that the practice of inbreeding was not uncommon. The price paid for Stylish Boy proved to be money well spent, as he sired many litters, which were to make an impact on the breeding stock of several kennels. He was also the sire of three Champions – Rowsley Conquest, Dolly Gray, and Kenvil Blinkers.

BRITISH IMPORTS

At this time, American enthusiasts were prepared to pay enormous amounts of money for adult Old English Sheepdogs who were well-bred, preferably having been shown and used for breeding in the UK before going over to the US. Many well-known English stud dogs came to America, the most famous two being Ch. Shepton Hero and Ch. Tip Top Weather. This explains why so many present-day pedigrees can be traced back to show the same ancestors appearing in both the UK and America. It may seem strange that British breeders allowed well-proven dogs, and bitches, for that matter, to go overseas. However, most British breeders of that time were farmers, who bred livestock for their living. They bred, showed, and sold cattle, sheep, pigs, other farm livestock and dogs. Sentiments were not allowed to come into it.

By the time that Tilley came back to America a year later, in 1904, to show again at Westminster, the OES entry had multiplied, and as the breed was mostly owned by prominent people, the crowd around the ring was unprecedented. In fact, the officiating judge, James Mortimer, was told to take his time, as the dogs in the ring belonged to some of the most influential people in America. For the second year Bouncing Lass was Winners Bitch, and Winners Dog was Mr and Mrs Steadman's Wilburforce. On this trip to America, Tilley encouraged the OES owners and breeders to form their own club. It took until 1905 for the AKC to formally recognise the club, and it was 1921 when the club held its first Specialty show.

The history of the Old English in the USA was greatly influenced by the status of those early enthusiasts of the breed. The famous and wealthy were constantly in the spotlight, and this obviously gave the breed a lot more public recognition than would have happened if the breed had been owned by farmers and by the middle classes, as it was in England. Personalities like Mrs Tyler Morse with her successful Beaver Brook kennel, James A. Garland, owner of the North Prudence End kennel, R. C. Vanderbilt with the Sandy Point Farm kennel, C. Frohmann and C. Dillingham, from the Hidden Brook Farm kennel, and many others, all had enough money to run large, well-kept kennels. They hired kennel managers who were responsible for deciding on breeding programmes, and the general care of the dogs.

NORTH PRUDENCE END

In fact, James A. Garland, was so interested in breeding that he played a major part concerning all the decisions about his dogs. His kennel manager was Arthur Merrill, who knew a lot about coat care, and eventually worked for Mrs Tyler Morse after Garland's sudden death. Four Champions were shown by Garland to their titles. The most notable was Dolly Gray, who had come from the Shepton kennel, sired by Ch. Stylish Boy out of Dolly Daydream. She was considered to be one of the best bitches in England before she left for America. In Tilley's book *The Old English Sheepdog*, there are photographs of two different Dolly Grays. One was called Shepton Dolly Gray, sired by Ch. Southridge Rodger out of Pensford Blue Mist, and from the photograph, she looks very much like her sire, short in body with a nice balance. The other Dolly Gray photograph shows a well-bodied bitch, with a tremendous topline and excellent reach of neck. The caption below the photograph reads: "Champion Dolly Gray. Sire International Champion Stylish Boy, dam Dolly Daydream, purchased when a puppy by Messrs Tilley Bros of Shepton Mallet."

BEAVER BROOK

When Arthur Merrill, Garland's former kennel manager, came to the Beaver Brook kennel, he found the best possible conditions. Both Mr and Mrs Morse were interested in pure-bred dogs, and they were in an excellent financial position to provide their new manager with the best facilities and best dogs available in England. All this, combined with Merrill's own skills, resulted in the kennel soon becoming known for the best-conditioned and heaviest-coated Sheepdogs in the US.

Among their imports from the UK were two well-known stud dogs who came over in 1909. These were Ch. Shepton Hero (Lord Cedric – Avalon Lass) and his son, Ch. Brentwood Hero, out of Brentwood Country Girl. Through Stylish Boy and Bouncing Lass (sire and dam of Lord Cedric), both their pedigrees went back to Watch Boy and Young Watch. Brentwood Hero was to become a very successful show dog in America, culminating in a Reserve Best in Show at Westminster in 1915.

In 1909, the Morses also imported a bitch called Nightmare, in whelp to John O'Dreams. Again, the pedigree featured Stylish Boy and Young Watch. The litter was born in June 1909, and all nine pups were kept. One of the pups, a bitch called Slumber, was to become the most successful OES of her time. In fact, John Mandeville in his book *The Complete Old English Sheepdog* writes that Slumber may have been the greatest OES ever. She was Winners Bitch at Westminster in 1912, 1913, 1916, and again in 1917 when she was almost eight years of age. In 1914 she won Best of Breed and then went Best in Show, with a Reserve Best in Show also at Westminster in 1916.

The Best of Breed wins in 1916 and 1917 resulted in Slumber becoming the first OES to win the prestigious silver Challenge Bowl. This perpetual trophy was donated to the OESCA by Mr Tyler Morse, and was originally given to the Best of Breed winner at Westminster. It is now given to the BOB at the annual OESCA Specialty show.

Unfortunately Mrs Tyler Morse died very young, leaving the kennel to her husband who was a well-respected judge, not only for OES but for several other breeds as well. He judged the second Specialty show held by the OESCA in 1922, and he was one of the five Best in Show judges at Westminster in 1926.

THE BREED DEVELOPS

In the years leading up to First World War and for a few years afterwards, several new kennels bred and imported some very influential dogs, although they were not on the same scale as Beaver Brook or North Prudence End kennels. However, a number of these dogs can be traced back from present-day pedigrees. They included: the Tenacre kennel, which were registered to Messrs P. Hamilton Goodsell and P. Hamilton Goodsell Jr, Morris Kinney's Kinnelon kennel, the Willinez Weather kennel, owned by Mr Jamison, and Mrs Wilbur Kirby Hitchcock with her Hitchcock OES.

HITCHCOCK

Mrs Hitchcock bred and showed a number of excellent dogs, but she never registered an affix with the AKC. Her husband was the treasurer of the OESCA and an AKC delegate for several years. Mrs Hitchcock was responsible for a monthly column on Old English Sheepdogs in the *American Kennel Gazette* for almost eleven years. She was also highly regarded as a judge, despite a reputation for being very outspoken! Mrs Hitchcock did not believe in showing dogs too young. She wanted them to be fully mature and proven as studs or brood bitches before they competed in the ring. This explains why most of her exhibits did not finish until almost six or seven years old – and she also did not like males or females to be bigger than 25 ins to the shoulder. However, many Champions came from her kennel, most of them homebred. They included: Ch. Lassie of the Farm, Ch. Beau Brummel, Ch. True Lady, and Ch. Lovely Weather, to name but a few.

Beau Brummel was Winners Dog and Best of Breed at Westminster in 1926. Lassie of the Farm, a daughter of Beau Brummel, was Winners Bitch at Westminster in 1926, 1928, and 1929 when she was BOB and fourth in the Working Group as well. Her date of birth was July 30th 1922, so she was almost seven years of age when she won the breed.

KINNELON
Another very interesting character of this era was Morris Kinney, with his Kinnelon kennel. He was a true doggy man, with an eye for dogs in general. His name was also connected with Great Danes and Mastiffs. For many years he was involved with the American Kennel Club as a director; he served several terms as a secretary, delegate, vice-president and also president of the OESCA. Kinney had another hobby, which did not really go with breeding and keeping dogs. He loved to travel – and taking off for several months at a time was nothing unusual for him.

It was therefore surprising that he was so successful with his breeding. One reason for his success was his knowledge of the breed, and the ability to assess his own dogs honestly. Champions which were made up by him included the imports: Ch. Shepton Spark, Ch. Tip Top Weather, Ch. Night Rider, and the homebreds: Ch. Kinnelon Milkmaid, Ch. Kinnelon Mother Carey, Ch. Kinnelon Tower and Ch. Kinnelon Hallowe'en.

Tower and Hallowe'en were sired by Kinney's import stud, Ch. Night Rider out of Wangler. Night Rider's pedigree included Stylish Boy, Young Watch, and Watch Boy through his sire, Ch. Brentwood Hero, and his dam, Lady Rider. Hallowe'en went Best of Breed at Westminster in 1923. Tower was originally used to work on a farm, which belonged to his kennel manager's parents. However, due to his excellent potential as a show dog and stud, he was later brought back to the kennel and the records speak for themselves. He became an important sire with Best in Show winning offspring.

WILLINEZ WEATHER
The Willinez Weather kennel were officially registered with the AKC in 1920 by Mr W. Jamison, a very wealthy man, who was able to hire staff to see to all the kennel management. His kennel were soon making a big impact on the breed, and Westminster 1920 saw all four major awards going to his Weather OES. International Weather was Winners Dog, Clovelly Weather was Reserve Winners Dog, Victory Weather was Winners Bitch, and Lucky Fair Weather was Reserve Winners Bitch.

THE HEIGHT CONTROVERSY
Looking at the OES today and tracing its history, it is very interesting to note that due to the success of one OES, Ch. Cliffwold Sweet William, who stood 26 ins at the shoulder, the OESCA decided against a size limit in the Breed Standard. Sweet William was considered to be too big, but he was so good in every other respect that the decision fell to a mere recommendation of height, instead of a limitation. Breeders at that time considered size a most important aspect when discussing type.

One of the very few people who did not put too much emphasis on size, was Arthur Tilley. He felt that, depending on the environment where the OES was supposed to work, dogs who were less than 20 ins at the shoulder were needed as much as dogs who were more than 28 ins at the shoulder. However, this opinion was not shared by the OESCA committee.

The eventual recommendation was accepted by all the members, and to emphasise the importance, it was printed in italics: *"A height of twenty-six inches or over for dogs or bitches to be considered objectionable and not to be encouraged."* This was part of the Standard until 1953 when the OESCA decided to remove it.

THE THIRTIES TO THE SEVENTIES
Like so many OES Clubs of the present time, the Old English Club of America went through a period when they had problems. According to their president, there was a lack of co-operation among the members, with exhibitors being more interested in the results of dog shows, than in the breed itself.

MERRIEDIP
The person mainly responsible for the club becoming more effective again, was Helen Margery Renner (formerly Lewis, and Roesler), a highly respected breeder and judge of OES and Welsh Corgis. Her Merriedip OES, especially Ch. Merriedip Master Pantaloons and Ch. Merriedip Duke George (the last Merriedip Champion), had a great impact on the breed in general. Unusually for a woman at that time, she loved to travel. She was equally well-known in England, Canada and the USA for her knowledge, her success and her respected judging ability.

Many of her English imports came from the Downderry kennel, owned by Mrs W. Durham Waite. They included Ch. Downderry Irresistible, Ch. Downderry Volunteer, Ch. Downderry Voyager, to name just a few. Homebred Champions were Ch. Merriedip Kitty and Ch. Merriedip Ethel Ann. Several of the Merriedips were also Group and Best in Show winners. One of these Group winners, Merriedip Tiny Tre, sired by Ch. Downderry Irresistible out of Shelia of Ways Green, eventually took residence in the White House with Mrs Franklin Delano Roosevelt.

Contrary to breeders in the past, and the breeders she imported her dogs from, Mrs Renner had very strong views against inbreeding. Her belief was that poor temperaments resulted solely from inbreeding. In fact, she was even opposed to line-breeding. Considering that most of her imported dogs resulted at least from line-breeding if not inbreeding, these views seem rather surprising, especially as most of her imported dogs did extremely well in the show rings. From 1931 to 1938 her stock took most of the major awards at Westminster.

Her English import, Ch. Downderry Volunteer (Walleyed Bob – Glittering Cascade) was not just an All Breed BIS winner, but also an important stud. Names of his Champion offspring were: Ch. Mistress Merrie O Merriedip, Ch. Mistress Vindex, Ch. Merriedip Silverdale, Ch. Merriedip Ethelyn, plus the record-winning Ch. Merriedip Master Pantaloons. Pantaloons went Winners Dog and Best of Winners at less than a year old, at Westminster in 1937. He was Best of Breed at Westminster in 1939, 1940 and 1942. In 1939 he was second in the Group, and in 1942 he did even better by winning the Group. Pantaloons was also a Champion producing sire. His offspring included: Ch. Merriedip Mistress Monnie, Ch. Merriedip Flare for Victory, Ch. Merriedip Tag-A-Long, and several Champions for the Rosmoore affix.

Mrs Renner's most prolific stud dog was one of the English imports, Ch. Merriedip of Pastorale (Peterkin of Halliwick – Jasmine of Halliwick), bred by Mrs E. Sanders. Looking at present-day pedigrees, you can find this dog behind the breeding and show stock of a great number of OES kennels. He was whelped in 1937, but it was not until the sixties that another stud dog bettered his record for Champion offspring.

His two Champion sons, Ch. Kings Messenger and Ch. Black Baron (out of Ch. Mistress Opal of Pastorale), were bred by Julius Kraft. They became top-winning OES of their time with many Groups and Best in Shows to their credit. Messenger was Best of Breed at Westminster in 1944 and 1946. He was also Best of Breed at the OESCA Specialty in 1944. Black Baron was Best of Breed at Westminster in 1945, and did even better in the Working Group when he was placed second, his litter brother having come third the year before.

Many other Merriedip Champions deserve to be mentioned, such as Ch. Merriedip Mr Personality, Ch. Merriedip Mr Topper, Ch. Merriedip Frilly Petticoats, Ch. Merriedip Cracker Jack, and most of all Ch. Merriedip Duke George, the last Champion to carry the Merriedip prefix.

MOMARV

After the Second World War the most famous dog in the breed was again a Merriedip, Ch. Merriedip Duke George. He was not bred by Mrs Renner, but by Hope Norton, still carrying the Merriedip prefix. Sired by Ch. Merriedip Mr Personality out of Merriedip Pamela, his pedigree went back on both sides to Ch. Merriedip of Pastorale. He was owned and handled by one of the truly great OES lovers, Mona Kucker (later Berkowitz), owner of Momarv OES kennel.

Among many other wins, Mona handled Duke George to Best of Breed at the OESCA Specialty Shows in 1956, 1957, 1958 and 1959. He went second in the Westminster Working Group in 1957 and 1958, and in 1959 he came third. In fact, 1957 was also his most successful show year, ending with Top winning Working Dog in the United States and No. 3 All Breeds.

Mona came from a dog-orientated family: her father was on the Board of Governors of the OESCA in the forties. Her first OES was Ch. Crest of the Wave, born in 1933, and her second show dog became the second OES to achieve an Obedience Companion Dog title. Top-winning OES bred and owned by the Kuckers included: Ch. Momarv's Mistletoe, Ch. Momarv's Blue Devil, Ch. Merriedip Cracker Jack, and Ch. Momarv's Hi-Wide.

Mona's impact on the breed as a judge, handler, and importer, cannot be measured. It is believed that she has owned and shown in her time more OES Champions than anyone else. She has been honoured many times, and the magazine *Kennel Review* awarded her the title of best female handler of the year.

The well-known Ch. Prospectblue Rodger, and the top-winning bitch Ch. Shepton Surprise were owned and imported by Mona, adding two more great dogs to her list of Champions. Rodger was sired by Eng. Scan. Am. Ch. Prospect Shaggy Boy out of Farleydene Peggotty, and was bred by Isobel Lawson, owner of the Prospectblue kennel in England.

Now living in California, Mona is still very much involved in the breed, and is in great demand as a judge. She officiated at the OESCA Specialty Show in 1990, where she awarded Best of Breed to Ch. Bahlambs Broadway Billboard, handled by his breeder and owner, Caj Haakansson.

ROSMOORE

Many kennels started in the breed with a Merriedip OES, and of these, Claude Crafts, with her Rosmoore affix, became the most well-known. She owned Merriedip Mary and Merriedip Trouble. The first litter which carried the Rosmoore affix was whelped in 1937, sired by Ch. Merriedip Master Pantaloons out of Ch. Naughty Marietta. One of the dog pups went to Mrs Renner, and became a Best in Show winner. His name was Ch. Rosmoore Saint John. Naughty Marietta was also the dam of other Group and Best in Show winning offspring, such as Ch. Rosmoore Smarty

Pants, sired by Ch. Merriedip of Pastorale. The Rosmoore kennel later became the home of a very important stud dog called Beckington Reprint, who was imported from England. Reprint did not finish his title, but he sired seven Champions: two for the Merriedip kennel, one for the Rivermist affix, and four for the Shayloran's affix, with Mona Berkowitz's Ch. Shayloran's Billy Hayseed, being the best known.

Hayseed was out of Rosmoore Pink Lady, and was first owned and shown by Mrs Craft. At the OESCA Specialty Show in 1964 he went Best of Winners. The judge was Mona Berkowitz. She liked Hayseed so much that she purchased him from Mrs Craft, and later showed the dog during the mid-sixties in California, where he became most successful, and the sire of several Champions.

ROYAL
The Royal kennel was yet another kennel which started with a Merriedip OES. Mr and Mrs Walton owned Mistress Merrie O'Merriedip, the litter sister to Ch. Merriedip Master Pantaloons. Like her litter brother, she was a very successful show dog and producer. Mated to Ch. Merriedip of Pastorale, she produced the multi Group winning males, Ch. Royal Prince Topper and Royal Prince Peterkin. Many other Champions were bred and owned by the Royal kennel, including: Ch. Royal Prince Snowman II, Ch. Royal Prince Topper II, Ch. Royal Princess of Crestwood, Ch. Royal Princess Bonnie, and Ch. Royal Prince Victor.

Ch. Royal Prince Victor was owned and shown by Mr and Mrs Gilg of Pittsburgh. He won several Groups and a record five Best of Breeds at Westminster – 1948, 1949, 1950, 1951 and 1953. Victor's sire, Ch. Royal Prince Topper, went Best of Breed in 1943, and one of Victor's sons, Marbert Highland Tuffy, took the BOB in 1952.

PATCHWORK
Louise and Barclay Acheson first became involved in Old English Sheepdogs in 1948. Their first three OES were English imports – Shepton Blushing Maid, Laddie of Bashurst, and Peggy Ann of Bashurst – and all three became American Champions. Ch. Shepton Blushing Maid produced Patchwork Bluebirds, sired by Laddy of Bashurst. Laddy was also the sire of Patchwork Phoebe, who was out of Merriedip Mopsie Merrie. In October 1953 Phoebe whelped a litter (sired by her half-brother, Patchwork Bluebirds), and this produced the foundation bitch for Hendrik and Serena Van Rensselaer and their Fezziwig OES. In 1952 Ch. Paul of Squarefour – considered to be one of the best males in England at the time – took up his new residence in the Patchwork kennel. He was soon made up, winning several Groups on the way. He sired two Champions for his new owners: Ch. Patchwork Blue Belinda (out of Ch. Shepton Blushing Maid), and Ch. Patchwork Mother Nachree (out of Patchwork Phoebe).

MOBLA
Mrs H. Schloss's Mobla kennel, based in Baltimore, was very active during the forties. In fact, Mrs Schloss was as much known for her imports as for her own breeding. She imported Ch. Shepton Dolly Gray (Ch. Southridge Rodger – Pensford Blue Mist). This bitch did a tremendous amount of winning, and her photograph was used for several years to illustrate the Bobtail in the AKC all-breed book.

FEZZIWIG
The Fezziwig kennel was owned by the late Hendrik and Serena Van Rensselaer. The Van Rensselaers had OES all through their life, starting with a four-legged wedding present from

Serena's uncle, which they received in October 1932. They registered their first prefix with the American Kennel Club.

After the Second World War Louise and Barclay Acheson of the Patchwork kennel asked Serena and Hendrik to whelp a litter for them. The bitch was Patchwork Phoebe, the sire Patchwork Bluebirds. The two OES were half-brother and sister through their sire, Ch. Laddie of Bashurst. Many well-known dogs from before the war were in Bluebirds and Phoebe's pedigree – the early Pickhurst, Shepton and Mrs Fare-Fosse's Weather OES.

On Phoebe's dam's side (Merriedip Mopsie Merrie) all the famous Merriedip names appeared, including Ch. Merriedip Master Pantaloons. Bluebird's dam was Ch. Shepton Blushing Maid (Ch. Shepton Surf King – Shepton Bluette). These two dogs went back to the early Pastorale dogs of Miss Tireman, and on the dam's side back to Shepton Moonshine. Blushing Maid had had a successful show career, with a Best of Opposite Sex at the OESCA Specialty show in 1952 to her credit.

Out of this litter, whelped on October 29th, 1953, Serena and Hendrik picked the best bitch puppy to start their own breeding with. Patchwork Gillian of Van R. was exactly the type of OES the Van Rensselaers liked, and she gained her title in 1956. Having very strong opinions about the way an OES should look, the Van Rensselaers found it very difficult to select a suitable stud dog for Gillian. So, when they found a male they liked while on a business trip in England, they tried their utmost to buy the dog. He was bred by George Gooch of the Farleydene kennel.

At first, George Gooch did not really want to let the promising young male go, as he had won classes at several shows including Crufts. However, eventually £70 changed hands, and one of the most important transactions for the American OES scene had taken place. Farleydene Bartholomew crossed the ocean to live in America, and his impact on the breed is virtually impossible to calculate, as so many of his offspring became record producing sires and dams.

Like Gillian, 'Barty' represented the type which he had inherited from his ancestors, the Pickhurst and Watchers dogs. He was sired by Ch. Shepton Surf King (already to be found in Gillian's pedigree) and his dam was Shepton Misty Light. Barty was shown to his American and Canadian title by E. J. Carver, picking up many Groups in both countries, and a BIS in Canada on the way. In 1957 Gillian whelped the first Fezziwig litter sired by Barty. World-famous dogs were the result of this successful combination, which, over the years, produced eleven American Champions and one Canadian Champion. The first litter produced probably the best-known Fezziwig of all, Fezziwig Ceiling Zero, and Fezziwig Blackeyed Susan, both to become Champions.

'Ceilie's' influence on the breed was tremendous; he sired sixty-three Champions, which is still the breed record. In 1966 he was No. 1 sire in the breed, No. 1 in the Working Group, and third overall. His great showmanship earned him numerous admirers in and outside the dog world. His outline was used for many years to illustrate the American Breed Standard. He was a Champion when still not eighteen months old.

At the OESCA Specialty in 1958 he won Best of Winners at fifteen months of age. Other BOBs, Best American-Bred in Show, and Group firsts followed. Handled by Anne Rogers (Clark), one of the best-known all-rounders today, he went to win the Working Group under the late Percy Roberts. He found Ceiling Zero at two years of age "almost perfect, even in the finest points", and expected him to last indefinitely.

In fact Ceilie was retired at just under seven years of age, having won fifteen Best in Shows, fifty Group firsts, six wins at Specialty shows, and on seven occasions he won the OESCA Challenge Bowl. He was the No. 5 Working Dog in 1959, No. 6 in 1960, No. 7 in 1962, and No. 2

*ABOVE: Ch. Fezziwig
Andrea and offspring.*

John L. Ashbey.

*RIGHT: Ch. Fezziwig
Artful Dodger: A son
of Ch. Fezziwig
Andrea.*

Evelyn M. Shafer.

in 1963. He was also No. 5 of all breeds that year. Most breeders would rate Ceilie a dog-in-a-lifetime and be happy with it. Not so Serena. She was always looking for the ultimate perfection, and, favouring inbreeding, she bred Susan back to her father, which produced Fezziwig Raggedy Andy. Due to Ceilie being shown until almost seven years of age, Andy's career was held back a little. However, by the time that Andy retired he had won the Working Group at Westminster in 1966 and 1967, becoming the first OES to gain this honour since Ch. Ideal Weather in 1938 and Ch. Merriedip Master Pantaloons in 1942.

Andy continued the year with several more Groups and Best in Show wins, which gave him so many points in the Philips ranking system that even his annual summer break from showing did not make any difference to the end results of 1966: Andy was top Working dog, and No. 2 all

Breeds. In 1967 he won the Group at Westminster again, just for good measure. His wins also included four Best of Breeds at the OESCA Specialty shows. Throughout his career, Andy was handled by the famous Bob Forsyth, and even with Ceilie still in the ring, Andy overtook him with his wins, but he never managed to come close to Ceilie's record as a producer.

Although he was not widely used at stud, Andy is responsible for three more famous Fezziwigs. Following a mating to Amblehurst Daisy, a bitch, Fezziwig Andrea, was purchased, and she later became a Champion. She was put back to her sire, and she whelped three pups, sired by Andy, in 1967. All three became Champions – Ch. Fezziwig Artful Dodger, Ch. Fezziwig Vice Versa, and Ch. Fezziwig Andorra. Both males became Best in Show winners. Vice Versa won BOB more than ninety times, including Westminster in 1974, going second in the Working Group.

Many breeders might not agree with the amount of inbreeding the Van Rensselaer's have done over the years, but their overall record speaks for itself. Vice Versa ended his show career becoming another top winning Fezziwig. He was in the annual breed top ten list for six consecutive years, and he was the top producing OES male in 1972, 1973, 1974, and 1976. He sired fifty-six Champions, only seven short of the No. 1 top producing sire, which is, of course, Ch. Fezziwig Ceiling Zero.

There have been many more top winning Fezziwigs, too numerous to mention. However, three dogs made a great impact on the OES scene in Europe, and eventually also in England. These were Fezziwig Silver Lining (Ch. Fezziwig Hoodwink – Fezziwig Homeward Bound), Ch. Fezziwig Honey Bun (Ch. Fezziwig Artful Dodger – Ch. Fezziwig Spring Song), and Ch. Ellenglaze Ladies Choice (on the dam's side an Artful Dodger grandson, and on the sire's side a Ceiling Zero great grandson).

Silver Lining was the dam of one of Holland's top winning OES bitches, Ch. Reeuwijk's Care for Beauty (sired by Ch. Ellenglaze Ladies Choice) and several other Champions. Honey Bun produced my own Ch. Reeuwijk's Dew Fantasy (sired by Ladies Choice), who when bred to his half-sister, Care for Beauty, sired Ch. Reeuwijk's Filmstar in Silver, the dam of Ch. Zottel's Miss Marple of Lameda, England's top-winning bitch of all times and joint breed record holder with her son, Ch. Lamedazottel Flamboyant.

Looking at all these pedigrees, the Fezziwig story has come full circle, with Miss Marple's offspring being exported to countries all over the world, even back to America. In fact, the Fezziwigs appear in the pedigrees of dogs all over the world.

RIVERMIST

This kennel, owned by Mr and Mrs Barry Goodman has had a great influence on the OES in America. Their first OES came from Mona Berkowitz, named Momarv River Mist. She was shown to her title in 1960, and also gained an Obedience Companion Dog title. She was sired by the famous Ch. Merriedip Duke George out of Ch. Arnue Platinum Penny. In 1962 River Mist was mated to the English import, Ch. Shepton Bobbibingo.

This first Rivermist litter was born on May 20th 1962, and it included Ch. Rivermist Robber Baron, and Ch. Rivermist Frostflower. Robber Baron went to the Silvermist kennel in Brooklin, Wisconsin, owned by Beverley Katchmar Hildrith, and he became the sire of several Champions – Ch. Beowulf Tyrone, Ch. Silvershag Miss Debonair, Ch. Silvershag Miss Bustle N' Bows, Ch. Silvershag Robbin Rascal, Ch. Silvermist Snow Sprite, and Ch. Silvermist Snow Dance.

In the meantime, Frostflower became the foundation bitch for the Sunnybrae kennel, owned by Ann Penn, and produced several Champions in her two litters by Ch. Rivermist Dan Patch. One of them, Ch. Sunnybrae Jack Frost, was owned by the well-known artist Louisa Lopina and her husband Robert. Louisa's OES drawings are for sale worldwide – and some of them might just feature Jack Frost.

In the early sixties, the Goodmans bought the imported son of the English Ch. Beckington Tom Tod, who was out of the then breed record holder, Ch. Beckington Lady of Welbyhouse, bred by the late Mabel Gibson, and originally imported by the Rosmoore kennel. His name was Beckington Reprint. Reprint died very young and was never shown in the USA, even though Barry Goodman rated him a great OES. He was used twice on Rosmoore Pink Lady, who was bred by Mr and Mrs Harold Richards, and he sired several Champions for the Shayloran kennel, including: Ch. Shayloran Penny Plain Rosmoore, Ch. Shayloran Little Beaver, and Ch. Shayloran Billy Hayseed, who was later purchased by Mona Berkowitz and became the most popular stud dog on the West Coast.

Due to his early death, Beckington Reprint produced only a few OES for his own kennel. One of them was Rivermist Laurel (out of Nan of Rokeby), who became a Champion, having won a Best of Opposite Sex at seven months of age at the New England OES Club Specialty show in 1965 on her way to the title.

Unfortunately, the next English import to Rivermist did not live long either, but she is responsible for the worldwide fame of the kennel. Baroness of Duroya (Eng. Ch. Fernville Fernando – Azuree Queen of Duroya) was by bred by Audrey Woodiwiss, and was whelped on January 17th 1962. Baroness was the top-winning OES bitch, with Winners Bitch at Westminster in 1964, Best of Opposite Sex at the same show in 1965, and Best of Opposite Sex at the 1964 OESCA Specialty show. On top of that, she won Groups and a BIS at Salisbury, North Carolina. She won this BIS when her pups out of her only litter were just four months of age.

This litter was sired by the great Ch. Fezziwig Ceiling Zero; it was whelped on the May 5th 1964, and it proved to be one of the most famous litters ever. Out of the eleven pups, nine became Champions and, in turn, great producers for many other kennels.

However, before all this success was achieved, the Goodmans had to undergo a long and hard struggle. As often happens with large litters, the puppies were small, and two were so weak they were not expected to survive. Baroness was not an excellent mother, and this meant that the pups had to be supplement-fed from birth. Anyone who has supplement-fed a litter will know what this means – constant work day and night.

In fact, this was probably an advantage for the puppies, because if they had not had additional feeds, they might not have been strong enough to survive the next crisis, as they became seriously ill within a few days. The vet discovered that Baroness had infected milk. He recommended a diet of small pellets of lean minced beef, the use of heating pads, and a wet nurse, who came in the form of Ch. Rivermist Frostflower, and the litter managed to recover their strength.

But the bad luck continued; the tail-docking was found to be faulty, and the whole litter had to be redone. Then, at four weeks of age, one puppy after another went lame due to a presumed calcium deficiency, producing brittle bone. A week after being treated with calcium injections, all the pups developed abscesses on their shoulders. These wounds had to be cleaned regularly, but they healed well, and nine of the pups went to their new homes.

Nosegay, the first puppy to have gone lame with two broken legs, was eventually sold to a pet home as no-one expected her to be sound. However, at seven months of age she had outgrown all her early problems, and later on she finished her Champion title and became a great producer. Hollyhock was kept after the original buyer opted out, and this worked out well for the Goodmans. She became the top-winning bitch while she was shown, beating, on occasion, every top-winning OES male, including Ch. Fezziwig Raggedy Andy. She was Best of Opposite Sex at OESCA

Int. Am. Ch.
Unnesta Pim: One
of the greatest
sires in the history
of the breed.

Specialty shows in 1967 and 1968, and at Westminster in 1966, 1967, and 1968.

Hollyhock was mated several times to Ch. Unnesta Pim, producing a total of twelve Champions, including: Ch. Rivermist March Flower, Ch. Rivermist Blue Trio, Ch. Rivermist Blue Chip and Ch. Rivermist Pied Piper. When Hollyhock won the Best of Opposite Sex at the OESCA Specialty show in 1967, her litter brother Galahad was Best of Breed, just beating another litter brother, Dan Patch. The Winners Dog was Knightcap Moody Blue, and Winners Bitch was Fezziwig Ruffle and Flourish. All four top winners at this large show were sired by Ch. Fezziwig Ceiling Zero.

Dan Patch amassed some of the greatest wins for a Working dog in 1966, 1967 and 1968. He was owned by Howard and Celeste Payne, and his professional handler, Jack Funk, showed him to almost two hundred BOBs, countless Group firsts, many more placements, and seventeen Best in Shows. He also won Best of Breed and second in the Group at Westminster in 1968. The same year he ended with the titles No. 2 Sheepdog and No. 9 Working dog, despite having been shown for only the first five months of 1968.

Apart from being an excellent show dog, Dan Patch sired a total of twenty-three Champions. Among them was Ch. Rivermist Dan Tatters (out of Miss Muffit of Tatters, a bitch who was leased for breeding by the Goodmans), and he proved to be an even more influential sire than his father. Dan Tatters sired a total of thirty-seven Champions. He was co-owned by Bob and Sheila Ziccardi and Jim McTernan.

At first, Dan Tatters was handled to his title by his breeder, Barry Goodman, but when Jim McTernan brought him back out, after a retirement of eighteen months, he took over as handler. The two together became a successful team, winning Best of Breeds, the Canadian Champion title, a Working Group 1st, and other Group placements. Unfortunately Dan Tatters died when he was just over six years old, which makes his tally of Champion offspring even more impressive.

One other bitch out of the Ceiling Zero – Baroness litter deserves a special mention, as she also produced Champion offspring. She was owned by Captain and Mrs T. E. Rich of the Jendower affix, and in her litters to Ch. Unnesta Pim, Ch. Prospect Shaggy Boy, and her nephew, Ch. Rivermist Dan Tatters, she produced fifteen Champions. Ch. Unnesta Pim was the sire of Ch.

Jendowers Rivermist Tobi, Ch. Rivermist Forgetmenot, Ch. Jendower Rivermist Storm, Ch. Jendowers Rivermist Smoke. Dan Tatters was the sire of Ch. Jendowers Lady Bromwich, Ch. Jendowers Jubilee, and Ch. Jendowers Blue Beard. Prospect Shaggy Boy sired Ch. Jendower's Blue Max, Ch. Jendowers Cloud Nine, Ch. Jendowers Spencer and Ch. Jendowers True Grit.

One other dog helped the Rivermist kennel to go down in history, and this was Ch. Unnesta Pim, bred by Mrs M. Korfitzen of the Unnesta kennel in Sweden. He was sired by Ch. Reeuwijk's Cupid (by Ch. Shepton Grey Idol, a son of Ch. Shepton Wonder) out of Ch. Shepton Sally Ann (who was also sired by Ch. Shepton Wonder). Unnesta Pim was bought when he was one year old by Caj Haakansson, who showed him to his International title and later took him to England, where he won a CC under Percy Whitaker immediately after he came out of quarantine.

Due to personal circumstances, Caj let Pim go to the Goodmans, and in his new home Pim became one of the greatest sires ever. He could not be described as a glamorous dog, because of his dark markings; he was dark-legged, his head markings were heavy, with a short white collar and a white bib. He was five years old when he came to the USA, and his first litter was whelped in December 1965 out of Rivermist Nosegay. He went on to sire a total of forty-six Champions, with many of his progeny producing Champion offspring themselves.

THE SEVENTIES TO THE NINETIES
BAHLAMBS
The Bahlambs kennel, owned by the Swede, Caj Haakansson, has probably had the greatest impact on the breed in America during the last twenty-five years. This prefix can be found in so many present-day pedigrees, more so than any of the other leading breeders.

Caj's interest in the breed started in 1961 when he attended the International Show in Stockholm. He had been asked by the vet he worked for to handle an OES bitch. Later on at the show, a very heavily-marked Bobtail, called Pim, kept going to Caj asking for his attention. By the end of the day Caj had fallen in love with him, and when he heard that the dog was for sale as the owners were emigrating, he cancelled an appointment to pick up a German Shepherd Dog and bought Pim instead. This decision later proved to be of extreme significance for the breed in America.

In 1963 Caj and Pim went to live in England, where Caj worked for the famous all-rounder judge, Joe Braddon. Pim gained his first English CC under Percy Whitaker, the same day he left quarantine. Considering that six months quarantine means six months confinement to a kennel, it can be imagined what excellent coat-care Pim must have had. The first Bahlambs litter was born in 1964 out of a working OES bitch named Bahlambs Gospelgirl. The sire of this first litter was the famous Ch. Reculver Christopher Robin.

Then, in 1964, due to personal tragedy, Caj went back to Sweden. As he did not want to put Pim (now Scandinavian and English Ch. Bahlambs Unnesta Pim) through another six months of quarantine, Caj let him go to Barry Goodman's Rivermist kennel in America. From then on, Pim's records speak for themselves – he was to become one of the all-time top producing sires in the American history.

While Pim started his new career in America, Caj went back to England. Before he had left for Sweden in 1964 he had seen a mature male he really wanted to buy, but Ch. Prospect Shaggy Boy (Ch. Bluebrigand of Tansley – Ch. Blue Glamour Girl) had not been for sale. Now back in England, Caj went to the breeder/owners, Mr and Mrs Lawson, and made an offer which they couldn't refuse. He also bought one of Shaggyboy's daughters, Bahlambs Prospectblue Fair Lady (out of Farleydene Peggotty). This combination also produced the well-known Ch. Prospectblue Bulk, Ch. Prospectblue Cindy and Mona Berkowitz's famous Ch. Prospectblue Rodger.

LEFT: Ch. Rollingsea Viceroy: Imported from the UK, and a Champion producing sire for the Bahlambs kennel.

Pearce.

BELOW: Ch. Bahlambs Beachboy (sire of thirteen Champions) and Ch. Bahlambs Balletomane.

Martin Booth.

Not long after buying the two Prospectblue OES, Caj had to return to Sweden, taking his dogs with him. There, Pim's daughter, Ch. Teddy Bear Angela (a litter sister to Ch. Teddy Bear Bobo) was bred to Shaggy Boy, and she produced one of Caj's most important early brood bitches, 'Millie', who was later to become a US Champion.

In Sweden Gospelgirl was mated to Ch. Teddy Bear Bobo, resulting in Ch. Bahlambs Brilliant Blue Barrister, and Ch. Bahlambs Bleak Blue Blackguard. Blackguard was originally sold as a pup. He went on to win Groups and BISs, but later on he was bought back and sent to America, soon to become American Champion.

Finally in 1968 Caj and a total of eighteen dogs crossed the Atlantic for a new life in the New World. These eighteen dogs included OES, Champion Pugs and Champion Poodles. Bahlambs Prospectblue Fair Lady's first show in America was Westminster in 1969, where she took Winners Bitch and Best of Winners over sixty-nine dogs.

While Fair Lady was doing well in the show ring, Ch. Millie produced Caj's first famous US litter sired by Bahlambs Brilliant Blue Best Band. In fact, this was Best Band's only litter, as, unfortunately, he died young of acute hepatitis. Three Champions were produced in this litter: Ch. Bahlambs Beloved Birgitta, Ch. Bahlambs Blue Baritone, and Ch. Bahlambs Brass Band – the first flashed Champion, who did an enormous amount of winning. Baritone became a Specialty Best in Show winner, and the fourth puppy of this litter, Bahlambs Bewitched Barbara, although unshown, produced two Champions to Ch. Bahlambs Burly Bushman. Brass Band sired seven Champions to various bitches.

One of the most significant decisions for the Bahlambs breeding programme was made by breeding Shaggyboy back to his two daughters, Ch. Millie and Ch. Bahlambs Prospectblue Fair Lady. This resulted in Millie producing Ch. Bahlambs Blue Book, who was to become the sire of five Champions, and Fair Lady producing Ch. Bahlambs Burly Bushman, who also sired five Champions, three of them for the Bahlambs affix: Ch. Bahlambs Bouncing Bubbles and Ch. Bahlambs Bushy Bushman, both out of Bahlambs Bewitched Barbara, and Ch. Bahlambs Blue Billy Boy out of Ch. Millie.

Looking at the Bahlambs records, Ch. Millie has to be rated as the most valuable brood bitch, as she produced seven Champions, the most notable being the record-breaking sire, Ch. Bahlambs Brazen Bandit, who was also Top OES for two years, and sire of thirty-six Champions. Brazen Bandit was sired by Bahlambs Big N Bountiful (Ch. Bahlambs Bene – Farmarens Candy).

In 1976 the Bahlambs kennel saw a new arrival in Ch. Rollingsea Viceroy (Rollingsea Hawthorne Pride – Ch. Rollingsea Twotrees Aurora), who was already seven and a half years old when he came to America. Bred to a Ch. Bahlambs Brass Band daughter, Bahlambs Brass Bed, Viceroy sired a new record-breaking dog, Ch. Bahlambs Beachboy. Beachboy achieved twenty-one Best in Shows all Breeds, two BIS at Specialties, eighty-five Working Group firsts, over two hundred Best of Breeds, No. 1 Working Dog, and No. 3 all Breeds.

Thirteen Champions go to Beachboy's credit. In fact, the all-time top winning OES bitch, Ch. Rholenwood Taylor Maid, is closely line-bred back to him. Beachboy bred to Ch. Bahlambs Baroness Belinda (Ch. Rollingsea Viceroy – Bahlambs Brassy Broad) produced Ch. Bahlambs Beachboy Bleu, who was to become the next important Bahlambs sire, with seven Champions to his name. Beachboy Bleu's daughters and sons were: Ch. Bahlambs Battle Besieged and Ch. Bahlambs Bishop Becket (both out of Ch. Bahlambs Beach Bunny), and Ch. Bahlambs Back on Broadway, Ch. Bahlambs Barnum on Broadway and Int. Ch. Bahlambs Broadway Bonanza (out of Showtimes Box Office Sellout, who was sired by Bahlambs Big N Bold).

Broadway Bonanza is the sire of the well-known Champions Int. Nord. Ch. Unnesta Pluto and Int. Nord. Ch. Unnesta Halligang. Ch. Bahlambs Barnum on Broadway was to become a multi Group winner and went Best of Breed at Westminster in 1983 at only seventeen months of age. He is also the sire of eight Champions, notably Ch. Rholenwood's Taylor Maid (out of Ch. Rholenwood's Enjoli) and her litter sister, Ch. Bahlambs Bathed N Brushed, another multi BIS winner. Showtimes Box Office Sellout mated to Ch. Bahlambs Baltimore Banker resulted in Ch. Bahlambs Baltimore's Best, who in turn sired World Ch. Am. Ch. Bahlambs Baltimore Blues.

Another highspot for Caj Haakansson was the 1983 National Specialty when Ch. Bahlambs Bobby Brown (Liverbobs Olympic Warrior – Ch. Bahlambs Brassy Broad) won Best Dog from an entry of 232 OES, including fifty-two Champions. Bobby Brown, at ten and a half years old, was mated to Ch. Bahlambs Back on Broadway and the result was: Ch. Bahlambs Biloxy Blues, Ch. Bahlambs Broadway Blast, Ch. Bahlambs Broadway Ballad and Ch. Bahlambs Broadway Billboard – and all three Broadways became OESCA award of merit holders.

The latest Bahlambs success was in 1993 at Westminster when Ch. Bahlambs Barnyard Banner,

ABOVE: Ch.
Rholenwood's
Tailormaid: Top OES
bitch of all time in
the USA.

RIGHT: Ch.
Bahlambs Barnyard
Banner: BOB and
Group third,
Westminster 1993.

Ashbey Photography.

sired by Ch. Moptops Lambluv Master Plan (a Barnum on Broadway grandson) out of Ch. Bahlambs Barnyard Beauty (Ch. Sniflik Warwyck Darwin – Bahlambs Bouncing Beachball) won Best of Breed, and later came third in the Herding Group.

WHISPERWOOD

There is nothing to whisper about this kennel – Joyce and Robert Wetzler's achievements deserve to be shouted from the rooftops! At the present time, they have a tally of seventy-eight Champions, including Group and BIS winners, to their name. Whisperwood OES have been BOB at the prestigious Westminster Show and at National Specialities. Their dogs have frequently been in the top 25 list – often as many as five or six dogs at the same time.

   Joyce got involved with Bobtails in 1964, and her first OES was called 'Homer'. The first litter was born in 1971, and since then the Wetzlers have been rated as the Top OES Show Kennel on many occasions. They owned one of the all-time top producing sires, Ch. Bahlambs Brazen Bandit (Bahlambs Big N Bountiful – Ch. Millie), bred and co-owned by Caj Haakansson. Bandit produced Champion stock for many well-known kennel, such as the Aphrodite kennel, Moptops, Warwyck and, of course, for Whisperwood.

   When mated to Ch. W. Welborne, by Am. Can. Ch. Bahlambs Brass Band, he produced Ch. W. Warrior, who later sired Ch. W. War Lord, the Best of Breed winner at the 1991 National Specialty, out of Ch. Capricorn's Amazing Amalia (Ch. W. Wise Guy – Canterbury Adventures of Amy). Other Warrior Champion offspring include: Ch. W. Rich N Famous and Ch. W. Blue Mist (both out of Ch. W. Wealthy N Wise), Ch. W. Windfall and Ch. W. Wins of War (both out of Ch. Warwick Wendy of W.). Ch. Warwick Wendy is also dam of Ch. W. Wallstreet and Ch. W. War Party (both sired by Warrior), and Ch. W. Wise Guy and Ch. W. Whispering Wind (both sired by Ch. Pim's Brazen Churchill).

   Ch. W. Wildwon (Ch. Warwyck Tommy Tittlemouse – Ch. W. Blue Velvet) also proved to be a top-producing male for the W. kennel. His offspring include: Ch. W. Wildflower, Ch. W. Wild

Ch. Whisperwood War Lord: BOB Westminster 1990 and 1992. Top male in the USA 1990 and 1991.

Ashbey Photography.

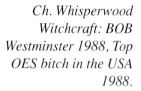

Ch. Whisperwood Witchcraft: BOB Westminster 1988, Top OES bitch in the USA 1988.

Ashbey Photography.

Oats, Ch. W. Amiable Won, and Ch. W. Professor Patches (all out of W. Wildwood), and several other Champions both for W. and other affixes. Ch. W. Wise Guy also made his mark as a sire, with Ch. W. Scarborough Fair, Ch. W. Woman of One Year, and Ch. W. Midsummer Snow (all out of Ch. W. Our Miss Brooks) to his credit, plus several Champions for other kennel.

A top-producing Whisperwood female was Ch. W. Blue Velvet, who produced Ch. W. Our Miss Brooks, Ch. W. Whippersnapper, and Ch. W. Wildwon (all by Ch. Warwyck Wildfire O Aphrodite), plus two Rollingmist Champions (by Ch. Mistyisle Captain Hawkins). Ch. W. Wildwood is another female worthy of mention, producing Ch. W. Professor Patches, Ch. W. Amiable Won, Ch. W. Wildflower, and Ch. W. Wild Oats (all by Ch. W. Wildwon).

Other well-known W. Champions include: Ch. W. Winning the Blue (Ch. W. War Lord – Ch. W. Winning Ticket), and Ch. W. Sir Lancelot (Ch. W. Wise Guy – Ch. W. Well to Do).

The Wetzlers' OES used to be handled by Robert Forsyth, but when he retired, Joyce decided to have a go at it herself. Watching her in the ring today and keeping track of the results confirms that this was a good decision.

TO-JO

Joy and Tom Kelley got involved with Old English Sheepdogs in 1974. Joy saw her first Bobtail in full coat and fell in love with the breed, and so Tom decided that a puppy would be a nice Valentine's present for her. This first pup came from a pet shop, but it took only four years for the Kelleys to get seriously involved in OES and start breeding. Since then, their enthusiasm has taken them right to the top. By the end of 1991 they achieved a staggering total of seventy-nine Champions, which gave them a joint first place in the top 25 kennel list, together with Harriet Poreda's Greyfriar kennel.

The present To-Jos are based on the two foundation OES, Ch. Maidstone Debutante of To-Jo (Ch. Whispering Oaks Tuff'n Stuff – Ch. Chatelaines Exuberant Elsa) and Int. Am. Can. Mex. Ch. Warwyck Oscar Performance (Ch. Bahlambs Brazen Bandit – Ch. Shaggiluv's Special Angel).

Debutante broke the record for the all-time top-producing bitch in 1985. She was also top-producing Working bitch in 1981. When mated to Am. Can. Ch. Aphrodite Snow Scooter, she produced: Ch. To-Jo's Toot Toot Toobie, Ch. To-Jo's Gadabout Gabby, Ch. To-Jo's Flying Dutchman, Ch. To-Jo's Toot She Rolls of Tomalee, and the famous Int. Am. Can. Mex. Ch. To-Jo's Root'N Toot'n Cowboy, owned and handled to tremendous fame by Michael Larizza. Cowboy, in turn, sired just three litters but still produced eight Champions, including the aforementioned Ch. Lamblue Moptop Show Stopper, out of Ch. Rholenwood's Taylor Maid.

Debutante's other Champion offspring include: Ch. Barrister Shadow of To-Jo, Ch. To-Jo's Only the Shadow Nose, Ch. To-Jo's Shadow in the Moonlight, Ch. To-Jo's Shadow Box, Ch. To-Jo's Shadow of your Smile – all by Ch. Aphrodite's Snow Sniflik. When mated to Ch. Warwyck Oscar Performance, she produced Ch. To-Jo's Ease on Down the Road, Ch. To-Jo's Folo Th Yelo Brik Rhode, Ch. To-Jo's Sweet Azzalena of Oz, and Ch. To-Jo's Wizard of Oz. Mated to Ch. Fargaze Willie Wonka, she produced Ch. Sniflik's Sambler of To-Jo and Ch. To-Jo's Hot Chocolate.

The Kelleys' foundation male, Int. Am. Can. Mex. Ch. Warwyck Oscar Performance, has got an equally impressive record. As well as all his Champion titles, he also won the Ch. Fezziwig Ceiling Zero Award in 1982. During this time he sired twenty-four Champions – fifteen for his own kennel. The most successful are: Am. Can. Ch. To-Jo's High Performance, Ch. To-Jo's Matinee Performance, Ch. To-Jo's Performance Co O'Russmar, Ch. Warwyck To-Jo Champagne Blues (all out of Ch. To-Jo's Crescent Moon), and Int. Am. Mex. Ch. To-Jo's Oscar Th' Grouch, Ch. To-Jo's Oscar Nominee, and Ch. To-Jo's Chatty Cathy (all out of Ch To-Jo's Gadabout Gabby).

Oscar Performance is also the sire of the 1979 National OESCA Sweepstakes Winner Ch. To-Jo's Sweet Azzalena of Oz and Ch. To-Jo Folo Th' Yelo Brik Rhode out of Ch. Maidstone Debutante of To-Jo. Oscar was very precious to the Kelleys as he was the sire of the first To-Jo Champion and their first Best in Show winner. He had fifty-five Working Group placements, three Best in Shows at Specialties, and two BIS. Several of Oscar's offspring went on to produce more To-Jo's Champions. Other top-winning To-Jo's are: Int. Am. Can. Mex. Ch. Barrister's Shadow of To-Jo (Ch. Aphrodite's Snow Sniflik – Ch. Maidstone Debutante of To-Jo), Int. Mex. Am. Ch. To-Jo Light My Fire of Piroska (Ch. To-Jo Solo Contender O'Sniflik – Ch. To-Jo Shadows in the Moonlight), and the No. 1 OES for 1988, Int. Am. Can. Mex. Ch. To-Jo's Nice N'Easy (Aphrodite's Snow Sniflik – To-Jo's Toot She Rolls of Tomalee).

Easy won several Best in Shows and Specialties, as well as taking Best of Breed at Westminster in 1989. As a sire, he was equally successful, with twelve Champions to his credit – five for his own kennel out of Ch. To-Jo's Dust Ruffles. This litter of five bitches proved to be so successful that the Kelleys have repeated the mating, and eight pups have been produced. Looking at all the past records, I am sure that there will be many more To-Jos Champions, as well as valued breeding stock for the Kelleys and many other leading kennels.

LAMBLUV

Jere Marder, the owner/breeder of the Lambluv OES, is one of the best-known exhibitors today. She used to be a dancer with her own studio, and she feels that showing dogs is like being on stage. Jere started exhibiting in 1978, and her first five Old English Sheepdogs came from Caj Haakansson, owner of the internationally famous Bahlambs kennel. She handled Ch. Bahlambs Beaming Beauty and Ch. Bahlambs Balletomane to their titles.

After that came Am. Can. Ch. Bahlambs Beachboy, who was No. 1 OES in 1979 and 1980. Beachboy was sired by Caj's English import, Ch. Rollingsea Viceroy, out of Bahlambs Brass Bed,

Ch. Lambluv Moptop Showstopper: No. 1 OES in 1990, 1991 and 1992.

Ashbey Photography.

and was to become the grandsire of Jere's multi Group and Best in Show winning Ch. Rholenwood's Taylor Maid (Ch. Bahlambs Barnum on Broadway – Rholenwood's Enjoli, a Beachboy daughter). Taylor Maid was campaigned by Jere Marder and Woody Nelson, of Moptop fame, from 1984 to 1987. In this time she accumulated twenty-two Best in Show, over 150 Group firsts, over 250 Group placements, nine Specialty Best of Breeds – two of which were National Specialty wins (1985 Virginia, under Linda Jordan, Loyalblue kennel, and 1986 Illinois, under Donald Booxbaum). All these wins added together made Taylor Maid the top-winning bitch in the history of the breed in America.

She had two litters, producing four Champions: Ch. Lambluv's Winning Easy (winner of the National Sweepstakes in 1990), Ch. Moptops Lambluv Master Plan, Ch. Lambluv Moptop Luvem N Levem, and Ch. Lambluv Moptop Show Stopper (National Sweepstakes winner in 1989), sired by Int. Am. Can. Mex. Ch. To-Jo's Root'n Toot'n Cowboy. Cowboy was sired by Ch. Aphrodite Snow Scooter out of the all-time top-producing dam, Ch. Maidstone Debutante of To-Jo.

Ch. Lambluv Moptop Show Stopper was retired at Westminster 1993 having been No. 1 OES in 1990, 1991, and 1992, No. 2 Herding Dog in 1992, with fifteen BIS, eight Specialty BIS, Winner of the Herding Group at Westminster in 1991, and over 125 Group firsts.

SILVERSHAG

Dr Louise Forest based her breeding on an English imported male, Ch. Shepton Bobbibingo (Beau Geste – Burford Belle), and a bitch from the Greyfriar kennel, Greyfriar Jenny (Greyfriar's Woody Bobbibingo – Ch. Greyfriar's Bar Maid). Jenny produced Dr Forest's first main brood bitches, Ch. Silvershag Ruffles and Ch. Silvershag Frolic. When Ruffles was mated to Ch. Fezziwig Faintheart Falstaff she produced Ch. Silvershag Snowlace, Ch. Silvershag Snowfrills and Ch. Silvershag

Snowtatters, whelped in 1963. Falstaff was a full, but younger brother of Ceiling Zero. Unfortunately, he died young having sired only two litters. His son, Snowtatters, also died young at only three years of age, but he left more offspring, including eleven Champions.

His son, Ch. Silvershag Snowbright out of Ch. Silvershag Madcap Margot (Ch. Lillibrad Sir Lancelot – Ch. Silvershag Frolic) sired a total of sixteen Champions, none of which carried the Silvershag prefix. Ch. Silvershag Donnemerry (Ch. Downeylane Donnybrook – Silvershag Maida) became the foundation bitch of the Droverdale kennel, owned by Pat and Sandi Baker. She produced ten Champions: five were sired by Ch. Rivermist Marco Polo, and three were by Ch. Rivermist Dan Patch.

Like Harriet Poreda's Greyfriar kennel, the strength of the Silvershag kennel seems to lie in the females. Thirty-two bitches with the Silvershag prefix produced almost one hundred Champions, in comparison to sixteen Silvershag males producing forty-nine Champions for Silvershag and many other kennels. The different bloodlines in the Silvershag pedigrees is probably more extensive than those of most other kennels, even though the individual pedigrees are either very closely line- or in-bred.

Ch. Silvershag Ruffles, Ch. Silvershag Frolic and Silvershag Sweet Sue (owned by the Van Rensselaers) were the main brood bitches with the Silvershag prefix. Ruffles produced a total of nine Champions. Her two Champions by Ch. Rivermist Dan Patch were, of course, similar breeding to the three Champions by Fezziwig Faintheart Falstaff, through Dan Patch's sire, Ceiling Zero. Her litter to Ch. Rivermist Robber Baron was a half-brother/sister mating through Robber Baron's and Ruffles' sire, Ch. Shepton Bobbibingo. Robber Baron was the result of the first-ever Rivermist litter, bred by Mr and Mrs Barry Goodman. In this litter Ruffles produced three more Silvershag OES who were made up. Finally, a mother/son mating to Ch. Silvershag Snowtatters resulted in Ch. Silvershag Snowdrifting.

Ruffles' sister, Frolic, mated to Ch. Lillibrad Sir Lancelot (Ch. Lillibrad Prince Charming – Ch. Beckington Aristocrat) produced two Champions, Ch. Silvershag Madcap Margot and Ch. Silvershag Honorbright. Margot later became the dam of another five Champions in her litters to Ch. Silvershag Snowtatters. Snowtatters is also the sire of four other Champions out of Frolic: Ch. Jolly Old Nick, Ch. Silvershag Little Prudence, Ch. Silvershag Pembroke and Ch. Silvershag Wyndham.

The third Silvershag bitch mentioned, Silvershag Sweet Sue, produced seven Fezziwig Champions. They were: Ch. Fezziwig Bluejohn Wilhemina, Ch. Fezziwig Fringe Benefits, Ch. Fezziwig Nosey Peeper, Ch. Fezziwig Ruffle And Flourish and Ch. Fezziwig Sir John Falstaff – all by Ch. Fezziwig Ceiling Zero; and Ch. Fezziwig Billian and Ch. Fezziwig Kara, sired by Ch. Fezziwig Sir Brasil (Farleydene Bartholomew – Patchwork Gillian of Van R.). These seven Champions made Sweet Sue ('Taffy') one of the most important producers for the Van Rensselaer's Fezziwig kennel.

Many of the Silvershag OES were not just made up, they also became Group winners and top sires or brood bitches for their new owners, helping newly established kennels to get off to a great start in terms of breeding and showing.

WINDFIELD
The Windfield kennel, formerly owned by Dennis and Margaret Gordon, later by Margaret Gordon-Haslett, of Michigan, are mainly Rivermist-based. More than fifty-two Champions have been finished since the early sixties, giving the affix the number five spot in the ranking of top-producing kennels.

Margaret Gordon's most successful sire was Am. Can. Ch. Windfield Barrister out of Ch. Windfield Holly (Ch. Rivermist Dan Tatters – Shaggyshire's Tiffany Star) and sired by Ch. Rivermist Pimson. Pimson was out of Ch. Rivermist Nosegay (a daughter of the famous Ceiling Zero – Baroness of Daroya litter) and sired by the great Ch. Unnesta Pim. Barrister's twenty-nine Champions included seventeen for his own kennel. Six out of these seventeen were out of the same female, Windfield Ivy. They were: Ch. Windfield Benjamin Scottbar, Ch. Windfield Coriander, Ch. Windfield Oliver, Ch. Windfield Sam, Ch. Windfield Tulip and Ch. Windfield Scarborough Jill, who was Best Opposite Sex at the 1981 OESCA Specialty Hills, Michigan, under Eileen Pimlott.

Bred to his sister, Ch. Windfield Magnolia, Barrister produced Ch. Windfield Mancho Man, who in turn sired three Champions for the Sleepy Hollows prefix. The combination Pimson and Holly, which produced Barrister, resulted in a total of twelve Champions, which is not surprising, looking at the beautifully line-bred pedigree of Ch. Windfield Amy of Scottbar, Ch. Windfield Barrister, Ch. Windfield Chaucer, Ch. Windfield Magnolia, Ch. Windfield Pimpernel, Ch. Windfield Samantha, Ch. Windfield Scotch Mist, Ch. Windfield Semper Fidelis, Ch. Windfield Vitablue Lullabye, Ch. Windfield Willy Wonka, Ch. Windfield Windjammer and Ch. Windfield Baron Blu Cascade.

A more recent Champion finished in 1992. This was Ch. Windfield Kande Cane CD (Ch. Windfield Jack Daniels – Blue Misty Lady Amanda). 'KC' is owned by the Misty Morn OES kennel.

LOYALBLUE

Owned by Dr Hugh Jordan and his wife, Linda, this kennel is based on English imports, mainly from the Prospectblue kennel. One of the first imports was Ch. Prospectblue Samuel (Am. Eng. Ch. Prospectblue Rodger – Fernville Fashion), whelped on August 4th 1966. Samuel quickly finished his Championship by winning two California majors at his first few shows, followed by two consecutive five-point majors at the KC of Beverly Hills and the Golden Gate KC show.

Looking at the early Loyalblue pedigrees, Samuel, and through him, Ch. Prospect Shaggy Boy and Ch. Fernville Fernando, are behind most Loyalblue breeding stock. His excellent pedigree, which bred for type and substance on one side, and elegance and coat on the other, is evident in the early Loyalblues. Later additions to the kennel were Prospectblue Elizabeth (Gwehelog Welsh Tammie – Prospectblue Ladye Jayne) and Rollingsea Vanessa (Rollingsea Hawthorne Pride – Ch. Rollingsea Twotrees Aurora). 'Lizzie' was also bred by Isobel Lawson, and like Samuel, she had no problem finishing her title with four and five point major awards in a very short time. Vanessa's dam was a grand-daughter of Shaggy Boy, the great sire of Prospectblue Rodger. Combining the offspring of 'Lizzie', Samuel and Vanessa resulted in almost pure-bred Prospectblue offspring – no wonder the Loyalblue affix figures high in all the rankings.

One of the important Champions bred in the kennel was Ch. Loyalblue Hendihap (Loyalblue Right Time – Ch. Mistress Mary of Taralane). Hendihap sired sixteen Champions, including three for his kennel. They were: Ch. Loyalblue Hendihap Dearly (out of Ch. Loyalblue Hendihap Carrie), Ch. Loyalblue Hendihap Once Again (out of Ch. Prospectblue Elizabeth) and Ch. Loyalblue This One Too (out of Ch. Loyalblue This One is Mine).

Ch. Loyalblue Fascinatin Rhythm (Ch. Cheerio Poetry in Motion – Rollingsea Vanessa) sired an amazing thirty Champions, including eleven for the Loyalblues. They were: Ch. Loyalblue Hendihap Sadie and Ch. Loyalblue Hendihap Carrie (out of Ch. Loyalblue Hendihap Charlotte), Ch. Loyalblue Hendihap Sugar Cain and Ch. Loyalblue Hendihap Th' Bold One (out of Ch.

Prospectblue Elizabeth), Ch. Loyalblue Christy Minstrel and Ch. Loyalblue Scalawagg Amy Too (out of Ch. Loyalblue This One Too), Ch. Loyalblue Hendihap Sound A Best (out of Ch. Loyalblue Hendihap Once Again), Ch. Loyalblue Hairyhood Surprise, Ch. Loyalblue This One is Mine and Ch. Loyalblue Henry Morgan (out of Ch. Snowbear Loyalblue Lisa), and Ch. Loyalblue Painted Lady (out of Ch. Loyalblue Hendihap Once Again).

Ch. Loyalblue This One is Mine (Ch. Loyalblue Fascinatin Rhythm – Ch. Snowbear Loyalblue Lisa) was No. 1 OES Bitch in 1977 and 1978, No. 2 all OES in 1978 and is also a Best in Show winner. Her offspring include the following Champions: Ch. Loyalblue This One Too (by Ch. Loyalblue Hendihap), Ch. Loyalblue Peg Of My Heart (by Ch. Pinafore Drummer Boy), and Ch. Loyalblue Artistic Rhythm, Ch. Loyalblue Such Sweet Thunder and Ch. Loyalblue The Right Stuff (all by Ch. Loyalblue Hendihap Sound A Best).

GREYFRIAR

One of the most successful kennels in the last forty years is undoubtedly Harriet Poreda's Greyfriar OES kennel. By the end of 1991 a total of seventy-two OES had gained their titles, giving Mrs Poreda the joint No. 1 place of top-producing kennels. The most obvious achievement, and this might just be the clue to the kennel's success, is the fact that there is a distinct female dominance in the Champion-producing records. Forty-three different Greyfriar bitches are listed in the record books as having produced Champion offspring, in comparison to thirty-one males. These thirty-one males produced a total of one hundred and two Champions. The forty-three bitches are responsible for one hundred and eight Champions, which they produced for kennels all over the USA. These unbelievable figures are only counted from dogs which carried the Greyfriar affix. Breeding stock which was bought in, and not registered with the Greyfriar prefix, is not included. Top-producing sire for the kennel was Ch. Greyfriars Chumley O'Moorland (Greyfriar Parsley Sam Chumley O'Moorland – Greyfriars Miss Muffin), who was responsible for twelve Champions, four for his own kennel. They are: Ch. Greyfriar Bentley (out of Ch. Greyfriar's Matilda), Ch. Greyfriar's Yankee Paddler and Ch. Greyfriar's Xan of Willoby (out of Ch. Greyfriar's Tochiko) and Ch. Greyfriar's Lord Chufley (out of Greyfriar's Chatelaine Chalet).

Top-producing dam in the kennel was Greyfriar Royal Show Off. Show Off did not finish her Champion title, but she made up for it by producing eight Champions to four different Greyfriar males. Her litter to Greyfriar Fancy Pants resulted in Ch. Greyfriar Missy Bevan, Ch. Greyfriar Sir Fang, Ch. Greyfriar Unsinkable Molly and Ch. Greyfriar Tareyton of Majon. Her earlier litter to Greyfriar's Woody produced the two Champions – Ch. Greyfriar Royal Peggy and Ch. Greyfriar's Lord Fauntleroy. Ch. Greyfriar Royal Powder Puff was sired by Ch. Greyfriar Little John and Ch. Greyfriar Trafalgar Square by Greyfriar's Alfie.

WARWYCK

Owned by Melvin and Vinita Smith, this kennel has bred some outstanding animals by using the right dogs from their own breeding in combination with the right partners from other kennels. In the Warwyck pedigrees are the famous affixes of Bahlambs, Aphrodite, Sniflik, Droverdale, Shaggiluv and others.

The kennel has had some outstanding sires, which has resulted in the Warwyck name appearing in a great number of pedigrees. They include Ch. Warwyck Tommy Tittlemouse (Ch. Aphrodite Snow Sniflik – Warwyck Surprise Party), sire of seven Champions, Ch. Warwyck Duesenberg (same breeding as Tittlemouse), sire of four Champions, Ch. Warwyck Oscar Performance (Ch. Bahlambs Brazen Bandit – Ch. Shaggiluv Special Angel), sire of twenty-four Champions, Ch.

Warwyck Wildfire O Aphrodite (Ch. Bahlambs Blue Book – Ch. Shaggiluv's Special Angel), sire of twenty-five Champions, and Ch. Sniflik Warwyck Darwin (Ch. Aphrodite Snow Sniflik – Ch. Warwyck Bonnie Bandit), sire of thirteen Champions.

Highlights for the kennel were the OESCA Specialty Shows in 1982 in Denver, Colorado and the 1983 OESCA Specialty in Los Angeles, California. At the Denver Specialty Show, under David Lee, Ch. Warwyck Tommy Tittlemouse went Best of Breed, Winners Dog went to Warwyck Charles Dickens (Ch. Aphrodite Snow Sniflik – Shaggiluv Special Angel) and Best Brood Bitch was given to Warwyck Surprise Party (Ch. Bahlambs Blue Book – Ch. Droverdale's Lady Barbella). One year later at the Los Angeles Specialty, under breed specialist Caj Haakansson, the Warwycks repeated their success by sweeping the board again. Best of Breed went to the three-year-old Sniflik Warwyck Darwin (Ch. Aphrodite Snow Sniflik – Ch. Warwyck Bonnie Bandit), owned by Susan Davis, who gained his title on the day. Bonnie Bandit went Best Opposite Sex and Best Brood Bitch. The American-bred Dogs Class was won by Warwyck Sniflik Stetson (Ch. Warwyck Duesenberg – Ch. Warwyck Bonnie Bandit). To round off this special day, several class placements also went to Warwyck dogs. Darwin became a Multiple Group and Best in Show winner. His total of Champion offspring currently stands at thirty-eight.

MOPTOP
The Moptop kennel has been responsible for more than forty OES Champions. It was owned by Woody Nelson and Buddy Satterfield, but following Buddy's tragic death, Woody is now in sole ownership. The kennel was best-known in the late seventies for the No. 1 OES in 1979. This was the multi Group and Best in Show winning Ch. Atherstone Perfect Melody. 'Biddy' was sired by the great Ch. Fezziwig Artful Dodger out of Ch. Moptop's Melody of Ragbear. Due to her early death at the age of five, Biddy produced only one litter. Sired by Ch. Stonehenge Clarence of Clyde, the litter produced six Champions: Ch. Moptop's Snowbird Symphony, Ch. Moptop's Lady Diana, Ch. Moptop's Semi Tough, Ch. Moptop's Splish Splash, Ch. Moptop's Tycoon and Ch. Moptop's Upper Crust.

Semi Tough, like his father, became a useful sire with eleven Champions to his name. Two years before Perfect Melody's great achievement, Woody Nelson handled Ch. Moptop Bombadil to the top-winning OES for 1977, 10 Group 1st, 1 Best in Show (all breeds) and many more group placements. Bombadil sired a total of fourteen Champions, seven of which were registered with the Moptop prefix.

OTHER TOP-CLASS KENNELS
Many other affixes in America deserve to have their kennels reviewed; over the years they have also contributed to an excellent high standard of the breed with mainly sound and typey dogs, which all can be proud of. In the following, I include a few breeders whose influence on the breed has been invaluable.

TAMARA: Owned by Marvin and Tammy Smith, this kennel was active from the early sixties to the early eighties. It was the home of a great English import, Ch. Tempest of Dalcroy. Together with Ch. Tamara's Patches of Perse he produced nine Tamara Champions, and overall he sired twenty-one Champions. A total of thirty-nine Champions are credited to the kennel. The Smiths also imported the Belgian dog, Shaggy Wonder Prince Charming, bred by Yvonne Mevis de Ryck.

LOVE 'N STUFF: The two sisters Marilyn and Kristi Marshall are the owners of the Love 'N

Stuff OES. They have been involved in the breed since the early seventies. In 1992 their Ch. Love 'N Stuff Parlor Party (Ch. Love 'N Stuff Obsession – Ch. Love 'N Stuff Izza Dorable) went Best of Breed at the OES of Central Arizona Specialty Show, under breed specialist Sue Richey. At the same show Love 'N Stuff Go'n Bonkers (same breeding as Parlor Party) went Winners Dog. Ch. Love 'N Stuff Grand Illusion (Ch. Love 'N Stuff Big Stuff – Love 'N Stuff Hot Stuff) was the sire of five Champions, and in total, more than forty Champions have been connected with the kennel.

COTSWOLD: Owned by Dr James and Elizabeth Layman. This couple have kept OES since 1951, but they did not start showing and breeding until their children were grown up. They were able to purchase an unshown bitch, OFA certified, and already sixteen months old. She became Ch. Buttonwoods Magic of Tatters ROM. She was based on Rivermist lines and was a Ceiling Zero grand-daughter. Of her eighteen puppies, five became Champions. Her two daughters, Ch. Squarecote Cotswold Buttons and Ch. Cotswold Magic Touch both became ROM producers. The Laymans are also very interested in Obedience work and have finished Obedience Champions as well as more than thirty show Champions.

DANDALION: Janice McClary's Dandalions are probably amongst the most titled dogs in the USA. Her Ch. Dandalion's Dreamweaver Patty gained the International American, Mexican, Dominican, Champion of the Americas 1987 and 1988, and the Peruvian, Bi-Peruvian, Grand Peruvian, South American and World 1988 title. On top of these eleven titles, Patty is also a Best in Show winner. She is bred out of Ch. Wooly Bully of Dreamweaver sired by Ch. Dandalion Sunday's Devil. Sunday's Devil was sired by Ch. Dandalion's Chunky Chicken out of Ch. Dandalion's Hot House Pansy. Top sires for the kennel are Ch. Dandalion's Lord Tanker (Ch. Momarv That's My Boy – Bobmar Noelle) with ten Champions to his name, and Ch. Dandalion's Spiffy Chicken (Lord Tanker – Aniesbury Maggie Girl) who sired nine Champions. More than thirty Champions carry the Dandalion affix.

JENDOWER: Owned by Capt. F.E. and Elizabeth Rich, the kennel is based on Droverdale and Rivermist lines in combination with some outcross matings, in particular using Ch. Prospect Shaggy Boy. Top brood bitches were Ch. Jendower's Cloud Nine, with six Champions to her credit, and Ch. Jendower's Queen Victoria, who produced seven Champions. Several Jendower males ensured that the affix figured high in the ranking of Champion sires. Ch. Jendower's Paddy sired twenty-two Champions and Ch. Jendower's Spencer was the sire of twenty-one Champions. The Jendower's foundation bitch was Ch. Rivermist Gentian out of the famous Ceiling Zero – Baroness of Duroya litter. In her time Gentian was the all-time top-producing dam, with fourteen Champions from matings to Ch. Unnesta Pim, Ch. Prospect Shaggy Boy and Ch. Rivermist Dan Tatters.

TALISMAN: Owned by Carol Moss, more than forty Champions have been bred over the years. The Fort Lauderdale's top Herding dog in 1985 and their 1986 show dog of the year was Am. Ch. Talisman's Jay Silverheels (Talisman Folies A Bit of Blue – Ch. Talisman's Bluer Than Blue). 'Jay-Jay' is a Best in Show winner who was retired at three and a half years of age, with a record twenty-six Group firsts and sixty-eight Best of Breeds. Seven champions were sired by the top-siring Talisman OES male, Ch. Talisman's Dunder Blue (Ch. Talisman's Sir Wulfgar Blue – Ch. Talisman's Tinsel Top). Top Brood Bitch is Ch. Talisman's Snoshu Crescendo (Ch. Winnoby's Dictator of Talisman – Talisman's Out of the Blue). Five Champions, all to Ch. Brightcut Limited

Edition, registered with the Crescendo prefix, are to her credit.

TROSAMBE BLUE PANDA: Owned by Diane McKee and her daughter, Lita Long, this kennel is known as much for Show Champions as for Obedience Champions. Established in the early seventies, by the time they reached their twenty-fifth anniversary the kennel's record stood at:
45 American Championships, 19 Canadian Championships, 21 American Companion Dog Degrees, 8 Canadian Companion Dog Degrees, 4 American Companion Dog Excellent, 2 Canadian Companion Dog Excellent, 9 European Championships, 1 Mexican Championship, 23 Herding Instinct Certificates and 8 Register of Merit Certificates. These great records speak for themselves. They were achieved by dogs with the Trosambe Blue Panda kennel name, or produced by their sires or dams.

Top Trosambe Blue Panda sire is Am. Can. Ch. Trosambe Blue Panda St Owly Am. Can. CDX, ROM, a multiple Best in Show Winner. He was sired by Am. Can. Ch. Blue Panda Snow Knight, ROM out of Misty Blue of Aaron, ROM. Top brood bitch is Ch. Blue Panda's Party Doll, who is the dam of six Champions; three out of these were Register of Merit holders, two were Group winners and one was a Specialty winner. Party Doll was sired by Dee-Dee's Noble Lord (Ch. Polar Paw Blue Panda – Am. Can. Ch. Bluedover Beau Aaron) out of Mistihills Thule Fog (sired by Ch. Bluedover Lord Baron). Lord Baron lived from 1972-1986 and was the kennel's foundation sire, with ten Champions to his credit.

The following prefixes are by no means less important than the affixes named before. They belong to the band of the dedicated breeders who tried to do their best by breeding our lovely Old English Sheepdogs. They are: Rolling Gait, Lillibrad, Barrelroll, Bugaboo, Limey Lane, Pinafore, Dollhouse, Double JJ, Canterbury, Sniflik, Squarecoat, Ambelon, Bobmar, Knottingham, Loehr, Banbury, Cheerio, Tanglewool, Wallyweather, Droverdale, Pettibone, Pidiwick, Sleepy Hollow, Brightcut, Gainsboro, Hug, Jen-Koris, Tales End and Su-Gran.

CANADA
EARLY HISTORY
In the late twenties Old English Sheepdogs bred in Canada were meeting with a lot of attention from admirers in America. One of the first Bobtail lovers in Canada was Mr F.T. James from Ontario, and he bred one of the most successful litters ever whelped in Canada, which was, in fact, English bred. He had bought a bitch from England, who was in whelp by Tenet Spook. The pedigree of the bitch, Bhurra Snow Bunting, and of Tenet Spook went back to Shepton Moonshine and some of Mrs Fare Fosse's Weather dogs.

Snow Bunting whelped her litter in June 1929, producing three bitches and two dogs. They were Snowflake, Snow Bunting of Merriedip, who went to Mrs Lewis Roesler (Merriedip), Snowball, Snow Lady, and the male, Snowman, were kept by Mr James. All five dogs were made up, and apart from Snowball, all were multiple Group winners. The two males took the Breed and the Group at Westminster. Snowman won this in 1932 when he was less than three years old, and Snowflake repeated the triumph in 1934. Snow Lady later became the dam of Walleyed Snow Bobs O'Merriedip, sired by Downderry Irresistable. Snow Bobs can be found in many present day pedigrees. Two others of Snow Lady's offspring, Snowdrift and Snowflurry (by Boxer of Vacoas) carried on by producing top-winning OES, which were admired by many well respected OES fanciers.

The most famous OES to come from Canada at this time was Am. and Can. Ch. Ideal Weather out of the English import Moonbeam Weather, and sired by the English import, Lucky Jean. Ideal

Weather was bred by Leonard Collins of Toronto. His pedigree contained some of the most famous Weather dogs, plus Blue Knight. Not many OES will ever enjoy a career like Ideal Weather. He was quite heavily marked with two dark front legs, eye and ear patches, and a short white collar. He was of perfect size for his time, standing 25in at the shoulder. During his short show career of only two years, he was always handled by Alf Loveridge, who took him to Best of Breed every time out, multiple Group firsts and eleven Best in Shows. Most of his wins must be very highly rated, as he had to beat many of the top winners at the time under the most well respected judges.

THE SEVENTIES TO THE NINETIES
Many kennels were founded during the seventies. In common with other countries, the popularity of the breed among Canadians increased enormously during this time. A very successful Old English in Canada in the early seventies was the Am. Can. Ch. Sir Lancelot of Barvan. He was shown to thirty-nine Canadian Best in Shows, sixty-three Group firsts and just under 200 Best of Breeds. His handler was Malcolm Fellows.

APHRODITE
One of the most successful kennels during the last twenty years is owned by Bette and Ken Maxwell. They started showing in 1971 and breeding in 1974, using the Aphrodite affix. They have, on average, only one litter a year, which makes the amount of Champions bred almost unbelievable. In the list of the top 25 kennels in America, published in *The Old English Times,* December 1992 the Aphrodite kennel is ranked fifth, with fifty Champions finished from 1952 to 1991. It is interesting to see that many of Ken's and Bette's OES go back to Bahlambs breeding. This includes Canada's Number 1 for 1978, Can. Am. Ch. Aphrodite Snow Frost (Can. Am. Ch. Bahlambs Brazen Bandit – Can. Am. Ch. Blenheim Far Fan Fan). Fan Fan is also by Brazen Bandit out of Ch. Tarfelu Tiny Snowflake. Frosty went BOB under breed specialist Earl Jacobson at the OES Club of Canada National Speciality Show December 1979. He was also a multiple Best in Show winner.

Frosty's full sister, Am. Can. Ch. Aphrodite Snow Flirt, was mated to Am. Can. Ch. Warwyck Wildfire O'Aphrodite (Am. Ch. Bahlambs Blue Book – Am. Ch. Shaggiluv's Special Angel), and produced Am. Can. Ch. Aphrodite Snow Scooter, who eventually became the sire of top-winning Int. Am. Can Mex. Ch. To-Jo's Root'n Toot'n Cowboy (out of the top-producing dam, Ch. Maidstone Debutante of To-Jo (Am. Ch. Whispering Oaks Tuff'n Stuff – Am. Ch. Chatelaines Exuberent Elsa), who had eighteen Champion offspring to her credit. Elsa was sired by Am. Ch. Brazen Bandit, who was also the sire of Can. Am. Ch. Snow Dude at Aphrodite (out of Can. Ch. Aphrodite Snow Bird). Dude was the No. 2 OES in 1981 in Canada. At the Canadian National Specialty November 1981, under Sheldon Rennert, he went BOB, which was a repeat of his Best of Breed at the Chicagoland Specialty Show in June 1980, under David Lee.

Dude sired Best in Show winners in Canada and Chile. He was the sire of Can. Am. Ch. Aphrodite Snow Pebbles (out of Can. Am. Ch. Snow Dumpling Aphrodite) winner of the Canadian Specialty Show in 1982, under Phil Marson. He also sired the Canadian National Specialty winner in 1985, Am. Can. Ch. Aphrodite Snow Dancer (also out of Am. Can. Ch. Snow Dumpling Aphrodite). Snow Dancer's half-sister, Am. Can. Ch. Aphrodite Snow Tara Tara (by Am. Can. Ch. Warwyck Wildfire O' Aphrodite) was Best Opposite Sex at the same Specialty Show. To round things off, Dumpling's daughter, Can. Ch. Aphrodite Dare Devil, took the Best Puppy and Reserve Winners Bitch at only seven months of age. Dare Devil was sired by Am. Can. Ch. Warwyck Wildfire O'Aphrodite.

Snow Dumpling was Ken and Bette's foundation bitch, whelped on August 15th 1974 (Can. Ch. Farfelu Facsimile – Can. Ch. Canterbury Misty Maxwell). Dumpling lived to the good age of eleven and a half. She died on January 21st 1988, leaving a total of twenty Champions, which gives her the title of the top-producing dam of all time. Together with Am. Can. Ch. Warwyck Wildfire O' Aphrodite she produced Am. Can. Aphrodite Snow Crystal, Am. Can. Ch. Aphrodite Dare Devil, Am. Can. Ch. Aphrodite Dare To Be Different, Can. Ch. Aphrodite Snow Trix, Am. Can. Ch. Aphrodite Snow Fall at To-Jo, Am. Can. Ch. Aphrodite Tuff Act to Follow, Am. Can. Ch. Aphrodite Road Runner, Am. Can. Ch. Aphrodite Snow Sniflik, Am. Can. Ch. Aphrodite Snow Fresh, Am. Can. Ch. Aphrodite Snow Tara Tara, Am. Can. Ch. Aphrodite Snow Sassy Warwyck, Am. Can. Ch. Aphrodite Snow Candy Cane, Am. Can. Ch. Aphrodite Snow Crisp, and Am. Can. Ch. Aphrodite Snow Toot Toobie.

All of Dumpling's other Champions were sired by Ch. Snow Dude at Aphrodite: Am. Can. Ch. Aphrodite Snow & Sky, Am. Can. Ch. Aphrodite Snow Pebbles, Am. Ch. Aphrodite Snow Pixie, Am. Can. Ch. Aphrodite Promise to Paris, Am. Can. Ch. Aphrodite Snow Dancer and Am. Can. Ch. Aphrodite Snow Puddin. Many of Dumpling's Champions became Group and BIS winners, as well as being top producers for the Maxwells or for their new owners.

Snow Sniflik, owned in partnership with Bette Maxwell and Linda Burns, ranks amongst the first five top-producing sires of all time, with thirty-seven Champions to his credit. One other top producer bred by this kennel was Am. Can. Aphrodite Snow Scooter (Ch. Warwyck Wildfire O' Aphrodite – Am. Ch. Aphrodite Snow Flirt). Eleven Champions, mainly for the To-Jo's kennel, go to his credit.

SOME BUDDY
Owned by Dr Gary and Terry Carter of Calgary, this kennel was established in 1966. Together with the well-known Jim McTernan, who handled many Rivermist and Fezziwig dogs, they owned the No. 1 OES in Canada in 1970-71, Can. Am. Ch. Rivermist Feather Merchant CD (Ch. Unnesta Pim – Ch. Rivermist Nosegay). Feather Merchant became the sire of many Champions, notably Am. Can. Ch. Some Buddy's Cotton Candy (out of Can. Ch. Peace Hill's Princess Michelle) who in turn became one of the top-producing dams for the kennel. In her litters to Can. Ch. Some Buddy Ready to Ruffit (Can. Ch. Bobtail Acre's Rough N Ready – Am. Can. Ch. Windfield Friendly Fiancee CD) she produced the top-winning sires, Am. Can. Ch. Some Buddy Bring on the Clowns and Am. Can. Ch. Some Buddy Leading The Parade, a multiple Group winner in Canada. Cotton Candy is also the dam of Can. Ch. Some Buddy's Tall Flower (sired by Ch. Rollingait's Buttonwood), who was another top producer. Her offspring included a Canadian Specialty Breed Winner, and most notably Can. Am. Ch. Some Buddy I'm a Believer (by Ch. Jendower's Spencer) who was a Specialty Breed winner. When bred to Ch. Wiggans Little Bear she produced Can. Ch. Some Buddy Believe It Or Not and Can. Ch. Some Buddy's Mr Cool, who became a Group winner from the puppy classes.

One other top-producing male of the kennel was Am. Can. Ch. Some Buddy Catch the Action. His offspring included: Ch. Some Buddy Just a Doll (out of Some Buddy's Razzle Dazzle), Ch. Some Buddy's Great Expectations and Ch. Some Buddy's Promises Promises (out of Ch. Some Buddy's Just My Style), and Int. Danish Ch. Some Buddy Canadian Ambassador (out of Can. Ch. Some Buddy Love in Symphony).

OTHER TOP-CLASS KENNELS
FRENESIE: Owned by Eliane and Pascal Lo Bianco of Montreal, with Can. Ch. Frenesie First in

Line, Can. Ch. Aphrodite Finders Keepers, Can. Am. Ch. Frenesie Corey Hart, all sired by Am. Can. Ch. Frenesie Reach for the Top, a multiple Group and BIS winner, and No. 1 OES in Canada in 1983.

AURIGA: Owned by Martin and Cathy Doherty of Orangeville, Ontario. This kennel is partly based on Bahlambs lines. Can. Am. Ch. Auriga's Magnum Fargaze, out of Can. Am. Ch. Blenheim Auriga Avec Casque (Am. Can. Ch. Bahlambs Brazen Bandit – Can. Ch. Farfelu Tiny Snowflake), sired by Can. Am. Ch. Fargaze Willy Wonka (Can. Am. Ch. Farfelu Fearless Fido – Silverwood's Low Overhead) took Best of Winners at the SIKC Show on June 26th 1983, under the breed specialist Woody Nelson. Can. Am. Ch. Auriga's Peter Pan mated to Can. Ch. Fargaze Jenny produced the Group winner, Can. Am. Ch. Muriga. Fargaze's dam, Avec Casque, had been BIS under the world-famous Florence Tilley (Shepton) at the OESCA National Specialty, with a record entry of more than 300.

BARVAN: Owned by Barbara Vanword-McGregor and Alan G. McGregor, Newmarket, Ontario. Their Champions include Can. Ch. Barvan's Afternoon Delight, Can. Ch. Barvan's Count Tancredi and Can. Ch. Windfield Prayers & Promises (Ch. Windfield Barrister – Ol'targhee's Proud Shepherd), Can. Ch. Barvan's Forever in Blue Jeans (Ch. Barvan's Park Avenue Playboy – Am. Can. Ch. Barvan's Pilgrim Apple Dumplin), and Am. Can. Ch. Barvan's Officer & Gentleman (Ch. Barvan's Park Avenue Playboy – Am. Can. Ch. Barvan's Pilgrim Apple Dumplin.

Park Avenue Playboy is also the sire of Am. Can. Ch. Barvan's Chairman of the Board (out of Ch. Rodyke's Lady Diane Barvan), who went BOB at 1985 Westminster Kennel Club, under breed specialist Hendrick Van Rensselaer, and Best of Winners in 1984 at Westminster Kennel Club, under Virginia Hampton. 'Drew' is a multiple Group winner in Canada, under the respected judges, Robert Forsythe and Robert Wills, among others.

Chapter Seven

THE OES IN SCANDINAVIA

SWEDEN

The first two OES registered in Sweden were the English imports Bonny Nell of Bullfighter, owned by Lady Birgitta Bennet, and Lord St. Levan, owned by Lt. Stjemsvards. They were shown at a Championship show in 1907 with the bitch going BOB. This pair also produced the first OES litter born in Sweden, 1909.

The leading kennel in the thirties was Opp's, owned by Olga Brusell. During the Second World War the breed almost died out. It was saved by the famous Sara Leander, who imported a dog from Germany, named Banco of Windermere. This dog and a bitch from the Opp's kennel kept the breed alive.

In 1950 Mrs F. Backx-Bennink from Holland exported a litter brother and sister to Sweden. These were Reeuwijk's Charming Girl and Reeuwijk's Cupid, who was later to become the first International and Nordic Champion. He was later owned by Maine Lundell-Olsson of the Farmarens kennel, and became very influential as a sire. A mating of these two Reeuwijk dogs produced a litter of seven puppies, four of which were to become Champions.

UNNESTA

In 1957 Shepton Sally Ann was imported to the Unnesta kennel, owned by Marta Hult-Korfitsen. Together with Ch. Reeuwijk's Cupid, she produced several good litters. The most important puppy from this pairing was Ch. Unnesta Pim, later also to become the kennel's most famous dog. Marta had first seen the breed in Denmark, and Shepton Sally Ann was her first OES. In Sally Ann's first litter with Ch. Reeuwijk's Cupid, she produced two puppies – Unnesta Pussy and Unnesta Pim – and both became Champions. Pim was later sold to Caj Haakansson, owner of the world-famous Bahlambs kennel. He took Pim to England and later to America, where he gained both titles. Sold to the Rivermist kennel in USA, he became one of the all-time top-producing sires in America.

Pim's litter sister, who was mated back to her father, Cupid, produced Unnesta Holyday, who became the foundation bitch of Anita Olsson's Holymans kennel. Pussy's last litter was sired by another import, Ch. Rollingsea Gordon Pride, and this produced Unnesta Hoppsan. In the meantime, Sally Ann was mated to Blue Crest Happy Fella and the result was three bitches. One bitch was exported to Holland, one to Denmark, and the third, Unnesta Piccolo, was retained by the kennel. Piccolo was mated to another import from the Reeuwijk's kennel, Reeuwijk's Fernville Fair Friday, and produced Unnesta Stormogul. When Stormogul was mated to Hoppsan, the result was Unnesta Verdi. Marta considers Stormogul and Verdi the most important stud dogs in her kennel.

ABOVE: The Unnesta
OESs: pictured left to
right) Hasard, Pussy, Pilo,
Happy and Ch. Unnesta
Pim, later to become one of
the all-time top-producing
sires in America.

LEFT: Int. Ch. Unnesta
Pluto, top-winning OES in
1986, 1987 and 1988.

Two other imports, Reeuwijk's Lady Lucy and Gracia of Roselodge, were very important for the future of the Unnesta Old English Sheepdogs. When Stormogul was mated to Lady Lucy, the result was Ch. Unnesta Aurora, and when she was put to Ch. Don Juan, they produced Unnesta Grandios. She was later mated back to her father, resulting in Unnesta Katinka. Katinka put to Farmarens Angus produced Unnesta Niklas.

Niklas and Lapaloma were the parents of three Champions: Ch. Unnesta Richarda, Ch. Unnesta

Regina and Ch. Unnesta Rival. Rival was sold to the Farmarens kennel, and he became the top OES in 1983 and 1984. Both bitches, Regina and Richarda, were later mated to Ch. Bahlambs Broadway Bonanza, Richarda becoming the dam of Ch. Unnesta Pluto, top-winning OES in 1986, 1987, and 1988. He was also among the five top-winning dogs all breeds in 1987 and 1988. Bonanza mated to Regina produced Ch. Unnesta Halligang, the top-winning OES in 1989 and 1990. Halligang was No. 2 and No. 3 top-winning dog all breeds in these years.

FARMARENS

The Farmarens kennel is owned by Maine Lundell-Olsson. Her first OES was a gift from Mr and Mrs Cedergen, who had imported Ch. Reeuwijk's Cupid from Holland. The second OES in the kennel was Unnesta Chooli. She was the mother of the first litter born with the Farmarens affix, which was sired by Rollingsea Gordon Pride. Farmarens Cynthia, a bitch from this litter, later gained her International Champion title. In 1965 Mrs Lundell-Olsson imported her next female, Amberford Hygd, known as 'Lucy'.

Lucy became the mother of a total of twenty-one puppies, by different sires. Ten of her puppies were exported: one to the USA to Caj Haakansson (Bahlambs), four went to Denmark, and five to Norway. Ch. Don Juan was also a gift to the kennel. He was mated to Lucy, resulting in Farmarens Samantha. Samantha mated to the English import, Ch. Prospectblue Tommy Tucker, was a very successful combination for the Farmarens kennel and other European kennels. Their offspring included Ch. Farmarens Apollo, who became the top-winning OES in East Europe in 1977, Ch. Farmarens Angus the No. 1 OES in Sweden in 1976, and Ch. Farmarens Amanda, top-winning Bobtail in Sweden in 1977, and No. 1 Veteran in 1984. When Samantha was mated to a dog called Obelix, a bitch called Farmarens Raggedy Rascal was kept. She became an Int. and Nordic Ch. and the top-winning Veteran in 1986.

In 1981 Maine acquired Unnesta Rival, later to become Int. and Nordic Champion, and also No. 1 OES in 1983 and 1984. Ch. Farmarens Raggedy Rascal was mated to Ch. Unnesta Rival twice, and in the second litter these two Champions produced a puppy whom Maine rated as the best bitch born in her kennel. This was Int. and Nordic Ch. Farmarens Bring On The Clown, known as 'Clownie'. Rival's last litter produced a dog puppy, Farmarens Wery Well Winston. He was two years old when he was shown for the first time, but he went BIS at an all breed Championship show. He later finished his title, and went on to become the No. 1 OES in 1988.

Believing in the regular introduction of new blood, the Farmarens kennel imported Boundalong Blithe Spirit, bred by Mrs Sinclair Day of the Boundalong kennel in England. He was sired by Rollingsea High Spirit and his dam was Boundalong Beautiful Dream. In 1987 he was used on Ch. Farmarens Bring on the Clown. She produced a fine litter, and Ch. Farmarens Jasper of Spirit was kept by the kennel.

When docking was banned in Sweden, this highly successful kennel stopped breeding OES, but it is a top-winning kennel for Bearded Collies with over one hundred homebred Champions.

OLD FASHION

Eva Fabiansson-Jonsson's first OES was Unnesta Hamlet, but it was not until the late sixties that she started her own breeding programme. For this she imported a male and a closely related female from the English Prospectblue kennel, owned by Isobel Lawson. These were Ch. Prospectblue Mary Anne (Prospectblue Andrew – Whitefall Mig Midnight) and Andrew's litter sister, Prospectblue Angelique, sired by Eng. Am. Ch. Prospectblue Rodger. Ch. Prospectblue Mary Anne was put to Ch. Holymans Obligness, resulting in several Champions.

Another import for the kennel came from Shaggy Wonder kennel in Belgium, which was based on the early Reeuwijk's dogs. Shaggy Wonder Lord X Copy was used on Ch. Prospectblue Mary Ann, and the only puppy born was Ch. Old Fashion A Touch of Gold. When she was mated to another English import, Ch. Oldash Sea Fabel, she produced Int. & Nordic Ch. Old Fashion Doctor Special, No. 10 Dog of the Year 1980, and Ch. Old Fashion Dancing Queen. Dancing Queen had three litters, producing a total of six Champions, notably Ch. Old Fashion Sky is the Limit, sired by Ch. Askelepios. 'Fame' as she was known, was a great winner for the kennel, with several Groups and BIS going to her credit.

Eva, who is a vet, decided to look outside the country for a suitable stud dog. The male she chose was Den. Ch. Somebuddy Canadian Ambassador, owned by another vet, Birgitte Schjoth. Both vets worked out the plans for an artificial insemination, and this resulted in Ch. Old Fashion Canadian Way and Ch. Old Fashion Crack the Sky, known as 'Pamela'.

In 1983 a new English import came to the Old Fashion kennel – Raynham Viscount (Raynham Scaramouch – Rollingsea Alice Blue Gown) bred by Jenny Joice. Viscount put to Pamela produced a few more Champions for the Old Fashion kennel. Ch. Old Fashion Sky is the Limit whelped her second litter (sired by Ch. Old Fashion to the Manor Born), and this produced the twenty-fifth Champion for the kennel, named Ch. Old Fashion Cloud Nine.

Three years later Eva looked out for some new blood to be introduced to her lines. She found it in her new English import, Lamedazottel A Star is Born (from my own kennel). This dog later became a Champion, a Group winner, and a Best in Show winner. He is sired by Ufo-Star a. d. Elbe Urstromtal out of Int. Germ. Swiss. Ned. Ch. Zottel's Estee Lauder. 'Theodor' has not only made his mark in the show ring, but he has also sired several Champions.

TEDDY BEAR

Elin Vanner Salin started with OES in the mid-fifties. Her first Bobtail, 'Dorothy', came from Mrs Grahl. 'Dorothy' was made up and later mated to her half-brother, Ch. Unnesta Pim. Out of that combination came Ch. Teddy Bear Bobo, a male who was to become an influential stud dog in the breed. He gained his Int. and Nordic Champion title and was also dog of the year in 1964.

Other Champions from this pairing were: Ch. Teddy Bear Oliver, Ch. Teddy Bear Angela, Ch. Teddy Bear Gentle Gregory, Ch. Teddy Bear Fair Fhilip, and Ch. Teddy Bear Dorothy Doll. This kennel has never done a lot of breeding, but through 'Bobo' it is represented in many present pedigrees.

SHAGGY DOGS

Anita Zetterstrom had her first OES puppy out of the Ch. Dorothy – Ch. Unnesta Pim litter, and this was Ch. Teddy Bear Bobo. He was shown for the first time at ten months of age and proved to be an excellent show dog, winning the CC and BOB, and then added a Group second for good measure. He ended his show career with the Int. Dk. Ch title and Dog of the Year 1964. In the same year Anita imported a bitch called Raywill Rowena, who gained the same title as Bobo. The two dogs produced their first litter in 1966. It proved to be a very successful combination, and over the years they produced: Ch. Shaggy Dogs Bingo Star, Ch. Shaggy Dogs Bamse Bear and Ch. Shaggy Dogs Cheerie Dream Girl.

One of Bobo's daughters, out of Prospectblue Tinkerbell (bred by G. Niskas), came to the Shaggy Dogs kennel. Her name was Chanelle, later to become Ch. Chanelle. Her first litter, sired by Ch. Big Deal of the Embages, produced three successful dogs – Ch. Shaggy Dog Chan Brasse Baron, who went to Karen Larsen in Denmark, Shaggy Dogs Bernhard, who went to Germany, and Shaggy Dogs Beautiful Boggie, who went to Norway. Big Deal ('Bigs') came to live with the Shaggy Dogs in 1970. He was sired by Raidor Bundle out of Bess of the Embages, bred by Dorothy Malins in England. For five years (1970-1975) Bigs was the No. 1 OES in Sweden. Raywill Rowena was mated to Big Deal for her last litter and she produced three puppies. One bitch, Shaggy Dogs Happy Girl, was mated to the ten-and-a-half-year-old Bobo, and this resulted in five puppies. One of them, Shaggy Dogs Happylix, later became an Int. and Nordic Ch. When she was mated to Big Deal, three more Shaggy Dogs Champions resulted: Ch. Shaggy Dogs Bambarie Try Again, Ch. Shaggy Dogs Bang Wish Me Luck, and Ch. Shaggy Dogs Brilliante Best of All, who was exported to the USA.

Two more imports came to the kennel. In 1980 Shendar Silver Star arrived, later to become Int. and Nordic Champion, and the top-winning OES Veteran in 1985 and 1988. The second import came from England from the famous Wenallt kennel. Wenallt Contender (Eng. Am. Can. Ch. Tynycoed Caradog ap Tegwch – Wenallt Ben Girl Contender) was imported in partnership with a Finnish kennel, but when Finland changed its quarantine law and opened its borders to Europe, Sweden closed its borders to Finland. Contender was in Sweden at the time and never went back to Finland, and so was shown to his title in Sweden.

HOLYMANS

Anita Olsson who owns the Holymans affix got her first OES from the Unnesta kennel in 1964. Unnesta Holyday, who later became a Champion, was mated to Shaggy Wonder Oblingness. From the resulting litter a dog puppy was kept, Ch. Holymans Obligness. He sired several Champions and was later sold to Mrs Garvin in the USA. In 1968 Mrs Olsson imported Nancy of Embages from England. Nancy was a daughter of the famous Ch. Bevere Proud Monarch out of Nan of the Embages, bred by Dorothy Malins. She later imported Avenger of Oldash (Silver Image of Oldash – Bridlepath Blue Mist), a two-year-old male, from Jill Harwood in England. Both dogs went on to become Champions.

In 1973 Ch. Rollingsea Comet was imported from Jean Gould's famous Rollingsea OES. He was mated to Ch. Old Fashion Mistress Choice, resulting in Holymans Baby Doll, who was sold to Denmark. When Nancy of Embages was mated to Ch. Avenger of Oldash, a dog pup, named Holymans Adamson ('Mao'), was kept, but after he gained his title he was sold to the USA. A litter sister to 'Mao' mated to Comet produced Ch. Holymans Askelepios, who later sired several Champions: Ch. Old Fashion Thunder of the Sea, Ch. Old Fashion Sky is the Limit, Ch. Mandy's Master Mind, Ch. Likeabear Attention Please, and Ch. Likeabear Abracadabra, who was purchased by Anita Olsson and went BIS at two Specialty shows two years in a row.

Other homebred Champions were Ch. Holymans Legacy of Adam (Ch. Askelepios – Old Fashion Mistress Choice), and Ch. Holymans Winston (Ch. Rollingsea Comet – Oldash Loving Legend).

MANDY'S

Margitta Ersson bought her first OES, Unnesta Jolanta, in 1973 from the Unnesta kennel. In 1977 she imported the English-bred Barnspring Mandy (Gwelelog Whelsh Gelert – Mistress Nobetta of Embages) from Mrs Allen. Mandy gained her title and for her first litter she was mated to Ch. Oldash Sea Fabel. A bitch was kept, Ch. Mandy's My Fair Lady. Her litter brother, Int. and Nordic Ch. Mandy's Midnight Express, was No. 1 OES in 1982, and he was very successful in the ring as a veteran.

Mandy and Ch. Askelepios produced Int. and Nordic Ch. Mandy's Master Mind, the top-winning OES male in 1985. Ch. Mandy's My Fair Lady had a litter by Ch. Likeabear Abracadabra, resulting in Ch. Mandy's My Kind of Lady. Unfortunately, Margetta, like many other top breeders, felt that when the docking ban came into force she did not want to breed anymore.

Two other homebred champions were Ch. Mandy's Master Mind (Ch. Askelepios – Barnspring Mandy), and Ch. Mandy's Midsummer Dream (Mandy's Magie-Noie – Ch. Mandy's My Fair Lady).

HONEYSUCLE
Kristina Purens has bred quite a few Champions over the years. Kristina started breeding with an imported bitch, Barkwith Lucy Manett of Oldash (Oldash Sea Legend – Shanwille Little Bo Peep of Barkwith). Lucy was later shown to her Int. and Nordic Ch. title. She was mated to Ch. Old Fashion Doctor Special and produced Ch. Honeysucle Lucky Lady. When Lucy Manett was mated to Ch. Askelepios (Ch. Rollingsea Comet – Holymans Blue Bird), she produced Honeysucle Mischief Maker, who was later to gain his title. When Honeysucle Lovely Liza was mated to Beowulf New Broom, the result was Ch. Honeysucle Near-My-Heart.

Another addition to the Honeysucle kennel was Old Fashion Summer Symphony, bred by Mrs Fabiansson-Johnsson. Mated to Ch. Raynham Viscount, she produced Honeysucle PS I Love You, who also gained her title, adding another Champion to the Honeysucle kennel. Ch. Rollingsea Viceroy is the sire of her English import Ch. Primadonna of Rollingsea, the dam is Rollingsea Starturn.

Ch. Tallyddans T Scramble (Old Fashion of the Sea – Pelajilo Bouquet), bred by Y. Hedin-Elg, later became the dam of Ch. Honeysucle Ready Steady Go (Ch. Lamedazottel A Star is Born).

GREAT DANISH
Yrsa Tranberg started her kennel with Wolly Wandering Star, later to become a Champion. This bitch was artificially inseminated by Den. Ch. Somebuddy Canadian Ambassador, which resulted in three Champions: Ch. Great Danish What-A-Guy, Ch. Great Danish Watch Out, and Ch. Great Danish Wanna Be Loved. In 1986 Yrsa imported Peaceful Dreams Lovely Lady, who, when mated to Ch. Lameda Zottel A Star is Born, produced Ch. Great Danish Leading Lady.

HJARTER ESS
The kennel's affix comes from Ingrid Thoren-Ahlstrom's foundation bitch, Ch. Unnesta Hjarter Ess. Her breeding is based on the Unnesta lines with five homebred Champions to her credit. Ch. Unnesta Hjarter Ess has been successful in the show ring, especially as a veteran, winning several BIS.

FOOTPRINTS
Anita Skoglund started with Farmarens and Fezziwig bloodlines. Her bitch, Sjorstrands Bluemasked Barbara, mated to Playmates Julius produced six Champions: Ch. Footprints After Me Dear, Ch. Footprints After Paul, Ch. Footprints After Please, Ch. Footprints After Me Sir, Ch. Footprints Barry McGuire, and Ch. Footprints Bonnie Jean.

When Sjorstrands Bluemasked Barbara was mated to Ch. Timmy (Playmates Julius – Wrightway Sweet Sue), the result was Ch. Footprints Evening Love. Emmerdale's Fancy Felicia mated to Ch. Footprints After Me Sir gave two more Champions: Ch. Footprints Daystar and Ch. Footprints Daybreak.

Ch. Bahlambs Bedazzling Bear: Number One OES in Sweden in 1991.

Per Unden.

DIZZNY'S

Until recently, Ingela and Per Wallstrom were better known as successful exhibitors. They own Ch. Unnesta Pluto and Ch. Unnesta Halligang, and the American import, Ch. Bahlambs Bedazzling Bear (Ch. Bahlambs Bobby Brown – Ch. Bahlambs British Begonia). All three OES made their mark in the show ring: Halligang and Pluto as mentioned before, and Bedazzling Bear was No. 1 OES in 1991, top-winning bitch all breeds in the same year, and No. 4 overall. She is a multi Group and BIS winner.

In 1992 Ingela and Per bred their first litter out of Bedazzling Bear, sired by Halligang. Knowing both animals, I am sure their offspring will do well.

NORWAY

The first OES to be registered in Norway was in 1910. The dog's name was Kiddy, but the pedigree is unknown. The next registrations were not until 1932, and they were a male and a female, bred by Olga Brusell in Sweden, using English imports. Opp's Teddy Bear and Opp's Lurva were sired by Ch. Sergeant Mutt out of Ch. Bess Steadfast, who were to become the parents of the first OES litter bred in Sweden. This litter out of the brother-sister mating was registered in 1933 by Lizzie Juul, who was the first OES breeder to officially register an affix – Svartskogen. Two pups out of this combination, Svartskogen Troll and Svartskogen Tufsa, did very well in the show ring. In 1937 two more imports arrived in Norway, this time from the UK. They were Floss Jackline (Shepton Chief – Shepton Delphinia) and Pensford Snowball (Piccadilly Dandy – Pensford Rosa) who was bred by H. E. Saunders. Due to the outbreak of the Second World War there were no litters registered or Bobtails shown until 1946, when Ch. Shepton Princess Charming was imported from the UK.

No progress was made in the breed for the next twenty years – no OES were registered in the fifties, and it was not until 1966 that an Old English Sheepdog made a name for himself. This was the Danish import, Jolly Bears Johnny (Int. Nord. Ch. Teddy Bear Bobo – Int. Ch. Lady MacDuff), who went on to become an International Champion. In the same year the Swedish import, Unnesta Sebastian (Int. Ch. Fernville Fair Friday – Int. Ch. Unnesta Piccolo) also became a Champion.

Thirty-six years after the registration of the first OES litter in Norway, the second litter was officially recorded in 1969. The sire was Int. Nord. Ch. Teddy Bear Bobo and the dam was Ch. White Mansion Snow Queen. A new English import from the Embages kennel also arrived in 1969. This was Nor. Nord. Ch. Barnaby of the Embages (Eng. Ch. Bevere Proud Monarch – Bess of the Embages), who was to become an active sire in Norway, with eight litters going to his credit.

The Norsk OES Klubb was founded in 1971. During the first ten years the club registered 650 Bobtails, with British imports playing an important role with forty new registrations. There are several kennels who had an impact on the breed, and it is because of the dedication of these breeders that the OES has become successful at International shows, with several dogs taking the No. 1 spot in Groups and Best in Show.

SNUTA

Laila Eggan Hansch started her well-known OES with two females based on English and American lines. These were Nor. Swed. Ch. Proper Duchesse (Nord. Ch. Rollingsea the Duke – Nor. Ch. Proper Lilane) and Nor. Ch. Sjostrands Blackeyed Belinda (Nor. Ch. Beowulf New Broom – Fezziwig Cinderella). Both bitches were whelped in November 1981. Proper Duchesse goes back to Rollingsea lines on her sire's side, and to Oldash and Embages lines on her dam's side. Blackeyed Belinda has Pockethall breeding on her sire's side, and her dam, Fezziwig Cinderella, was sired by Am. Ch. Fezziwig Hoodwink out of Fezziwig Bluemasked Barbara.

These two bitches were not just good show girls, they proved to be of even greater value as brood bitches. Belinda produced four Champions. Two of these Champion offspring were sired by Swed. Ch. Old Fashion To the Manor Born, who was bred by the well-known Swedish OES breeder, Eva Fabiansson. The other two Champions were by Nor. Ch. Peaceful Dream Sir Thomas. Proper Duchesse produced a total of six Champions. Two were sired by Nord. Ch. Holymans Legacy of Adam, two by Nord. Ch. Brinkley Sebastian, one each by Nor. Ch. Baylind Mister

Int. Nor. Swed. Ch. Snuta's Elegant Miss Agatha: Dam of the first undocked Norwegian Champion.

Mottram, and one by Swed. Ch. Old Fashion To the Manor Born. Both bitches have also been responsible for Champion-producing offspring. Nor. Swed. Ch. Snuta's Flitting Amanda (Nor. Ch. Peaceful Dream Sir Thomas – Nor. Ch. Sjostrands Blackeyed Belinda) was mated to Int. Nor. Swed. Ch. Snuta's Eminent Sir Roderick (Nord. Ch. Brinkley Sebastian – Nor. Swed. Ch. Proper Duchesse), which resulted in Nor. Ch. Snuta's Hillbilly Hector, and Nor. Ch. Snuta's Hearty Halima. When mated to Tuckles Treacle Toffee, Amanda also produced Nor. Ch. Snuta's Kind Kitty.

Int. Nor. Swed. Ch. Snuta's Elegant Miss Agatha (Nord. Ch. Brinkley Sebastian – Nor. Swed. Ch. Proper Duchesse), mated to Nor. Ch. Likebear Blueprint, became the dam of the first undocked Norwegian OES Champion.

ROSENHJORTH

Dr Leif Ragnar Hjorth and Steiner Rosenberg first became involved in OES in 1981 with the English import, Nor. Ch. Prospectblue Tessa (Prospectblue Brigand – Ch. Tinkebelle of Prospectblue), bred by the late Isobel Lawson. Having been lucky with their first import, they decided to bring over a male from England. This time they went to Pam Tomes's Brinkley kennel. Again their choice proved to be right, as Brinkley Sebastian (Pockethall Playboy of Brinkley – Brinkley Misty Blue) was soon to become Nor. Swed. Fr. Champion, and on top of that, he was one of the most influential studs in Scandinavia.

Sebastian achieved Best in Show and Res. BIS awards in Sweden, and sired several top-winning Champions. His daughter, Int. Nor. Swed. Ch. Rosenhjorth's Te-Ba Cornelia (out of Nor. Ch. Prospectblue Tessa) was the top OES in 1989. With a total of eighteen Champions to his credit, he most certainly proved to be an asset to the breed in Norway and Sweden. Sebastian's own show records also speak for themselves. He was among the top five OES in 1985, 1986, and 1987.

The Rosenhjorth kennel's best year was 1991, with three litter sisters in the limelight. Nor. Ch. Rosenhjorth's Ti-To Electra was No. 1 OES, Nor. Swed. Ch. Rosenhjorth's Ettie was No. 2 OES, and Nor. Ch. Rosenhjorth's Evita ended the year with the seventh place in the top ten list. This litter of five pups was by Swed. Ch. Rayham Viscount out of Nor. Swed. Ch. Rosenhjorth's Te-Go

Nord. Ch. Brinkley Sebastian: Imported from the UK and one of the most influential sires in Scandinavia.

Arabelle, and it produced four Champions. In 1992 Messrs Hjorth and Rosenberg imported a mature male from Holland, Das Beste a. d. Elbe Urstromtal (Int. Germ. Dk. Ned. Ch. Osborn a. d. Elbe Urstromtal – Int. Germ. Pol. Ch. Quality Street a. d. Elbe Urstromtal). 'Kevin' was originally sold to Rita Molhock of Barking Bears OES in Holland. However, following Rita's tragic premature death he went back to his breeder, Mrs C. Hartman (formerly Abicht). He was shown for a while with some excellent results, and was later sent in an exchange to the USA, to the famous Trosambe Blue Panda kennel. Kevin achieved some great show results in America, and he also sired some good litters for the Blue Pandas. He came back to Holland in 1989 and was shown to several more Champion titles by Mrs Hartman until 1992, when Leif and Steiner became his new owners.

To his impressive show record, he has now added the Nor. Champion title, which makes him probably the only OES to achieve the International, USA, German, Canadian, Danish, French, Netherland and Norwegian Champion titles. I am sure he will, in time, add a few more to the total of seven Champions bred by the Rosenhjorth kennel to date.

LIKEABEAR

In 1986 and 1987 Norway's OES scene was dominated by the Likeabear kennel, owned by the American, Diane Anderson. Nor. Ch. Likeabear Attention Please (Swed. Ch. Askelepios – Nor. Ch. Simberdale My Fair Lady of Raynham) was the No. 1 top-winning OES in 1986; No. 2 was his litter sister, Nor. Ch. Likeabear Anne's Choice, who took over her brother's No. 1 place a year later. Attention Please was also the top-winning OES in Scandinavia in 1986. Mrs Anderson is now living in America again.

SHAGGY

The Shaggy kennel is owned by Anne and Werner Hagun, and their many Champions go back mainly to the English Embages lines. In 1982 a bitch, born tail-less, was the top OES bitch. She was Nor. Ch. Shaggy's Wild Rose (Nor. Ch. Beowulf New Broom – Mistress Blue Mab of Embages).

Nor. Ch. Shaggy's She Belongs To Me: Top-winning female OES.

In 1983 another Shaggy OES bitch, Nor. Ch. Shaggy's She Belongs To Me (Int. Nord. Ch. Playmates Gordon – Shaggy's Rose Queen) took over the top-winning female spot. Her dam, Rose Queen, was the litter sister to Wild Rose. She had two litters by Int. Nord. Ch. Playmates Gordon (Farmarens Angus – Prospectblue Minibella) and she produced nine Champions. Two of these, Nor. Ch. Shaggy's Babusjka Sirkeline and Nor. Ch. Shaggy's Lovely Hannah, were number two and number three in the top ten list in 1984 and 1985 respectively.

The Shaggy kennel was the home of two imports. Nor. Ch. Beowulf New Broom (Ch. Pockethall New Shoes – Ch. Bamblebarn New Penny) was bred in England by the Coopers and became a popular and successful stud dog. The Haguns' other import came from Sweden. He was Int. Nord. Ch. Playmates Gordon (Int. Nor. Swed. Fr. Ch. Farmarens Angus – Swed. Fr. Ch. Prospectblue Minibella), bred by Vor Wiger. This dog stayed in Norway for about four years, becoming the first Norwegian Champion to gain the title of top-winning OES in Scandinavia. He is also the sire of several Champions.

Other Shaggy Champions worthy of mention are Nor. Ch. Shaggy's Black Muffin, and Ch. Shaggy's Black Meadow (Nord. Ch. Brinkley Sebastian – Nor. Ch. Shaggy's Lovely Hannah).

PEACEFUL DREAMS
Solweig Wang Kristianson has bred quite a few Champions. The best-known dogs are: Nor. Ch. Peaceful Dream's Pernille, Nor. Ch. Peaceful Dream's Blue Belinda, and Nor. Ch. Peaceful Dream's Lord Cedrik, all sired by Int. Nord. Ch. Playmates Gordon out of Searwell Peaceful Dream.

OTHER TOP-CLASS KENNELS
Other Norwegian OES kennels include A. Bergquist's Rock'n Roll kennel. She owns the top Scandinavian OES in 1985, Nor. Ch. Lord Peter Whimsey (Nor. Ch. Beowulf New Broom – Nor. Ch. Sjostrand Summer Song). The Baylind kennel, owned by Sue and Terje Holm-Nielsen, is based on Barnolby and Amblegait lines. They bred the foundation bitch for the Marshall kennel, owned by Anne-Britt Haakenstad. This was Nor. Ch. Baylind Lady Marchmain (Nord. Ch. Brinkley Sebastian – Nor. Ch. Amblegait Antarctica), who later produced Nor. Ch. Marshfield Artistic Amandus (by Nor. Swed. Ch. Memphis Blues).

DENMARK

The first OES to be shown in Denmark was a Swedish import called Raggylug Lavilla, and this was in 1912. In 1930 the first two Bobtails were registered with the Danish Kennel Club. Both dogs came from the Newcote kennel in England. But it took until 1935 for the first litter to be registered, and this was sired by Blue Boy out of Opp's Bessy. Blue Boy was an English import, and Bessy was imported from Sweden. Blue Boy and Bessy were also the sire and dam of the first Danish Champion – in 1939 a bitch called Lone gained her title. Until the late fifties/early sixties there were nine more Champions made up, with Bashurst Bellman siring four of them. Ch. Lone also produced two Champion children: Ch. Pernille (by Bashurst Bellman) and Ch. Fortinbras (by Opp's Jacob).

JOLLY BEARS
In 1965 one of the top-producing females gained her title when she was three years of age. Ch. Lady MacDuff (Ch. Halewyn – Zeta) was a Danish and International Champion, and she produced

a total of ten Danish Champions. Ch. Lady MacDuff was owned by the well-known Jolly Bears kennel. This top-producing OES kennel was originally owned by Mr and Mrs Christiansen, who first became involved in the breed in the early sixties. Ch. Lady MacDuff was their foundation bitch.

She was bred twice to the Swedish top-winning and producing Int. Ch. Teddy Bear Bobo, and she produced the Champions Jolly Bears Arne, Jolly Bears Hope, and Jolly Bears Bill from her first litter to Bobo, and Jolly Bears Blue Boy and Jolly Bears Blossom out of the second mating to Bobo. Four more Champions resulted out of the two matings to Int. Ch. Shaggy Wonder Obligeness (Ch. Shaggy Wonder Lord – Audrey van de Britjes). They were: Jolly Bears Esmeralda, Jolly Bears Expectation, Jolly Bears Shaggy Wonder, and Jolly Bears Gabriella. Lady MacDuff's fifth litter, which produced one more Jolly Bears Champion, was to Ch. Hannibal (Ch. Reeuwijk's Cupid – Bumblebarn Bramble).

The kennel's next Champion-producing female was the Belgian import, Int. Ch. Shaggy Wonder Patch of Blue. At that time the ownership of the kennel had changed from Mr and Mrs Christiansen to Gyda Ersgaard. She bred Patch of Blue to Sceaphirde Lone Traveller in 1971, which resulted in Ch. Lollybear and Ch. Lovelybear. Lollybear was to become a Best in Show winner and the sire of four Champions. These two Champions (out of Patch of Blue) did not carry the Jolly Bears affix. It was not until 1973 that Patch of Blue produced a litter with the Jolly Bears afffix. This litter was sired by her own son, Ch. Lollybear, and she produced Ch. Jolly Bears Up-to-Date. In 1974 she had a litter sired by Ch. Shaggy Wonder Stackolee (Bobtail Acress Shaggy Wonder Snowman – Shaggy Wonder Personal Jewel). This combination resulted in one more Jolly Bears Champion, Ch. Jolly Bears Guttorm.

Stackolee was imported by the kennel in 1969, and he was to become the sire of eight Danish Champions. One of the early Jolly Bears Champions, Ch. Jolly Bears Hope, was mated to Ch. Lollybear, producing the top-winning Ch. Jolly Bears Quasi Una Fantasia. One other import in the mid-seventies, Foggydews Yankee Doodle (Am. Can. Ch. Prince Andrew of Sherline – Foggydews Miss Fancy), was later to become a Danish Champion.

There have not been any litters bred for some years, and the ownership has changed again. The kennel is now co-owned in partnership by Gyda Ersgaard, Hans Ove Pedersen and Lis Thorup Hansen. They have just imported a new bitch puppy from the Pennylane kennel in Switzerland, and so perhaps they will start breeding again in the near future.

SHAGGY DANE

The Shaggy Dane kennel is owned by Lissie and Erik Juul, who registered their first litter in 1970. Originally the breeding was based on Jolly Bears lines. Jolly Bears Beloved Shaggy was mated to Charisma Chief Chincoteague (Ch. Happytown Ragamuffin of Card – Charisma Whimsical Fantasy Chief), who was an American import owned by the Cheerio kennel. This combination resulted in their first Champion-producing dam, Shaggy Danes Glittering Grace. She was mated to Int. Ch. Kassenknuller a.d. Elbe Urstromtal in 1984, and she produced Ch. Shaggy Danes Little Shoes. A repeat mating in 1985 produced Ch. Shaggy Danes Ninetynine.

In 1982 Lissie and Erik imported Q-Tip a. d. Elbe Urstromtal (Ch. Chris a. d. Elbe Urstromtal – He-Du-Da a.d Elbe Urstromtal) from Germany. Q-Tip was shown very successfully, becoming an Int. Danish Germ. and VDH Champion. When she was mated to Little Shoes in 1986, she produced Ch. Shaggy Danes Quecksilber. Her next litter was sired by Int. Am. Can. Ch. Das Beste a. d. Elbe Urstromtal, in 1987, producing Ch. Shaggy Danes Super Duper. In 1989 Ch. Ninetynine was mated to Ch. Quecksilber, and this resulted in Ch. Shaggy Danes Yndig.

The Shaggy Dane OES: Int. Ch. Shaggy Danes Lady Di, Ch. Shaggy Danes Little Shoes, Ch. Shaggy Danes Super Duper.

DANWILL BLUE

Karen Larsen's Danwill Blue kennel was the most successful during the seventies and the early eighties. Karen's foundation bitch was an English import, Int. Ch. Takawalk Enchantment (Somerstreet Chieftain – Shepton Silver Foam). Apart from being a top-winning bitch in her time, winning Best in Shows, the Danish Champion title and the International title, she is also the dam of no less than six Champions. They were: Ch. Aly (by Shepton Moorland Blue), Ch. Bountyblue and Ch. Bellowblue (out of her first litter by Ch. Shaggy Wonder Stackolee, in 1972), and Ch. Danwill Blues Darnella, Ch. Danwill Blues Deary and Ch. Danwill Blues Delany (a repeat mating with Ch. Shaggy Wonder Stackolee).

In 1972 Karen Larsen imported her top-winning Shaggy Dogs Chan Brasse Baron (Int. Ch. Big Deal of the Embages – Int. Ch. Chanelle). Bred in Sweden by Mrs Zetterstrom, he was to become a top-producing sire in Denmark, and in Germany, through the Elbe Urstromtal kennel. When he was mated to Beatyblue, the result was Ch. Danwill Blues Fascination and Ch. Danwill Blues Kings Comet. When mated to Danwill Blues Delight, he produced Ch. Danwill Blues Unusual Sweetie.

The Danish Delight kennel bred Karen Larsen's next addition to her household, Ch. Danish Delight Blue Chieftain (Int. Ch. Oldash Sea Fabel – Ch. Audrey). Blue Chieftain, who was the result of artificial insemination, carried out by his breeder/vet Brigitte Schjoth. Through his dam, Audrey, he was a Takawalk Enchantment great-grandson, and therefore of special interest to Karen Larsen. Bred to an Enchantment daughter, Dk. Ch. Cinderella Blue, he produced the Best in Show winning Ch. Danwill Blues Ziggy Stardust.

Karen Larsen's last import was Blueacre Bump in the Night (by Am. Ch. Barrelroll Blues in the Night – Blueacres Misty Morning), later to become a Danish Champion, and he was also the sire of several Champions in Germany. The kennel has now stopped breeding.

Dk. Ch. and World Winner Danish Delight Call Me Barbara.

DANISH DELIGHT

Originally owned by Birgitte Schjoth and Herdis Thuesen, this kennel bred their first litter in 1972. This first litter was sired by Ch. Danwill Blue Bountyblue (Ch. Shaggy Wonder Stackolee – Ch. Takawalk Enchantment) out of Ch. Bombadil Pretty Polly (Ch. Somerstreet Chieftain – Bevere Cleopatra), and the top-winning Ch. Audrey was the result of this combination. Later, artificially inseminated to Ch. Oldash Sea Fabel (Oldash Sea Legend – Shanwill Little Miss Muffet), Audrey produced the two Champions, Danish Delight Blue Chieftain, and Danish Delight Bombadil.

In the early eighties the kennel became the home of the Canadian import, Some Buddy Canadian Ambassador (Am. Can. Ch. Some Buddy Catch the Action – Can. Ch. Some Buddy Love in Symphony), bred by Terry Carter in Canada and later to become a Champion. He sired two Champions for his owners, Ch. Danish Delight Canadian Sound and the Danish Ch. and world winner, Danish Delight Call Me Barbara. When he was used by Free-Style OES kennel, Ambassador sired several more Champions. One of Blue Chieftain's daughters, Free-Style's Be the One, was also acquired and artificially inseminated to the Swedish-owned and English-bred Ch. Raynham Viscount. The result was yet another Champion for the Danish Delight kennel, Ch. Danish Delight Fuzzy Bear.

There have not been any litters bred for the last six or seven years, and Birgitte Schjoth has become the sole owner. However, a new English import was introduced in 1990 through Lameda Zottel Go Miss Sophie, and breeding is underway again. Sophie (Ch. Greyfell Storm Warning – Ch. Zottel's Miss Marple of Lameda) is out of a litter which has so far produced seven Champions. Sophie gained her Danish and Int. Champion titles, winning Best in Shows on the way.

CHEERIO

The Cheerio kennel, owned by Hanne and Ingrid Nissen, was the home of one of my most favourite OES bitches in Denmark, Ch. Candy. She was sired by Ch. Charisma Chief Chincoteague, a male which the Nissens brought back with them after several years living in

America, out of Allybirk. Candy didn't have a splendid start to her life as her first owners were divorced and her breeder did not want her back. When Hanne and Ingrid heard this, they offered to take the bitch and find her a new home. However, Candy was soon adopted as a member of the family, and she was to become one of the most successful OES in the Danish show ring, staying right up at the top for a decade.

When she was almost thirteen years old, I was judging the Club Show, and I will never forget the moment she came in the ring. She showed herself off supremely well, and her movement was better than any of the other bitches. So on that day she was only beaten by the Best in Show-winning male, Ch. Imposant v. d. Schwalbennestern, and ended up Reserve Best in Show. Candy's only litter was sired by Int. Ch. Kassenknuller a. d. Elbe Urstromtal. The result was two Champions, Ch. Cheerio Just A Tootsie Roll, and Ch. Cheerio Jennifer Juniper.

A later addition to the kennel was Moptop's Son of Liberty, in 1983. He was sired by Am. Ch. Sniflik Warwyck Darwin out of Am. Ch. Moptops Upper Crust, and he was made up in 1985. When he was mated to a Candy daughter, Cheerio Joy To The World, he sired two Champions, Ch. Champ and Ch. Charity, bred by Lindeblad and Lindskov. The next import was also from the American Moptops kennel, and this was Ch. Moptops All American Dream (Ch. Moptops Bombadil – Am. Ch. Rholenwoods Dust in the Wind). The Cheerio kennel has unfortunately stopped breeding.

SHAG-A-RAG

Birthe and Jorgen Brolykke bred and owned Ch. Shag-A-Rag Follow My Leader, the top-winning OES in Denmark for the years 1990, 1991 and 1992. Birthe and Jergen bred their first litter in 1981 out of a Swedish import, Old Fashion A Taste of Honey (Ch. Oldash Sea Fabel – Ch. Old Fashion A Touch of Gold). She was bred to the German-owned and English-bred Int. Ch. Rollingsea Sky Rocket. A male and a female were kept, with the male, Shag-A-Rag Blue Buccaneer, finishing his Danish title. The bitch, Shag-A-Rag Blessed Moments, was later mated to

Ch. Shag-A-Rag Follow My Leader (Symmetry Somebody To Love – Shag-A-Rag Blessed Moments).

a Norwegian import, Symmetry Somebody to Love, who carries a lot of Rollingsea blood through his dam, Rollingsea Sunday Special. This combination produced Ch. Shag-A-Rag Follow My Leader. In 1992 the Brolykkes imported a bitch puppy from the Pennylane kennel in Switzerland.

FREE STYLE

This is also a relatively small establishment with only five litters bred in the last fourteen years – but they included four Champions. The owners, Annette and Richard Ostergaard Mikkelsen, started breeding with the Swedish-bred Holymans Baby Doll (Ch. Rollingsea Comet – Ch. Old Fashion Mistress Choice). Her first litter was sired by Ch. Danwill Blues Bountyblue, producing Ch. Abbydream. Abbydream later produced three Champions: Ch. Free Styles Call Girl, Ch. Free Styles Cindylook and Ch. Free Styles Commander in Chief, all sired by Ch. Some Buddy Canadian Ambassador. The Free Style kennel is yet another which has stopped breeding.

BLUE BERRY

The Blue Berry OES kennel was established in the later seventies. Owned by Lene and Birte Fromberg, the kennel has bred six litters. Their foundation bitch was Krojerups Emilie. Two OES were imported, a male from England, Ch. Rollingsea Admiral Keegan (Liverbobs Olympic

Dk. Ch. Rollingsea Admiral Keegan: Imported from the UK.

Warrior – Springfield Wendy Mary of Rollingsea), and a female from Holland, Tuckles Blueberry Fame (Tuckles Tommy Tudor – Ch. Rollingsea Katie Bay). When mated together they produced Ch. Blue Berrys Daddy Darling. A more recent import from Holland is Vigilats Nuts Over Nana (Ch. Vigilats Different Yip – Int. Ch. Vigilats Wicked Lady).

SUMMARY

A number of OES kennels have now stopped breeding, and it is not easy to see the reason why. In 1991 the enforced docking ban was introduced, but this does not seem to have reduced the number of pups (about 100 per year) being registered. I would think this is because there is no law against breeders going to Germany to get their puppies docked. The Danish Club was founded in 1965 by the late Mrs Krostensen of the Jolly Bears kennel. The current membership stands at around the 300 mark. Denmark stages about twelve Championship shows per year, five international CACIB shows, five to seven National CC Shows, and one Club Championship Show.

Chapter Eight

THE REST OF EUROPE

GERMANY
In Germany only a very few OES kennels survived the Second World War. They included Ingelotte Knall (vom Bodensee), and Ruth Vorderstemann (vom Heydpark).

VOM BODENSEE
Many litters were bred by Ingelotte Knall, mainly for family pet purposes, until she stopped breeding in the early eighties. Some of the later Bodensee OES were Zotti v. Bodensee (Astor von Casa Ursae – Rhea u. d. Schelmenlache), Abranella vom Bodensee (Astor von Casa Ursae – Yvonne vom Bodensee) and Chita and Chantal vom Bodensee, out of Abranella by Zotti.

HEYDPARK
This affix was registered in 1945, and most of Ruth Vorderstemann's breeding stock was imported from England and America. Like Ingelotte Knall, she bred mainly for the pet market. OES imported by her included: Marayma Symphony (Ch. Oakhill Peter Pan – Sherry of Drub), Marayma Duchess Roubear sired by the Rollingsea-based Marayma Bodger Boots of Roubear out of Sherry of Drub (Shepton Favourite – Knotting Blue Cloud), Romance of Shepton (Kinlcomore Buster – Daniels Duchess), Wisebeck Forgetmenot and Wisebeck Love in the Mist, both sired by Barkwith Cassius of Oldash out of Wisebeck Adam's Lass.

One of her last imports was the American-bred, Sniflik Dotted Swiss. Whelped in 1979, Dotted Swiss was out of Ch. London Smoke Gets in Your Eyes (Ch. Jendower's Paddy – Ch. Rivermist Morning Glory), and sired by Ch. Warwyck Martinee Idyll (Ch. Bahlambs Brazen Bandit – Warwycks Surprise Party). Dotted Swiss was successfully shown for quite a while by Mrs Vorderstemann's daughter, Carola; she later became the dam of Fantasy vom Heydpark (by Int. Ch. Xiangxi Zizhizhou vom Onkenhof), who was also shown with some success. When Fantasy was mated to Ch. Marchenprinz vom Barenbruch, she produced, in 1985, Int. Ch. Ninotschka vom Heydpark.

VOM GLINDER BERG
This kennel, owned by Mr and Mrs. Punjer, produced a lot of important foundation stock. They bred Int. Ch. Cora vom Glinder Berg, who was to become one of the foundation bitches for the Elbe Urstromtal kennel, and also Basko vom Glinder Berg, the foundation stud for the Karhauser Hain kennel. Both dogs were sired by Shaggy Wonder Smart Guy out of Shaggy Wonder Sharon. The v. Glinder Berg kennel was also the home of the English import, Ch. High Lad of Jamboree

(Prince of Achetts – Slebech Blue Moon). High Lad was an often-used stud dog, not just for the Punjers but also for other kennels.

His daughter, Germ. Ch. Quecksilber v. Karthauser Hain (out of Playgirl of Shepton) was to become a Champion brood bitch. Most of the Glinder Berg's OES can be traced back to the famous Shaggy Wonder OES, bred by Mrs de Ryck Mewis in Belgium. Her stock goes back to the early Reeuwijk's breeding of Mrs F. Backx-Bennink in Holland.

ORPLIDS
The most successful show dog during the early seventies was undoubtedly Int. Germ. Ned. Lux. French Ch. World Champion Buckswood Desperado (Meadowblue Hercules – Ambassador's Pandorina). He was owned by the Hoyers and the Orplids OES kennels. Bred in England, he was the sire of Int. Ch. Orplids Andrella, out of the Hoyers' English import, Lameda Sugar Plum. Both Sugar Plum and Desperado went back to the well-known Somerstreet Chieftain.

The Orplids kennel did not breed many litters, but Andrella is behind most present-day pedigrees. One other English import the Hoyers used for breeding was Jeabor Holly Bunch (Tycehurst Valhalla of Jeabor – Jeabor Blue Bonnet of Glenabbey).

MIXED KENNELS
Most big kennels in the early seventies to mid-eighties were not just OES orientated. They had often started with Rough Collies or Shetland Sheepdogs, or both. Then when the so-called 'Bobtail boom' started, many of these Collie breeders also got involved with OES. The main reason for this was because the German Club represented all British herding breeds. This included: Rough Collies, Shetland Sheepdogs, Bearded Collies, Border Collies, Cardigan Corgis and Pembroke Corgis. This made it easy for breeders to gain knowledge of more than just one breed. Most of these big breeders had been appointed 'Zuchtwart' by the Club for many years. This is a kind of breeding control where experienced breeders go and check litters born in their area, ensuring that the puppies are being housed and reared correctly. Unless a litter has been formally checked in this way, the litter will not be registered. These breeders, therefore, had a very good idea about what was going on in the OES scene, and their knowledge of the breed was considerable, even though they specialised in more than one breed. Well-known kennels of this kind were, for example, Mr Kretzler (von der Schelmenlache), Mrs Villain (vom Wakenithof), Mrs Hofmann (vom Onkenhof), Mr and Mrs Blatt (vom Topferhof), Mr Jahn (Galgenheidjers), Mrs D. Leske (vom Silberbach), Mrs Altmann (vom Michaelis-Turm), and many more. Quite a number of the kennels established during the late seventies and early eighties based their lines on dogs from these kennels.

THE OESCD CLUB
In 1988 some OES fanciers split off from the main Club fur Britische Hutehunde and founded their own OES Club. This new Club solely represents the Bobtail, and membership is increasing rapidly. They hold their own Specialty Shows, and they share the organisation of the International CACIB Shows with the 'old' British Club. The first litter the OESCD registered was bred by the 'Of Prudence' Bobtail kennel – eleven pups sired by Ch. Zottel's Lady Killer out of Always Pretty from Beautiful Highland. The main difference between the two clubs is that the newly-founded OESCD limits the amount of brood bitches, and one breeder is allowed to own a total of three. This limit also applies to the number of litters bred in each kennel per year. Therefore, none of the larger kennels are members of the OESCD, and they have remained in the Club fur Britische Hutehunde, where restrictions on the individual breeder are not so severe.

BREEDING REQUIREMENTS

Both clubs have stringent requirements that must be fulfilled before a dog or a bitch is used for breeding. Every dog or bitch must be shown at least three times with either 'very good' or 'excellent' gradings. These gradings have to come from three different German judges. Together with the critiques from these shows, and the certified HD result, every OES has to be presented to a specially appointed judge, who assesses the dog for breed type points and decides if the dog is worthy to be bred from. If a dog fails this assessment, none of the offspring will be registered.

To my knowledge, Germany is the only country where the breed clubs are responsible for the registration of litters and individual dogs. Pedigrees are verified by the German Kennel Club – Verband Fur Das Deutsche Hundewesen (VDH) – but issued by the breed clubs. This obviously places a lot of power with the club committees, because it means that a code of ethics is enforced, whereas in many other countries clubs do not receive the backing from the national Kennel Club.

ELBE URSTROMTAL

The Elbe Urstromtal OES kennel, owned by Mrs C. Hartman (formerly Abicht) was, during the seventies and the early eighties, one of the most dominant kennels in Germany. Mrs Hartman started her breeding with her two foundation bitches, Cora vom Glinder Berg (VDH Ch. Shaggy Wonder Smart Guy – Shaggy Wonder Sharon), later to become an Int. and Austrian Champion, and Int. Germ. Ch. Orplids Andrella. Andrella was bred by Mrs Hoyer out of her English import, Lameda Sugar Plum (Somerstreet Chieftain – Whitefall Moonstone), and sired by Int. Germ. Ned. Ch. Buckswood Desperado (Meadowblue Hercules – Ambassador's Pandorina). Through Hercules, whose sire was also Chieftain, Andrella, was line-bred to Somerstreet Chieftain.

While Andrella was all-English breeding, Cora carried some English, but more American breeding in her pedigree. She was the result of a half-brother/half-sister mating, with Int. Belg. Ch. Bobtail Acres SW Snowman siring both her parents. Snowman was by Am. Ch. Rivermist Hornblower, an offspring of the famous Am. Ch. Rivermist Dan Patch, who was out of the successful Ceiling Zero – Baroness of Duroya combination.

Cora was the dam of the first litter in the Elbe Urstromtal kennel. The sire was the English import, Noakside Astronaut (Magic Morning of Oldash – Halsall Olde Peggotty). This litter produced, amongst others: Applesnut a. d. Elbe Urstromtal, who was to become the dam of Int. Ned. Den. Ch. Lohengrin a. d. E.U., who later sired the famous 'M' litter of the Zottel's kennel, and notably Eng. Ch. Zottel's Miss Marple of Lameda. Lohengrin's sire was Int. Ch. Hercules a. d. E.U. (Int. Ned. Ch. Ellenglaze Ladies Choice – Int. Ch. Orplids Andrella) out of the well-known 'H' litter, which also produced Int. Germ. Ch. Hullabaloo, and the top-winning OES bitch, Int. Germ. Lux. Ned. Belg. Ch. Hot-Dog a. d. Elbe Urstromtal.

Apart from winning so many titles and several Best in Shows, Hot-Dog ('Burste') was also an important brood bitch with ten Champions to her credit: Int. Ch. Rock 'n Roll a. d. Elbe Urstromtal, Int. French Ch. Rosarot, Int. French Ch. Rembrandt, Int. Ned. Ch. Uberraschung, Int. Ch. Umsobesser, Int. Ch. Ultimo, Int. Ch. U-Boot, Int. Ch. Bim-Bam, Int. Germ. Ch. Bezaubernd and Int. Germ. Ch. Burste II. The 'R' litter was sired by Ch. Blueacres Bump in the Night (Am. Ch. Barrelroll Blues in the Night – Blueacres Misty Morning), the 'U' litter was sired by her own homebred Int. Germ. Ch. Chris a. d. E.U. (Ch. Buckswood Desperado – Ch. Cora v. Glinder Berg), and the 'B' litter was sired by Germ. Ch. Marchenprinz vom Barenbruch (Int. Ch. Kassenknuller a. d. E.U. – Int. Ch. Princess Holly Bunch of Jeabor).

Other important Elbe-Urstromtal litters call for mention. The 'D' litter (Int. Dk. Ch. Shaggy Dogs Chan Brasse Baron – Int. Ch. Cora vom Glinder Berg), included: Int. Lux. Pol. Ch. Domino,

Int. Germ. Ch. Orplids Andrella: Foundation bitch for the Elbe Urstromtal kennel.

Int. Den. Belg. Dark Do-Do, and Int. Pol. Lux. Ch. Draussen. The 'Q' litter (Int. Germ. Ch. Chris a. d. E.U. – Int. Ch. Cora v. Glinder Berg) included: Int. Hol. Ch. Quality Street, Int. Den. Ch. Q-Tip, and Pol. VDH Ch. Quickborn. The 'W' litter (Int. French Ch. Rembrandt a. d. E.U. – Ch. Quality Street) included Ital. Ch. Weltweit and Int. Germ. Ned. French. Ital. Ch. Wunderschon. The 'M' litter (Ch. Chris a. d. E.U. – Ch. Orplids Andrella) included: Int. VDH Ch. Marzipan, Int. Ch. Moneymaker and Int. VDH Ch. Milky Way. Alongside Chris as a sire, mention must be made of Int. Ch. Kassenknuller (Chris – Andrella). He was a very frequently used stud dog and sired several Champions. Also important was Int. World Ch. Osborne a. d. E.U. (Int. Ch. Longdorhams Folly by George – Honeymoon a. d. E.U, litter sister to the Champions out of the 'H' litter). Several more Champions were bred over the years, starting off or adding to the breeding programme of several other kennels. They include: Happy Pandas (Mr and Mrs J. Pilz) with Ch. Marzipan and Ch. Umsobesser, Ko-Pi's 599 (Mrs B. Korn) with Ch. Moneymaker, Dodo Love (Mrs E. Lemke) with Ch. Dark Do-Do von den Barentazen (Mr and Mrs Bockenholt) with Ch. Hullabaloo, and several other kennels in Germany and abroad.

In 1986 the Elbe Urstromtal kennel imported their first Am. Ch., Trosambe Blue Spicer (Ch. Pembridge Cheerio T Rascal – Ch. Trosambe Blue Panda Winsome), bred by the Trosambe Blue Panda kennel, who in return gave Int. Ch. Das Beste a. d. Elbe Urstromtal (Int. Ch. Osborne a. d. E.U. – Int. Ch. Quality Street a. d. E.U.) a show home for two years. As previously mentioned, Das Beste now resides in the Rosenhjorth kennel in Norway. In terms of titles won, he is the most successful OES ever in the Elbe Urstromtal kennel. Spicer was joined for a while by another Trosambe Blue Panda OES, Am. Ch. Can. Ch. Trosambe Blue Panda Shawn (Am. Can. Ch. Bluedover Beau Aaron – Am. Can. Ch. Blue Panda's Pooh A Party of One). Both American imports gained their Int. Champion titles. and they were often-used stud dogs with Champion offspring, especially Int. Ch. Utopia by Spicer (out of Int. Ch. Coco Chanel a. d. Elbe Urstromtal), who was the top-winning OES female in Finland in 1990. Shawn eventually went back to the USA, and Spicer took up residence with Rene Parent and his French Lameda kennel.

Recently there have been several more Champions from this kennel, which is now based in Holland. They include Int. Ch. Uniclever a. d. Elbe Urstromtal who is a litter sister to Utopia, and Danish Ch. Vinh-Ninh a. d. E.U. (Ned. Ch. Pockethall Prince William – Marshmallow a. d. E.U.).

KARTHAUSER HAIN

The Karthauser Hain kennel, owned by Mr and Mrs Westphal-Giesenkirchen, was, like many other German kennels, originally known for their Rough Collies. They got involved with OES in the early seventies. The foundation bitches of what was to become one of the most successful kennels during the seventies and early eighties, were imported from England. They were Marayma Harmony (Marayma Favourite Lad – Brandy of Drub) and Playgirl of Shepton (sired by Kinlochmore Buster out of Daniels Duchess). From the beginning of their involvement with OES, the Westphals had their own stud dog. He was Basko vom Glinder Berg (Shaggy Wonder Smart Guy – Shaggy Wonder Sharon). He was the same breeding, but one litter earlier than Cora vom Glinder Berg, one of the foundation bitches for the Elbe Urstromtal kennel. These three dogs, in combination with a few outcross breedings with Int. Ch. High Lad of Jamboree (Prince of Acheta – Slebech Blue Moon) and Int. Germ. Ned. Ch. Ellenglaze Ladies Choice (Misselwaithe Squire Dickon – Ch. Ellenglaze Fleur Forsythe) were the basis for this extremely successful kennel.

Playgirl of Shepton was the dam of Germ. VDH Ch. Quecksilber v. Karthauser Hain (sired by Germ. VDH Ch. High Lad of Jamboree), and she was also the dam of the Best in Show winning Int. Germ. French Ch. Blue Arka v. Karthauser Hain (sired by Basko vom Glinder Berg). When Quecksilber was mated to Int. Germ. Ned. Ch. Ellenglaze Ladies Choice, the result was the kennel's most well-known homebred Champion stud dog, Int. Germ. VDH Ch. Why-Not vom Karthauser Hain, who later sired (in full brother/sister and mother/son combinations) several litters for his own kennel. He was also an often-used stud dog by other kennels. His Champion offspring included: Int. Ch. Blue Granada v. Karthauser Hain (out of his dam, Quecksilber), Ch. Blue Flaneur (out of Marayma Harmony), and Ch. Blue Enjoy (out of his litter-sister, White Wing).

Three other kennels started their breeding with Karthauser Hain bitches. They were aus der alten Noris with Ch. Blue Granada v. Karthauser Hain (Why Not – Quecksilber), of Crazy Family with Rube vom Karthauser Hain (Baske v. Glinder Berg – Marayma Harmony) and vom Tatzelwurm with Tanja v. Karthauser Hain (Basko v. Glinder Berg – Playgirl of Shepton).

The Karthauser Hain kennel has not bred many OES litters in the more recent past because they have concentrated on breeding some excellent Bearded Collies.

VON DER MASS

Owned by Hans-Erwin and Marliese Neisens, the von der Mass kennel has bred some excellent sound stock over the years. Their rate of OES free of hip dysplasia is probably the best in Germany. Their first litter was sired by Till vom Bodensee (Ch. Shaggy Wonder U' Blue Apollo – Reeuwijk's Queen of Diamond) out of Int. Ch. VDH Ch. Ra von der Schelmenlache. This combination produced the first homebred Champion, Int. VDH Ch. Aphrodite von der Mass.

Ra also produced the foundation bitch for the Of Cinderella's Baby kennel, Cinderella von der Mass. The sire of this litter was Int. Ch. Antonio a. d. Rappelkiste (Nifty of Jamboree – Atossa v. d. Mass). When Aphrodite was mated to Int. Ch. Argos v. Donaro she later produced Darling v. d. Mass, who, like her dam, had several litters to Int. Ch. Reeuwijk's Dew Fantasy. The v. d. Mass kennel has never bred many litters and their stock was mainly sold to be family pets. However, their dogs are known all over Germany as sound and typical for the breed.

PEEKABOO

The Peekaboo kennel is owned by Klaus Hubert and his English wife, Pat. Their lines are based on two English imports, Rollingsea Sky Rocket (Rollingsea Sirius – Springfield Wendy Marce), and Princess Hepzibar (Tuscan King of Fairydales – Fairydales Briar Rose). Sky Rocket was a very

*Int. Germ. Ch.
Rollingsea Sky
Rocket: Imported
from the UK.*

successful show dog, gaining the International German, CSSR and the VDH Champion title.

Pat and Klaus's first few litters came from these two OES. They kept Peekaboo Afternoon Dream from their first litter, and Peekaboo Bizzie Lizzie from their second litter, and both bitches were later bred back to their sire. They later acquired another daughter of Sky Rocket, bred by B. Baumeister, out of her English import, Int. Germ. Lux. Ch. Princess Holly Bunch of Jeabor, and she was called Oktopussy Peekaboo vom Barenbruch. This bitch was to become the dam of the most successful female for the kennel. Int. Danish Ch. Peekaboo Victorian Lace was sired by Int. Ch. Dodo Love's Fleetwood Mac (Int. Ch. Xiangxi Zizhizhou vom Onkenhof – Reeuwijk's Elien).

A later addition to the household was another Rollingsea OES, and this was the male, Rollingsea Secret of Magic, imported from the UK. Currently, the kennel's most frequently used stud dog is Peekaboo Unforgettable Udo. Udo is a CC and BOB winning Peekaboo, whose career was held back due to Victorian Lace. His sire was Pat and Klaus' second English import, Secret of Magic, and his dam was Peekaboo Bizzy Lizzy.

DODO LOVE
Mrs E. Lemke's first OES, Wodka vom Bodensee, who arrived in 1972 from the v. Bodensee kennel, was a much-loved pet. Mrs Lemke's first show dog was Int. Ch. Dark Dodo a. d Elbe Urstromtal (Int. Ch. Shaggy Dogs Chan Brasse Baron – Ch. Orplids Andrella). Wodka and Dodo were soon joined by Reeuwijk's Elien (Int. Ch. Ellenglaze Ladies Choice – Fezziwig Silver Lining). The kennel's few litters came out of these two bitches, with the two most well-known males being Ch. Dodo Love's Bright 'n Breezy (by Ch. Reeuwijk's Dew Fantasy), and the Champion-siring Int. Ch. Dodo Love's Fleetwood Mac (Int. Ch. Xiangxi Zizhizhou vom Onkenhof), both out of Reeuwijk's Elien.

HAPPY PANDAS
Owned by Joachim and Christina Pils, this small kennel bred their first litter in August 1983, sired by their own Int. Ital. Ch. Button Nose Amadeus – 'Happy' – (Int. Ch. Domino a. d. Elbe

Urstromtal – Elijah Blue a. d. Elbe Urstromtal) out of Int. Ch. Marzipan a. d. Elbe Urstromtal. Marzipan was sired by the multi-Champion producing Int. Ital. Ch. Chris a. d. Elbe Urstromtal. Her dam was Int. Ch. Orplids Andrella. 'Happy', and Marzipan ('Panda'), who was two years younger, were the kennel's first OES. Happy, through the sire of both his parents, Int. Ch. Shaggy Dog's Can Brasse Baron, came out of a half-brother–sister mating. Bred to Marzipan, the litter was closely line-bred back to the two foundation bitches of the Elbe Urstromtal kennel, Cora vom Glinder Berg and Orplids Andrella. Marzipan's sire, Chris, was out of Cora, as was Amadeus's sire, Domino, and Elijah Blue's dam was the same as Marzipan's, Orplids Andrella. Marzipan and Amadeus were joined in 1982 by another Elbe Urstromtal OES, Umsobesser a. d. Elbe Urstromtal, highly successful as a youngster and later to become an International Champion. Her sire was Chris a. d. Elbe Urstromtal, and her dam was the multi-Champion Hot Dog a. d. E.U. Based on these three closely related OES, this small kennel bred some excellent litters.

The most successful homebred Champion was Ch. Happy Panda Cornflower (Dewy vom Tatzelwurm – Marzipan), who went Best in Show at the second European OES Show in 1989, held in Switzerland. I was invited to judge this show, along with Mrs D. Brocklesby Evans of the Danum kennel in England. The next successful Happy Pandas' litter was their 'D' litter, again out of Marzipan. This time the sire was one of Amadeus's Champion sons, Int. Ned. Vigilat's Woody Allan. Woody was bred by Mr E. Ter Mors from the Dutch Vigilat's kennel. He was out of Vigilat's Pretty Thing (Reeuwijk's Dear Tom Tod – Reeuwijk's Fabulous Lady). This litter (Amadeus – Pretty Thing) also produced the Vigilat's most successful homebred Champion, Int. Ned. Ch. Vigilat's Wicked Lady, a multi-Group and Best in Show winner. The Happy Panda's 'D' litter produced Happy Panda's Don Giovanni, Happy Panda's Dark All Over, and Happy Panda's Dolly Parton. Due to the regulations of the OESCD, this kennel is breeding just a few litters, but it is still doing its best for the breed.

HOHENLOHEN FRANKEN

Owned by Mr and Mrs Otterbach, this kennel bred their first litter in 1986 sired by Int. Ch. Dodo Love's Fleetwood Mac (Xiangxi Zizhizhou vom Onkenhof – Reeuwijk's Eileen) out of Int. Soheka Catch-as-Catch-Can (Int. Ch. Kassenknuller a. d. Elbe Urstromtal – Abunja von den Schwalbennestern). This combination produced the kennel's first homebred Champion, Ch. Aeneas von Hohenlohen Franken. Aeneas is not only a top-winning male, he is also proving to be an important sire, producing Int. Germ. Austrian Ch. Barking Bobby's Dumpling Boy (out of Dodo Love's Join the High Society) and the Austrian German Ch. Dangerfreaks Izzy-Bizzy (out of Dangerfreaks Chocolate Chappy).

The second litter in the kennel was also sired by Fleetwood Mac, but the dam was the kennel's second foundation bitch, Burste II a. d. Elbe Urstromtal (Int. Ch. Marchen-Prinz vom Barenbruch – Int. Ch. Hot Dog a. d. E.U), bred by

Int. Germ. VDH Ch. Bhuteschwara von Hohenlohen Franken: Best in Show winner.

Mrs C. Hartman. Bruste is a multi-CC and Best in Show winner. Like her kennel mate, she has produced Champion offspring in her first litter. They include the Best in Show winners Int. Germ. VDH Ch. Bhuteschwara, and Ital. Int. Ch. Barbarossa. Bhuteschwara and her litter sister Berenike were kept, while Barbarossa was exported to Italy.

DANGERFREAKS

Kerstin Hemminger started her Dangerfreaks kennel with four OES. The male was Ch. Ilscha von Topferhof (Durus vom Topferhof – Gilles Pie's Meadow April), born in 1981. Ilscha is a multi-Best in Show winner and also gained an Obedience title. He was joined by three females from the Karthauser Hain kennel. They were: Blue Panda (Blue Flaneur v. Karthauser Hain – Cinderella v. Karthauser Hain), Carolina Moon (Ilscha – Cinderalla v. Karthauser Hain), and Blue X'zzy-Bizzy (Int. Ch. Why Not vom Karthauser Hain – Ch. Quecksilber v. Karthauser Hain). Ilscha was to sire several litters for the kennel, producing the Dangerfreaks Champions Ch. Artis Sunbeam and Ch. Eddy Murphy (out of Blue Panda), and Ch. Dumbling Ball (out of Carolina Moon).

A litter by Ilscha out of X'zzy Bizzy produced the 'C' litter, which included Chocolate Chappy. Bred to Int. Ch. Aeneas von Hohenlohen Franken, Chocolate Chappy produced the Austrian and German Ch. Dangerfreaks Izzy-Bizzy. Currently, Kerstin is showing Dangerfreaks Nosy Piper (Ch. Aeneas von Hohenlohen Franken – Ch. Dumpling Balls).

KO-PI'S 599

Owned by Barbel Korn, this kennel is based on dogs from the Elbe Urstromtal kennel with Jo-Jo Big a. d. Elbe Urstromtal (Ch. Domino a. d. E.U. – Ch. Orplids Andrella) and Ch. Moneymaker a. d. E.U. (Ch. Chris a. d. E.U. – Ch. Orplids Andrella). In addition, Barbel also owned a litter sister to the well-known Int. Ch. Button Nose Amadeus Button Nose Alpha (Ch. Domino a. d. E.U. – Elijah Blue a. d. E.U.). Alpha was to become the dam of the first litter in the kennel, and Ch. Moneymaker was the sire. The 'A' litter, whelped in 1983, included Ch. Apricot, and the well-known Asti Spumante. The kennel's second litter was also sired by Moneymaker, and the dam was Jo-Jo Big. Based on the three foundation OES, together with Apricot and Asti Spumante, the Ko-Pi's have had some excellent dogs. Most litters were either line or inbred, with only a few outcross matings. One outcross was to Ch. Moptops Son of Liberty, owned by Hanne and Ingrid Nissen from Denmark. Son of Liberty (Am. Ch. Sniflik Warwyck Darwin – Am. Ch. Moptops Upper Crust), was bred by the American, Woody Nelson. The dam of this outcross mating was Ch. Apricot, and the offspring included Ko-Pi's 599 Pastis.

TATZELWURM

This kennel, owned by Mr and Mrs Brickenstein, started in the early eighties with two bitches from the Karthauser Hain kennel. They were Tanja vom Karthauser Hain (Basko vom Glinder Berg – Playgirl of Shepton), and Blue Carina vom Karthauser Hain (Int. Ch. Why Not vom Karthauser Hain – Germ. Ch. Quecksilber vom Karthauser Hain). Tanja was the dam of the first litter in the kennel, whelped in 1981. This litter was by Int. Ch. Ellenglaze Ladies Choice. The second litter was by Int. Ch. Hercules a. d. Elbe Urstromtal out of Blue Carina. It produced, amongst others, Britta v. Tatzelwurm, who was kept and later used for breeding. Many litters have been bred over the years, mainly based on line or inbreeding.

VON DEN SCHWALBENNESTERN

Elke Standar has been involved with Old English Sheepdogs since the early seventies. Her first show bitch was Ch. Shaggy Wonder X'Carolyn (Shaggy Wonder V'Blue Apollo – Shaggy Wonder Titbit). Carolyn was mated in 1977 to the German Ch. High Lad of Jamboree (Prince of Acheth – Slebech Blue Moon), and she produced the first litter for the kennel. The third litter in the kennel was from the same parents, and produced Elke's next brood bitch, Contessa von den Schwalbennestern. When Contessa was mated to Int. Ch. Kassenknuller a. d. Elbe Urstromtal (Int. Ch. Chris a. d. E.U. – Ch. Orplids Andrella) she produced the famous 'F' litter, whelped in 1982, which included Ch. Fur Mich v. d. Schwalbennestern and Ch. Fassbrause v. d. Schwalbennestern. Also in 1982, Contessa produced Int. Ch. Erdbeben v. d. Schwalbennestern, also by Int. Ch. Kassenknuller a. d. Elbe Urstromtal.

Elke's most successful show dog was whelped in 1986. This was Danish Ch. Imposant von den Schwalbennestern (Big Mac a. d. Elbe Urstromtal – Golden Diva). Imposant is a multi CC and Best in Show winner.

ZOTTEL

Zottel was my nickname when I was still living in Germany, and the first thirteen litters I bred were registered with this affix. Old English Sheepdogs have been my great love since childhood. A number of American series on television featured the breed, and I decided that one day I would breed my own OES. As I came from a very dog-orientated family, where German Shepherds and Newfoundlands were bred and shown, it was just a matter of time before this ambition was eventually fulfilled in 1974. Several enquiries were made and letters were written to influential breeders. Finally two half-sisters from the famous English Rollingsea kennel took over our house and our lives. Despite their similar breeding, High Flyer of Rollingsea (Rollingsea Sirius – Mist of Torbay) and Winter Beauty of Rollingsea (Rollingsea Sirius – Bobalong Peek-A-Boo) were quite different in type. Both bitches were shown with great success by myself and my first husband. They gained their International, German and VDH Champion titles, as well as several Best of Breeds and a couple of Best in Shows at Club Show level, beating the BOBs of the other British herding dog breeds. This confirmed their quality in type and soundness.

After Bonny and Becky were retired for maternal duties, the next show puppy came from the Dutch Reeuwijk's kennel. Bred by Mrs F. Backx-Bennink, Reeuwijk's Filmstar in Silver was out of the only litter of the great Int. Lux. Ned. Germ. World Champion Reeuwijk's Care for Beauty, sired by her half-brother, Int. Germ. Ned. Swiss Ch. Reeuwijk's Dew Fantasy. 'Krumel' was only one year old when she and the two Rollingsea girls were joined by Krumel's sire. 'Dewy' had been living with his sire, multi Ch. Ellenglaze Ladies Choice, and he had refused to mate any bitches. The change of environment – without the domineering influence of his sire – soon got him on the right track, and he became one of the most often used stud dogs in Europe at the time.

His Champion offspring include: Int. Germ. Swiss VDH Ch. Reeuwijk's Filmstar in Silver, Int. Ned. World Champion Reeuwijk's Fancy Pants and Int. Ned. Ch. Reeuwijk's Fashionable Beauty (all three out of Int. Ch. Reeuwijk's Care for Beauty); Int. Austrian VDH Ch. Zottel's Ladykiller (out of Zottel's Bahama Girl, who was sired by Ch. Reeuwijk's Dew Fantasy out of Int. Ch. Winter Beauty of Rollingsea); Int. Germ. Monaco Ch. Zottel's Dolce Vita (out of Ch. Winter Beauty of Rollingsea); Int. Danish Ch. Dodo Love's Bright and Breezy (out of Reeuwijk's Elien); and Int. Ch. Bizzeeboots Chelsea Queen (out of Ch. Searwell Duchess Lady Day).

Both Dew Fantasy and his daughter, Filmstar in Silver, had great show careers. Dewy gained the International, Netherland, German, Swiss, Winner '79, VDH, Luxembourg Champion title, which was topped by winning the Working Group and Reserve Best in Show at the All Breed Championship Show in Bellagio, Italy in 1980, and Best in Show under breed specialist Stuart

Mallard at the British Herding Dog Show in 1980. Filmstar (Krumel)was not shown quite so often; nevertheless she finished her International, German, Swiss and VDH Champion titles.

The first homebred Champion was sired by multi Ch. Reeuwijk's Dew Fantasy out of Ch. Winter Beauty of Rollingsea. Zottel's Dolce Vita was owned by Birgit Hamm, who despite being a novice exhibitor soon became an excellent handler. By the time Dolce Vita was retired she had gained the International, German, VDH and Monaco Champion titles. Her greatest accolade was winning the Working Group in Monaco in 1983 under the late Catherine Sutton.

In 1981 Filmstar in Silver was bred to her grandsire, multi Ch. Ellenglaze Ladies Choice, who was the sire of both her parents. This mating resulted in a litter of six puppies, whelped on September 5th 1981. Two puppies were retained – Zottel's Eagle Has Landed and Zottel's Estee Lauder – one other male puppy went into a show home. He was Zottel Exclusive Relation, a multi CC and CACIB winner, who unfortunately died of torsion before confirmation of his title had come through. Meanwhile, Estee and Eagle developed into excellent specimens. Eagle was top-winning male in 1984. Estee was top-winning OES in Europe, also in 1984, with Group 1st, Reserve Best in Show and Best in Show wins in Germany, Italy and Switzerland. She achieved the International, German, Netherland, Swiss and VDH Champion titles, while Eagle gained the International, Luxembourg, Monaco, German and VDH Champion titles.

A repeat mating of Filmstar in Silver and Ladies Choice produced in 1982 the G-litter. Like the litter before, it included several puppies of excellent show quality. The two most important pups of this repeat mating were Int. Swiss, Italian and French Ch. Zottel's Grasshopper, who holds the breed record in Switzerland, and Int. Swiss, Italian and French Ch. Zottel's Get up and Boogie, top-winning female in France.

On January 6th 1985 Filmstar whelped her last litter. This time she had been mated to multi Ch. Lohengrin a. d. Elbe Urstromtal. Lohengrin was, through his sire, Ch. Hercules a. d. Elbe Urstromtal, a Ladies Choice grandson. The litter was therefore very closely bred back to the great multi Ch. Ellenglaze Ladies Choice. It was to become Krumel's most important litter, as it included a total of four Champions. They were: Group-winning Int. Swiss, VDH Ch. Zottel's Mosche, Int. Swiss, VDH Ch. Zottel's Magic Touch, and the two Champion bitches, Eng. Ch. Zottel's Moonlight Serenade of Lameda, a Group winner at the 1989 Southern Counties All Breed Championship Show, and the multi Group and Best in Show winning Eng. Ch. Zottel's Miss Marple of Lameda. In 1988 'Missy' became the new breed record holder in England, and she now has a total of fifty-one CCs. In 1985 Estee, Eagle, Miss Marple, Moonlight, and their dam, Filmstar in Silver, moved with me to England, where we all started a new life.

OTHER TOP-CLASS KENNELS
PANDA BEARS: Owned by Barbel Schellin, the first litter was bred in 1981 sired by Jumbo a. d. Elbe Urstromtal (Ch. Domino a. d. Elbe Urstromtal – Int. Ch. Orplids Andrella) out of Edda von Forsthaus Lanfermann (Ch. Domino a. d. Elbe Urstromtal – Biggi vom Forsthaus Lanfermann).
WHITE HEATHER: Owned by Mrs Mascher; her Germ. Ch. Angel was Top OES female in 1989, 1990 and 1991.
CHARIVARI: Owned by Mrs M. Aussendorf, home of the Champion stud dog, Int. Ch. Zottel's Magic Touch (Int. Ch. Lohengrin a. d. Elbe Urstromtal – Int. Ch. Reeuwijk's Filmstar in Silver), and his Champion daughter, Painter's Love Ariane (out of Smoke Mountain's Beautiful Day).
BEAUTIFUL HIGHLAND: Mesdames Siglinde and Annette Kirsch started this kennel in 1980 with Ch. Woodlane's Elliot (Reeuwijk's Desmond – Woodlane's Amber). They are now showing their Champion male, Sugar Bear from Beautiful Highland (Elliott – Scarlet O'Hara of Pelajilo).

Sugar Bear is the same breeding as two other Champions from this kennel, Always Pretty and All My Dreams.

VON DEN HOTTENTOTTEN: Owned by Ilona Lumberg, the kennel's first litter was whelped in 1981. It was by Int. Ch. Rollingsea Sky Rocket (Rollingsea Sirius – Springfield Wendy Marie) out of Ballerina III vom Wakeritzhof (Int. Ch. Ellenglaze Ladies Choice – Shaggy Wonder V' Born Free).

MIT DEN BARENTATZEN: Owned by Monika Bockenholt, the first litter was whelped in 1982 sired by Jumbo a. d. Elbe Urstromtal (by Ch. Domino a. d. E.U.– Ch. Orplids Andrella) out of Int. Ch. Hullabaloo a. d. E.U. (Int. Ch. Ellenglaze Ladies Choice – Ch. Orplids Andrella), litter sister to the multi Champion producing Hot Dog a. d. Elbe Urstromtal. The kennel also owns another Elbe Urstromtal female, Ojemine a. d. E.U. (Int. Ch. Longdorhams Folly by George – Honeymoon a. d. E.U.). Ojemine is the litter sister to the well-known Osborne a. d. E.U. She is also the dam of the homebred Int. Ch. Discjockey mit den Barentatzen, sired by the homebred Archie mit den Barentatzen – the first litter in the kennel.

FORSTHAUS LANFERMANN: This kennel is owned by Liesette Lanfermann, and it started breeding in the late seventies with the two foundation bitches, Sweet Gypsy Rose of Shepton (Lucky Charm of Shepton – Shepton Tramp), and Flock vom Wersestadtchen (Int. Ch. Buckswood Desperado – Nixe von der Schelmen Lache). From the second litter Mrs Lanfermann kept Biggi (Ch. Shaggy Wonder Smart Guy – Gypsy Rose) as her next brood bitch. She was later bred to Int. Germ. Ch. Blue Star (Wonder Boy of Shepton – Herbaceous Border).

ASTRO: Int. Germ. Ch. Blue Star was owned and shown with great success by Karin Seidel of the Astro prefix. Karin also owned the two English imports, Int. Ch. Pelajilo Pincushion (Ch. Aberfells Georgey Porgey – Pelajilo Lady Peggotty) and Int. & Germ. Ch. Pelajilo Master of Sparks (by Flockmaster John Barleycorn – Cobbicot Polly Flinders of Flockmaster). Both Pelajilos were as well-known as the older Blue Star.

WILD FRISIAN: Heidi Muller's first OES show dog was Int. Danish Ned. Germ. Ch. Lohengrin a. d. Elbe Urstromtal. 'Linus' was an often-shown Best in Show winner, and he was also the sire of the famous 'M' litter of the Zottel's kennel. He was sired by Int. Ch. Hercules a. d. Elbe Urstromtal out of Applesnut a. d. Elbe Urstromtal. Linus and his kennelmate, Ch. Rock 'n Roll a. d. Elbe Urstromtal (Ch. Blueacres Bump in the Night – Int. Ch. Hot Dog a. d. Elbe Urstromtal), produced the first litter in the kennel. Rock 'n Roll is also the dam of Heidi's most well-known homebred Champion, Int. Germ. Ch. Wild Frisian's Earl Grey (sired by Int. Ch. Zottel's Magic Touch, a Lohengrin son). Rock 'n Roll and Lohengrin were joined by the Dutch import, Ch. Tuckles Frisian Folly (Int. Ch. Reeuwijk's Dew Fantasy – Rollingsea Katie), bred by Stuart Mallard and Mark James.

SNOWBOOTS: Owned by Birgit Korting, the kennel's first litter was registered in 1986, sired by Int. Ch. Rollingsea Sky Rocket out of Gypsy Love of Wild Bunch. This litter produced Snowboots Admirable Beauty and the Germ. VDH Ch. Snowboots Averall. Admirable Beauty was mated to Int. Germ. Ned. Ch. Sparkles Square China Blue, and she produced the second homebred Champion, Ch. Snowboots Design of China.

AUS DER ALTEN NORIS: Owned by Vera Meyer, this is another kennel which started with Karthauser Hain bitches. Blue Granada vom Karthauser Hain (Int. Ch. Why-Not vom Karthauser Hain – Ch. Quecksilber v. Karthauster Hain) was whelped in 1981. As a young bitch, Granada was very similar to her sire, which explained her excellent show career. She ended the year 1982 with the No. 2 spot in the junior class. By the end of her show career Granada had gained the Int. Germ. and VDH Champion title. Subsequent litters proved that she also excelled as a brood bitch. The

two homebred Champions, Ch. Caribbean Queen and
Ch. Only You, are a daughter and a granddaughter of
Granada.

VOM WEIDENHOF: Owned by Ariane Meckmann-
Klein, this is one of the most fascinating kennels in
Germany. Ariane's dogs are the best proof that OES
are very intelligent and are capable of working. She
first became involved in the breed in the early
seventies, and for many years she has not only bred
for the show ring, but also for obedience training,
earthquake rescue, avalanche rescue, sniffer dogs and
schutzhund. What I find most amazing is the fact that
she keeps her dogs in full coats. Some of these highly
trained Bobtails have also done well in the show ring
and gained their Champion titles.

HOLLAND
REEUWIJK

The late Mrs H. F. Backx-Bennink established this
world-famous kennel, and from the mid-seventies to
the mid-eighties, Holland, arguably, boasted the best
breed specimens in Europe.

 Mrs Backx-Bennink was one of the first Dutch
breeders to bring back the Dutch Sheepdog, the
Schapendoes. This breed is similar to the Polish

*Liberta vom Weidenhof: Trained as a
rescue dog.*

Lowland Dog, and was almost extinct after the Second World War. I remember listening to her
many funny stories about the different breeds that appeared in her first so-called pure-bred
'Schapendoes' litters. However, the breeding experience she gained proved to be invaluable when
she started with Old English Sheepdogs. She developed an eye for a dog, and all those who knew
her will confirm that her opinion about OES was not gained through short-lived fashions, but by
interpreting the original Breed Standard. OES that were fine in bone, with small heads, unsound
dogs, or Bobtails with bad temperaments, would never have taken her fancy. She therefore strove
to breed only from the best dogs available.

 Her first Bobtails came from the famous English Shepton kennels, and she founded a dynasty of
top-winning and top-producing OES. Her dog, Ch. Reeuwijk's Cupid sired the famous top
producer, Ch. Unnesta Pim. Cupid was sired by Ch. Shepton Grey Idol out of Perrywood Blue
Bonnet. Blue Bonnet was sired by Prince Willow of Lyneal out of a Ch. Shepton Sonny Boy of
Marlay daughter, Perrywood Sun Bonnet. Cupid was a full brother to the great Ch. Reeuwijk's
Charming Masterpiece, who is behind all the Belgian Shaggy Wonder breeding and behind many
other European lines.

 In the early to mid-fifties, when Mrs Backx-Bennink started her famous line, most of her stock
resulted from full brother and sister, father/daughter, mother/son and other very close matings.
Famous dogs at the time were: Ch. Reeuwijk's Indiscreet Insider (out of an uncle/niece mating),
Ch. Reeuwijk's Charming Masterpiece (out of Reeuwijk's Filmstar, who was by Ch. Reeuwijk's
Cupid, a full brother to Masterpiece, out of Chang-Shi Charming Blue, who was all Shepton
breeding descended from the great sire, Shepton Wonder), Ch. Reeuwijk's Kiddy (Indiscreet

Ch. Ellenglaze Ladies Choice: An invaluable stud dog for European breeding lines.

Insider – Shepton Morning Pride), Ch. Reeuwijk's Grand Old Lady (Charming Masterpiece – Ch. Perrywood Blue Bonnet). Kiddy and Grand Old Lady are the sire and dam of Ch. Shaggy Wonder Main Attraction and Ch. Shaggy Wonder Meteorbright, who in combination with Ch. Rivermist Hornblower (Ch. Rivermist Hornblower – Miss Muffit of Tatters) were mainly responsible for many important European lines.

In 1968 Mrs Backx-Bennink imported a Shaggy Wonder bitch, Netherland, International Ch. Shaggy Wonder Rose Mary (Shaggy Wonder Perfect Gentleman – Ch. Shaggy Wonder Listless I Am), followed in 1973 by a litter brother and sister from the American Ellenglaze kennel. Ch. Ellenglaze Love and Kisses and Ellenglaze Ladies Choice were sired by Misselwaite Squire Dickon out of Ch. Ellenglaze Fleur Forsythe. Both their parents go back to the Van Rensselaers' Fezziwig breeding and also through Squire Dickon's sire, Ch. Giggleswyk Mardi Gras, back to the early Greyfriars and Tara-Woods, which were Shepton and Pickhurst based. Both 'Kissie' and 'Tristan' were easily made up into Int. & Dutch Champions. Tristan also gained his Luxembourg and German titles. Two years later two more American imports arrived in Holland. This time they came directly from the Van Rensselaers' kennel. They were Fezziwig Silver Lining (Ch. Fezziwig Hoodwink – Fezziwig Homeward Bound) and Fezziwig Honey Bun (Ch. Fezziwig Artful Dodger – Ch. Fezziwig Spring Song). Honey Bun was a very feminine bitch, with a compact body and nice angles. She finished her Int. and Dutch Champion title. Silver Lining was a completely different type, massive in bone and body. She was of too big a size to finish at that time in Europe, but she became one of the most useful brood bitches for the kennel. Her outstanding coat was passed on to most of her offspring.

One champion and many CC-winning dogs resulted from her litters to Ladies Choice, the most famous being Int. Ned. Germ. Lux. World Ch. Reeuwijk's Care for Beauty. 'Cary', bred to her half-brother, Dew Fantasy, produced three Champions in her only litter. They were Int. Ch. Reeuwijk's Fancy Pants and Int. Ch. Reeuwijk's Fashionable Beauty, who were kept, and my bitch, Int. Germ. Swiss Ch. Reeuwijk's Filmstar in Silver. Reeuwijk's Fabulous Lady was owned by E. ter Mors. When Honey Bun was mated to Ladies Choice she produced Int. Lux. Ned. Swiss Ch. Reeuwijk's Dew Fantasy, also owned by myself. These four American imports and their offspring had a great impact on the breed all over Europe.

Ch. Ellenglaze Ladies Choice proved to be invaluable for European breeding lines. He sired several Champions, especially when bred to German lines. All of his Champion offspring produced future breeding stock and show dogs of excellent type and soundness.

VIGILAT

Owned by Mr and Mrs Eef ter Mors, this kennel is based on the American Reeuwijk's lines. The foundation bitch was Reeuwijk's Fabulous Lady (Int. Ch. Reeuwijk's Dew Fantasy – Int. Ch. Reeuwijk's Care for Beauty), and the foundation sire was Reeuwijk's Dear Tom Tod (Int. Ch. Ellenglaze Ladies Choice – Fezziwig Silver Lining). When Mrs Backx-Bennink stopped breeding, offspring out of these two Reeuwijk OES became the most influential stock in Holland.

Vigilat's Pretty Thing (Reeuwijk's Dear Tom Tod – Reeuwijk's Fabulous Lady) was mated to the German-bred Int. Ch. Button Nose Amadeus (Int. Ch. Domino a. d. Elbe Urstromtal – Elijah Blue a. d. Elbe Urstromtal – both offspring of Ch. Shaggy Dogs Chan Brasse Baron). This combination of Pretty Thing and Amadeus in 1984 resulted, amongst others, in the top-winning Vigilat's Wicked Lady. 'Wicked' gained her titles in Germany, Belgium, and Holland together with the International Champion title, winning Groups and Best in Shows at Specialty and British Herding Dog Shows.

Reeuwijk's Dear Tom Tod: Foundation sire for the Vigilat kennel.

Wicked and her litter brother, Int. Dutch Belg. Germ. Ch. Vigilat's Woody Allan, played an important part in Eef Ter Mors's breeding programme, and in the last five years the Vigilats have been making important strides. They have exported dogs to various other European countries, and some have finished their titles. At the moment the most successful Vigilat males are Ch. Vigilat's Different Yip, who is probably the first undocked OES Champion, and his litter brother, Int. Germ. Dutch, VDH, World Champion 1991 and 1992 Vigilat's Dear Davy Jori. These two impressive males were sired by Int. Ned. Belg. Ch. Barking Bears Davy Belle out of Vigilat's Yoline (Reeuwijk's Dear Tom Tod – Reeuwijk's Fabulous Lady).

Jori's and Yip's litter sister, Int. Lux. Ch. Vigilat's Dropshot was retained, and when she was mated to Stoffel's Baloo (a Vigilat's Woody Allan son), she produced Ch. Vigilat's Latin Pluche. Int. Ch. Vigilat's Elliot Ozz was the result of Wicked Lady bred to Vigilat's Adonis. Adonis is also the sire of Ch. Vigilat's Checkpoint Charlie out of Vigilat's Zanne.

Ch. Pockethall New Shoes: Sire and grandsire of Champions.

Pearce.

BARKING BEARS

Due to the tragic death of Rita Molhock the owner of this affix, this kennel is not breeding any more. Only a few litters were bred, but the dogs resulting out of these litters made a great impact on the breed in Holland. Rita started showing in the early seventies with a Belgian-bred male, Int. Ch. Shaggy Wonder Tommy Atkins. He was sired by the English-bred Int. Ch. Loakespark Brandy Soda out of Int. Ch. Shaggy Wonder Personal Jewel, bred by Mrs Mewis of the famous Shaggy Wonder affix. Tommy Atkins was whelped on October 15th 1970. He was joined in 1976 by a litter sister to the great Int. Ch. Reeuwijk's Care for Beauty, Reeuwijk's Caprice in Silver (Ch. Ellenglaze Ladies Choice – Fezziwig Silver Lining). Caprice in Silver was to become Rita Molhock's foundation bitch.

When mated to her half-brother, Int. Germ. Dutch. Swiss, Ch. Reeuwijk's Dew Fantasy (multi Ch. Ellenglaze Ladies Choice – Int. Dutch Ch. Fezziwig Honey Bun), Caprice produced the kennel's first litter, which was registered under the kennel's first affix, 'Amble Gaits'. Out of this litter came Amble Gait's Arabella Bleu, who when later bred to Winner 1982 Shaggy Bear's Sugar Footstomp (Pockethall Silver Shire – Hairy Fellow Melody Pandora) produced the kennel's top-winning male, Int. Dutch Belg. Ch. Winner 1986, 1987 Barking Bear's Davy Belle. Other offspring out of this litter were: Barking Bear's Dainty Donja, Barking Bear's Daisy Dingle, Barking Bear's Daphne Diloa Penny, Barking Bear's Dew Blinnerd, Barking Bear's Dannish Bleu Belle, Barking Bear's Dillwyn My Dark Devil, Barking Bear's Din O My Bleu Eyes, Barking Bear's Davy Boy, Barking Bear's Danville Virginia and Barking Bear's Dorenthy Delightful.

One year later Arabella Bleu was mated to Netherland Ch. Pockethall Prince William (Ch. Pockethall New Shoes – Ch. Pockethall Silver Shoes). This mating resulted on July 8th 1984 in a litter which produced the top-winning bitch bred by the Barking Bears kennel. This was Int. Dutch. Lux. Germ. Ch. Winner 1986 Barking Bear's Eyeful April. Eyeful April was owned by Mrs J. van Riet (Sparkle Square OES), who also owned the top-producing Barking Bear's Dorenthy Delightful.

Barking Bear's Arabella Bleu's third litter was sired by Marks and Sparks of Pelajilo (Flockmaster John Barlycorn – Cobbicot Polly Flinder of Flockmaster), and this produced the Int.

French Swiss Ch. Barking Bear's Irresistible Boy. Both Irresistible Boy and particularly Barking Bear's Davy Belle, passed their excellent qualities on to their offspring. Davy was responsible for the top-winning Int. Ch. Vigilat's Dropshot, multi-Ch. Vigilat's Different Yip, multi-Ch. Vigilat's Dear Davy Jori, and the Int. Lux. Dutch Ch. Silver Mystery's Hoyden Hazel.

SHAGGY BEARS

Marieke and Herman Blom are the breeders of the Shaggy Bear Old English Sheepdogs. Their foundation bitch was Hairy Fellow Melody Pandora, sired by Int. Lux. Ch. Shaggy Wonder V'Blue Apollo out of Int. Ch. Shaggy Wonder Titbit, who was bred by Mr Joha of the Hairy Fellow prefix. In the early eighties, Marieke and Herman imported two Pockethall males from England, Pockethall Silver Shire and Dutch Ch. Pockethall Prince William, both out of Ch. Pockethall Silver Shoes and sired by Ch. Pockethall New Shoes.

Hairy Fellow Melody Pandora was mated to Pockethall Silver Shire, and this resulted in the Junior Winner and Winner 1982 Shaggy Bear's Sugar Footstomp, who gained his two winner titles under the late Bobby James. He did not finish his title but made up for it by siring the well-known Ch. Barking Bear's Davy Belle.

Silver Shire and Pandora are also the parents of Shaggy Bear's Ragtime Melody, who, when bred to Ch. Pockethall Prince William, produced the Dutch Ch. Shaggy Bear's Kiss in the Ring.

TRADEMARK

Denimblue Silver Lace (Eng. Ch. Tumbletop Trademark of Denimblue – Silver Susan of Denimblue) and her half-brother, Shapod Special Surprise (Ch. Tumbletop Trademark of Denimblue – Bliewalder Nilma of the Hills) were the foundation stock of the Dutch Trademark kennel. Owned by Wim and Annelies De Vries, this kennel produced a Best in Show winner in the first litter ever bred. Ch. Trademark's Tickle My Tummy (Baucott Blue Mr Humphry – Denimblue Silver Lace) went Best in Show at the all important Dutch Club Championship Show in 1984. To confirm this success, her younger sister, Trademark's Isn't She Lovely, did the same in 1985.

Isn't She Lovely, mated to Shapod's Special Surprise, produced Ch. Cartoon's Going Baloons in November 1987, who was to become top-winning female in Holland in 1990 and 1991. Silver Lace's third litter was to Shapod Special Surprise. One bitch was kept, and she was named Trademark's Fairy Tale. Fairy Tale was later mated to Ch. Sparkle Square's Carte Blanche, which resulted in a litter whelped February 16th 1990. Out of this litter Annelies kept her most successful Old English Sheepdog to date, Ch. Trademark's Dressed to Kill, top OES in Holland in 1992. The winner of many CCs, CACIBs and several Best of Breeds, she went BIS at the European OES Club Show in 1992, held in Denmark, under John Smith and Barrie Croft.

One other bitch, which was used for breeding was Blueville's Aint She Cute (Shapod Special Surprise – Baucott Blue Delft). One of her dog puppies, Trademark's Mr. Nice Guy (sired by Int. Ch. Zottel's Mosche), was exported to England and was shown with some considerable success.

SPARKLE SQUARE

Jacqueline Van Riet was the owner of the Sparkle Square kennel. Jacqueline was one of the best handlers in Holland, and all her dogs were always presented to perfection. Barking Bear's Dorenthy Delightful was her foundation bitch, who when mated to Jolly Joggler's Star Light produced two of the most successful males in the late eighties. They were Int. Ch. Sparkle's Square Carte Blanche, World Champion in 1989, and Int. Lux. Dutch Ch. Sparkle's Square China Blue, who went three times Best of Breed at the All Winners Show in Amsterdam 1988, 1989 and

1990, and (like his brother) went Best of Breed at the World Show in 1990. Apart from excelling in the show ring, both males became outstanding sires.

Jacqueline's most successful female was not bred by her, but by the late Rita Molhock. Int. Dutch Lux. Germ. Ch. Barking Bear's Eyeful April (Dutch Ch. Pockethall Prince William – Amble Gait Arabella Bleu). Unfortunately, Eyeful April died young before she was able to leave any offspring. Jacqueline does not breed Old English Sheepdogs any more, which is a great loss to the breed. She now breeds and handles Miniature Dachshunds in partnership with her husband.

SILVER MYSTERY
This kennel is owned by Mrs H. M. Tegelaar v. d. Moolen. The breeding programme is based on Vigilat's Unique Surprise (Reeuwijk's Dear Tom Tod – Reeuwijk's Fabulous Lady). She was mated to Int. Dutch Belg. Ch. Winner 1986 and 1987 Barking Bear's Davy Belle. The resulting litter, whelped on December 13th 1985, produced Int. Dutch Lux. Ch. Silver Mystery's Hoyden's Hazel.

Hoyden Hazel enjoyed an excellent show career and is now a useful brood bitch. Her daughter, Silver Mystery's Josie's Prime Time (sired by multi Ch. Sparkle Square Carte Blanche), owned by Mrs Debbie de Veer, became World Junior Champion in 1990. Hoyden Hazel was also the dam of the first litter produced by artificial insemination, sired by Eng. Ch. Bobbington Latin Lover.

OF FOOL'S PARADISE
This affix is registered by Sjaak and Nelleke Mejier. The foundation stock of this kennel were Pelajilo Camillo (Flockmaster John Barleycorn – Pelajilo Masquarade) and Mellowdee Hot Stuff (Cilla's Style Silver Lad – Orlon's Pride and Joy of Mellowdee). Mellowdee Hot Stuff ('Pepper')

The Fool's Paradise Bobtails: (pictured left to right) Dutch Ch. Hot Stuff Of Fool's Paradise (Reserve World Ch. 1992), Int. Span. Fr. Ch. Fairy Flirt Of Fool's Paradise (World Ch. 1992, BOB), and Frankie Boy Of Fool's Paradise (Reserve World Ch. 1992).

was mated to Sunlad's Raggedy Danish Snowball, and on February 28th 1988 she produced one of the kennel's most successful females, Int. Ch. J'Am Elsie of Fool's Paradise. In 1992 Sjaak and Nelleke's Fairy Flirt of Fool's Paradise gained the World Champion title and Best of Breed at the World Championship Show in Spain. Lynette Lewis (Nushayp) and Mark James (Tuckles) were officiating. Fairy Flirt is also the holder of the Spanish, French and International Champion titles. At the World Championship Show in Spain their Dutch Ch. Hot Stuff of Fool's Paradise and their Frankie Boy of Fool's Paradise gained the Reserve World Champion titles – what a successful day with three out of four titles going to one kennel. Sjaak and Nelleke are also the owners of one other English import, Int. Dutch Lux. Ch. Lamedazottel Good Gossip (Eng. Ch. Greyfell Storm Warning – Eng. Ch. Zottel's Miss Marple of Lameda).

OTHER TOP-CLASS KENNELS
CARTOONS: Owned by W. Rijnbeek den Dulk. This kennel's brood bitch, Isn't She Lovely (Baucott Blue Mr Humphry – Denimblue Silver Lace) comes from the Trademark's kennel. Bred to Shapod's Special Surprise (Ch. Tumbletop Trademark of Denimblue, who is also Silver Lace's sire, out of Bluewalder Nilma of the Hill), she produced Int. Dutch Ch. Cartoons Going Baloons, the top-winning OES bitch in Holland for 1990 and 1991.
SUNLAD: Owned by J. Zondag. The kennel's foundation brood bitch is Sheba of the Caitwick Sunnies (Int. Ch. Shaggy Wonder V'Blue Apollo – Hairy Fellow C'Blue Sacha). When Sheba was mated to Marks and Sparks of Pelajilo (Flockmaster John Barleycorn – Cobbicot Polly Flinder of Flockmaster), she produced Dutch Ch. Sunlad's Raggedy Biddy Bunting.
GONNAGITCHA: This affix is registered by Antoinette van Zwijndregt. Antoinette is the breeder/owner of Int. Ch. Gonnagitcha's Cacharell Lou-Lou (Ch. Lohengrin a. d. Elbe Urstromtal – Rowhide Dolly Dots). Lou-Lou gained the Reserve World Champion title in 1990, and she gained sixth place in the top ten list for 1990 in Holland.
ROWHIDES: Owned by Mrs V. Nieuwenberg, this kennel is based on Reeuwijk's lines. Mrs Nieuwenberg's foundation bitch was Reeuwijk's Frances Pride, bred by Mrs F. Backx-Bennink. This bitch was sired by Int. Dutch Germ. Lux. Ch. Ellenglaze Ladies Choice out of Reeuwijk's Audrey (Int. Dutch Belg. Ch. St. Trinian de Hond Alfie – Dutch Ch. Reeuwijk's Up to Victory). When Frances Pride was mated to Int. & World Ch. Reeuwijk's Fancy Pants (Ch. Reeuwijk's Dew Fantasy – Ch. Reeuwijk's Care for Beauty), she produced Rowhide's Big Mobey Dick, who was best male at the OES Young Dog Show in 1981.

These two OES are behind most of the Rowhide's breeding. Bitches bred by her have become brood bitches for several other kennels. Rowhide's Dolly Dot is owned by the Gonnagitcha's kennel and Rowhide's Everlasting Beauty belongs to the Ruchieng Beauty Dogs kennel.
v.t. SCHOKKERLAND: This kennel also based its breeding on Reeuwijk lines with their bitch, Reeuwijk's Farm Girl. A. J. Nieuwenhuis is the registered owner, who is now breeding from Shaggy Bears Silver Pandita out of Hairy Fellows Melody Pandora sired by Pockethall Silver Shire and Silvery Flower v. t. Schokkerland.
RUCHIENG BEAUTY DOGS: P. Janssen van Haandel registered this unusual prefix. The kennel's brood bitches are Rowhide's Everlasting Beauty, Dolly Dot Ruchieng Beauty Dogs, Doris Day Ruchieng Beauty Dogs and Lady Tatjoura Ruchieng Beauty Dogs.
HAIRY FELLOW: Owned by J. H. Joha, this kennel's breeding is based on Belgian imports from the world famous Shaggy Wonder kennel – Ch. Shaggy Wonder Raggedy Ann, Ch. Shaggy Wonder Blue Apollo, Int. Ch. Shaggy Wonder Titbit and Shaggy Wonder U'Love Story. Hairy Fellow OES are behind a number of other Dutch kennels, especially the Shaggy Bears kennel,

through Hairy Fellow Melody Pandora (Ch. Shaggy Wonder V'Blue Apollo – Ch. Shaggy Wonder Titbit).

Two Dutch-bred Old English Sheepdogs did a lot of winning in the mid to late eighties. Dutch Ch. Satchit's Daytripper, bred by Mrs M. Dierdorp, out of Bizzeboots I Betcha I Beat Ye (Ch. Danish Delight Blue Chieftain – Ch. Searwell Duchess Lady Day) sired by Ch. Dodo Love's Bright & Breezy (Ch. Reeuwijk's Dew Fantasy – Reeuwijk's Elien). Daytripper has been used widely at stud and produced some very successful offspring. Dutch Ch. Pocketpiece, bred by J. J. Oostenvijk, is out of Joky Jane v. t. Schokkerland (Shaggy Bears Sugar Footstomp – Reeuwijk's Farm Girl) sired by Dutch Ch. Pockethall Prince William (Eng. Ch. Pockethall New Shoes – Eng. Ch. Pockethall Silver Shoes). Pocketpiece, whelped on August 12th 1986, is owned by S. & J. Verhagen, and she and her owners enjoyed a tremendous show career.

FRANCE

The first OES to be registered in France was Old Nick of Pastorale, in 1933, owned by James Alain, and imported from the world-famous Pastorale kennel in England. Since then, the number of Old English Sheepdogs registered with the French Kennel Club has grown to an impressive 18,000 dogs. As in most other countries, the prime time for the breed was in the 1980s. In 1973 only one OES was born in France, twenty-seven in 1977, 230 in 1982, escalating to an amazing 2600 in 1986, and from then on going down again to about 1500 a year. The average number of OES entered at a Championship Show today is around twenty dogs, compared with the all-time record entry at the French Club Show in 1986 of more than 170 dogs. The judges on this occasion were Mrs B. Muller (Switzerland) and three English judges, Stuart Mallard, Mark James and Barry Croft. Recession and extremely high entry fees are probably the main reasons for this drop. In 1976 some Welsh Corgi enthusiasts, who were also interested in Bobtails, founded the first club, and this represents both breeds. Breeders of the late seventies and early eighties were Jean Paul Denis, who bred mainly with dogs imported from the English Shepton kennel. He was the first in France to present a Bobtail in the typical style of grooming. Georges (Jojo) Kraemer, a great character, was known all over Europe with his huge Int. Ch. El Padron of Jamboree. He also bred the Int. Fr. Ch. Gekabob Anada, who gained her titles in 1987 and 1988.

For a very long time France did not have breed specialist judges, relying on all-rounders only. This resulted in too much emphasis being paid to pigmentation and dentition. At the present time, the French club is educating a new generation of young and dedicated people to judge the breed. I have watched the development of the French Bobtails over the past nineteen years, and the improvement in the standard and quality is most apparent. The difficulty in making up a French Champion lies in the requirement to win a CC from the National Specialty Club Show, or a CC gained in Paris, which are of equal value. No matter how many national CCs are accumulated, unless a dog has won either of these CCs, he cannot become a French Champion.

LAMEDA

Rene Parent has bred several French Champions. Ch. Sir Scott de Lameda and Ch. Susie Q de Lameda both gained their French Championship title in 1983. He also owned Int. Fr. Ch. Rembrandt a. d. Elbe Urstromtal (Ch. Blueacres Bump in the Night – Int. Germ. Ch. Hot Dog a. d. Elbe Urstromtal), and later on Int. Am. Dk. Germ. Ch. Trosambe Blue Panda Spicer (Am. Ch. Pempridge Cheerio Rascal – Am. Ch. Trosambe Blue Panda Winsome. Spicer was originally imported from America and shown by the German OES breeder, Mrs C. Abicht/Hartman with the famous a. d. Elbe Urstromtal affix.

Ch. Rembrandt a. d. Elbe Urstromtal: A successful dog for the French Lameda kennel.

DES KORILS D'AMOR
This is one of the most successful affixes in France today. This kennel, owned by Messrs Prin and Thual, started breeding with Ch. Beldom Yves Panda and Ch. Maurin Snoopy (both imports), and six French Champions, bred in the last ten years, go to their credit.

EBONY AND IVORY
M. and Mme Claude and Daniele Ritter started showing in the late seventies with Nonours du Mont Sorcier and Nikita du Mont Sorcier. Since then, they have acquired four Zottel and Lamedazottel OES, and they have five homebred Champions to their credit. The two most successful dogs in this kennel are the top-winning OES female in France, Int. Swiss Ch. Zottel's Get Up And Boogie, born in 1982 (Int. Ned. Germ. Ch. Ellenglaze Ladies Choice – Int. Germ Swiss Ch. Reeuwijk's Filmstar in Silver) and the Int. Swiss Spanish Ch. Zottel's Freemason, born in 1989, litter brother to UK Ch. Lamedazottel Flamboyant (Ch. Pockethall J'Mashootoo– Ch. Zottel's Miss Marple of Lameda).

MARY PEOPLE
Mary People is the affix of another younger breeder, Guy Hubert. His breeding programme is based on dogs from the Koril d'Amor, Ebony and Ivory and Zottel kennel. His bitch, Int. Fr. Ch. Ephy of Mary People, was well placed all over Europe in 1992. He also owns a litter sister to Ch. Lamedazottel Flamboyant, named French Ch. Zottel's Fatal Beauty.

LES RIVES DE LA SAVOUREUSE
Owned by M and Mm Y. Droller, this kennel has enjoyed success in the ring. Ch. Romulus du Domaine des Deux Cedres gained his French title in 1984, and Until The End of Mink de Ville, bred by Rene Parent, also became a French Champion. Dominant in the show ring at the present time are several imports from the Dutch Vigilats kennel, bred by Mr E. ter Mors.

SWITZERLAND
The Swiss OES Club was founded in 1980 by a few dedicated Bobtail fanciers. Two of these founder members are still serving on the committee. Andreas Baumann, who has been the treasurer for the past 13 years, and Barbara Mueller of the Pennylane OES is responsible for all

breeding concerns. In Switzerland, like Germany, the Swiss Breed Club has the power to decide which dogs should be bred from. In order to be granted permission, the dog must meet certain criteria such as a minimum age for males and females and a maximum age for females. All breeding stock also has to be X-rayed for hip dysplasia and officially scored. Unlike Britain, the results are not published so it is up to the individual to decide whether to make a dog's score public or not. However, if the scored grade does not come up to the required result, breeding permission will not be granted. The first three OES mentioned in the Swiss stud book were whelped in 1910. Their coat colours were described as: white and yellow, dark steel-grey with a little white, and the third OES was white with dark steel-grey patches. Until the early fifties there were only a very few registrations. All registered dogs were kept as pets, and most came from the English Shepton kennel. Then, from the seventies, numbers started to increase: 1970, 9 OES; 1971, 7 OES; 1972, 18 OES; 1973, 9 OES; 1974, 16 OES; 1980, 36 OES; and 1981, 44. After that, the number of registrations increased to an average of 100 per year.

In 1968 one of the earlier OES litters was whelped. This was bred by O. Jegge of the St. Fridolin affix. The litter was sired by Bluecrest Happy Fella out of Shaggy Wonder New Idol, and six puppies were entered into the Swiss Stud Book.

THE SEVENTIES

One of the most well-known breeders in the seventies was Marina Grieder with the Ottenfels affix. She bred her first litter in July 1970, sired by Reeuwijk's Pattsy Progress out of Diva in St. Fredolin. Marina was also the first owner of Reeuwijk's Complete Tristan. Tristan was bred by Mrs F. Backx-Bennink from Holland, and he was one of the early winners at the dog shows. He was later sold to Mrs Blanc-Romance of the des Terreaux affix. Tristan was a brother to the famous World Winner, Int. Ned. Germ. Lux. Ch. Reeuwijk's Care for Beauty (Int. Ned. Germ. Lux. Ch. Ellenglaze Ladies Choice – Fezziwig Silver Lining). Two more imports in the seventies were Ellenglaze Maid of Honor and Unnesta Lord. Maid of Honor was mainly American Fezziwig breeding. Unnesta Lord came from Marta Hult-Korfitsen and her famous Swedish Unnesta breeding. I find the most interesting registration in the seventies is the litter with the affix Landstrasse, sired by Rossglen Meadow Romeo out of Rossglen Meadow Breeze. All the puppies out of this litter had an endorsement put on their pedigrees by the Swiss Kennel Club, stating that they were not allowed to be shown because they were left undocked!

LEADING KENNELS

Due to the small number of Championship Shows in Switzerland, there are not many Swiss-owned OES who have gained their titles. One of the first was Int. Swiss Ch. Quill v. Topferhof (Myriam v. Michaeli's Turn – Ch. Reeuwijk's Ursa Major), born in 1979, and bred by Mr and Mrs Blatt of the German Topferhof prefix. Quill was owned by Sylvia Stutz, of the v. d. Zollgasse affix, who started her kennel with him and with a bitch from the Victory OES kennel, owned by Mrs D. Ziegler-Vowinkel in Germany. This bitch was called Victory Nanuschka (Ch. Argos von Donaro – Yasabel Princess Sophie of Bobbingay). Sylvia is also the owner of the English import, Lamedazottel Best Man (Int. Dk. Germ. Ch. Lorengrin a. d. Elbe-Urstromtal – Int. Swiss Ch. Zottel's Get Up and Boogie).

Nanuschka's litter sister, Victory Nausikaa, went to the Meadow Breeze OES kennel owned by Lilly Zinniker. Lilly also used Quill for breeding, and her Meadow Breeze Cassiopeia (Quill – Nausikaa) was well-placed at the Swiss Shows. Cassiopeia is also the dam of Ch. Meadow Breeze Flibbertigibbet, who was sired by World Champion and Int. Ch. Osborn a. d. Elbe Urstromtal. The latest addition to the Meadow Breeze kennel is Ko-Pi's 599 U-Asti in Memory (Ko-Pi's 599 Hardenberg – Ko-Pi's 599 Asti Spumante), bred in Germany by Mrs Barbel Korn.

Mr D. Bill, who was one of the founder members of the Swiss Club is the breeder of Int. Ch. Bette of Yellowstone, sired by Int. Ned. Swiss. Ch. Reeuwijk's Dew Fantasy out of Idol v. Ottenfels. Other dedicated OES kennels include Marlies Mueller-Machler's of Bear Lake, based on Pennylane, Reeuwijk's, Zottel's and Rollingsea lines; Vreni Wyser of the Rosseville affix is dedicated to breeding OES with tails – her English import, Raydor Penelope, produced several undocked litters; Mr and Mrs M. Bays, owners of the De Claire Source kennel, have been involved with OES since the early eighties – they now own and successfully show Int. Ch. Lamedazottel Gershwin, sired by Eng. Ch. Greyfells Storm Warning out of Eng. Ch. Zottel's Miss Marple of Lameda.

PENNYLANE

The most successful kennel in Switzerland is Pennylane, owned by Barbara Muller. In fact, this kennel is not only well-known for their OES but also for English Cocker Spaniels. Barbara started breeding in 1979 with her English import, Rollingsea Daydream (Rollingsea High Spirit – Springfield Wendy Mary of Rollingsea). This first Pennylane litter was sired by Edward Davie v. Ottenfels. In 1982 the Pennylane kennel imported their first OES male, Zottel's Grasshopper, later to become Int. Swiss. Ital. Fr. Champion. 'GC' was sired by the famous Int. Ned. Lux. Germ. Ch. Ellenglaze Ladies Choice out of his granddaughter, Int. Germ. Swiss. Ch. Reeuwijk's Filmstar in Silver. Apart from becoming the most successful show OES in Switzerland, he is also the top-

Int. Swiss. Ital. Fr. Ch. Zottel's Grasshopper: Breed recordholder in Switzerland.

producing sire with three Champions to his credit. They are: Swiss Ch. Pennylane Chattanooga Choo Choo, out of Pennylane Orange Blossom (Ch. Reeuwijk's Dew Fantasy – Rollingsea Daydream), Ital. Ch. Pennylane I Love Italy, out of Pennylane Visa Vis (same breeding as Orange Blossom), and Int. Swiss Ch. Pennylane Love for la Vigie (same breeding as I Love Italy). The fourth Pennylane Champion is Int. Swiss. Ch. Pennylane Ragtime Baby, sired by Int. Germ. Ch. Zottel's Magic Touch, litter brother to the joint English breed record holder, Miss Marple, out of Pennylane Forever Lasting Love (Grasshopper – Orange Blossom). In 1990 the Pennylane kennel had a new addition to the household, Lameda Zottel Graffiti, litter sister to Ch. Lameda Zottel Gershwin out of a litter which produced seven Champions, sired by Eng. Ch. Greyfells Storm Warning out of Eng. Ch. Zottel's Miss Marple of Lameda. Graffiti finished her International title in 1992, winning several Groups and Best in Shows on the way, ending the same year with the top winning OES title in Switzerland. A more recently shown Champion is Int. Ch. Pennylane Penalty (Ch. Lamedazottel His Nibs – Aphrodite de Claire).

ITALY, SPAIN AND PORTUGAL

The population of Old English Sheepdogs in all three countries is rather small, with few reaching the standard of the dogs in other European countries. Nevertheless, all three countries have some very dedicated OES fanciers who do their very best to improve their own stock. Imports from the UK, Germany and Holland can be found in all three countries.

PORTUGAL: Dr Pedro Delerue with his da Quinta D'Abroeira kennel of Estoril keeps the OES flag going in Portugal. His top dog all Breeds in 1990 is the multiple BIS winning Port. Span. Ch. Crazy Lolla da Quinta d'Abroeira (Ch. Southview Colonel Bogey of Bartine – Ch. Pelajilo Maggy Meetlove) has helped the breed's popularity in this part of Europe. Her BIS and Reserve BIS awards came from the respected judges Nassi Assenmacher-Feyel (Germany), Ulla Erickson (Sweden), Madeira Rodrigues (Portugal), Carlos Saievich (Argentina) and Liz Cartledge (England). Ch. Pelajilo Maggy Meetlove is also the dam of Int. Port. Span. Ch. Darling Teddy da Quinta d'Abroeira (sired by Eng. Ch. Trushayp Eckythump of Jenards), who was Top OES in Spain.

SPAIN: The Spanish Club was founded in 1983 in Barcelona – El Club del Antiquo Perro Pastor de Ingles en Espana – (CAPPIE). The club held its first Championship show in October 1984, under the English judge, Christine Barber (Bartine) who had moved to Spain that January. There were twenty-one dogs entered. Best in Show went to Ch. Tuckles Timmy Teapot, bred in Holland by Stuart Mallard and Mark James. Since then the club has held a yearly Club Show in a different region of Spain. Christine Barber's presence in Spain, and for the last few years, Jenny and Richard Baker (Jenards), has helped to improve the quality of the OES in Spain, as all three gave invaluable advice concerning important imports. As a result homebred dogs are now a threat to foreign OES, who are exhibited at the International Shows to gain a last CACIB for the Int. Champion title.

ITALY: The Italian English Sheepdog Club was formed in 1978. It represented the English Sheepdog breeds: the OES, the Bearded Collie, and the Welsh Corgi (Cardigan and Pembroke). Early fanciers of the breed in Italy were Countess L. Barbolani di Montanto (S. Gervasio), who owned Ch. Jessica vom Ottenfels (bred in Switzerland), Ch. Rosalind of Reeuwijk and Ch. Moby Dick vom Ottenfels, who sired Ch. Cleopatra di S. Gervasio. All these dogs go back to Mrs Backx-Bennink's famous Reeuwijk OES. Mr G. M. Garlanda (Equinozio) owned Ch. Gweleog Blue Jackson, who became the first OES Champion in 1972. Blue Jackson sired Ch. Darling dell' Equinozio and Ch. Lola dell' Equinozio.

Mr N. Massobrio was the owner of Int Ital. Ch. Wisebeck Footlights George and Int. Ital. Ch. Oldash Tudor Magic. Mr and Mrs G. Pistolini, owned Int. Ch. True Blue of Mijoho (Wildahar Lynces Blue Diamond – Bluecrag Charlie's Girl) and Int. Ch. Bobbingay Super Dumpling (Rollingsea Dickory Dock – Baucottblue Beverley of Bobbingay). These two dogs produced Bruno Fuccini's Int Ch Star.

The first Speciality OES Show was held in 1976 in Vigevano, near Pavia. The officiating judge was the well-known all-rounder, Mr Luigiano Bernine, who gave Best of Breed to the English import, Ch. Applause of Amblegait, owned by Prof. Mille (Valkmanitu).

Chapter Nine

THE OES IN AUSTRALIA

THE EARLY IMPORTS

It is believed that the first OES came to Australia with British immigrant settlers in the 19th century. Subsequently, imported Bobtails came from a variety of English breeders, although most of them were registered with the Shepton affix and were also exported by the Shepton kennel. The first Shepton OES, Shepton Nell (Shepton Guardsman – Shepton Greymist), came to Australia in 1929. Earlier records of OES come mainly from the South of Australia, Victoria and Tasmania. Because of the grass seeds and burrs in the grasslands in the north and the west, OES could not be used to work the sheep and cattle there.

The shepherds and drovers preferred the shorter-coated cross-breeds, which were the result of matings between the native Dingo and the first imported OES, which later developed into the Australian Kelpi and the Australian Cattle Dog. These smaller-sized and shorter-coated breeds, together with the Border Collie, were much more suitable as working dogs in this part of the country. In fact, Smithfield dogs were still used for working sheep and cattle until the early sixties, especially in Tasmania. The first dog show in Australia was held in 1862 in Hobart Town, Tasmania. Records show that a so-called 'Smithfield Collie' was exhibited at this show. Not long after that, in 1871, nine English Sheep dogs and two English Sheep bitches were shown at an agricultural show in northern Tasmania. It is interesting that these dogs were shown fourteen years before the Breed Standard was approved by the English Kennel Club. However, it was not until 1898 that 'Old English Sheepdogs' were scheduled at the Melbourne Show, and also at the Adelaide Royal Show in the same year.

FRANKSTON

In 1914 the first OES litter bred in Australia was registered. It was bred by Lord Rothschild from the Chiltern Hills, near London, out of Homefarm Tring, an English import. Tring's pedigree went back to Young Watch, Ch. Cavendish Victor and Ch. Stylish Boy. The breeder of this litter was Douglas Picking, the owner of the Dromara Animal Park in Frankston, Victoria, and he used 'Frankston' as his prefix. Douglas Picking was to become the first really dedicated breeder of Old English Sheepdogs. Fortunately he was also a very particular man, who used to keep records about his breeding, which are now an invaluable part of the history of the OES in Australia. He continued breeding for almost sixty years and many Frankston OES became the foundation stock for other kennels in South Australia, Tasmania and New South Wales. One other important English import, Penzance Mack, bred by Robert Thomas in 1924, was sent out to South Australia and was used for stud work there and in Victoria. Mr Picking was mainly responsible for keeping the breed alive during the war years. Most of his breeding stock was imported from England by ship, and due to the length of the journey, some of his imports did not survive the trip. One of his most influential dogs was the English import, Shepton Blue Dragon, imported in 1948. He sired at least four Champions and many of his offspring went to other States. Aust. Ch. Frankston Esmond Surf King, his most successful show dog, went Best of Breed at the Melbourne Royal Show in 1951, 1952 and 1953. Mr Picking owned OES until the early seventies, although he did not breed a lot after the fifties. The first OES Champion in Australia, Llangollen of Kintora, was the result of a litter out of a Frankston bitch and a dog, Opihi John O'Gaunt, who was descended from Caedman of Pastorale and Big Grim Robbery, and imported to Victoria. Since then, many dogs have come to Australia from New Zealand and vice versa.

THE SIXTIES AND SEVENTIES

During the sixties and seventies the breed became really popular. Many OES were imported from England and used as breeding stock. The result of this sudden and really unwanted popularity was the same as all over the world. Too many so-called 'breeders' got involved with OES, even though they were lacking in knowledge, and this in turn meant that new owners were given very little advice on caring for the breed. As in the UK, Europe and America, Australia was suddenly faced with an immense rescue problem. The increasing number of abandoned OES, plus the need to co-operate between the many States, resulted eventually in rescue services being set up in most areas, and in the formation of regional clubs.

SOUTH AUSTRALIA: The first OES breed club was founded in South Australia in 1968. Many of the founding members are still involved with the club today, especially John Tremellen, who is now judging at all breeds level. His OES were registered with the Nellemerd prefix and based on Kersbrook and Fettlara lines. John is now patron of the club. The very successful Shaggywag prefix was originally owned by Judy Chapman and Trevor Watson, who both put a tremendous amount of work into the club. Judy was also instrumental in forming a National Breed body. Like John Tremellen, she is still a supporter of the club and a patron. Her prefix has changed to Cobbity, and Trevor Watson, an active supporter of the club, now breeds under the Trubshaw prefix.

Aust. Ch. Foamingsea Wots Portant: Top OES in Australia 1991 and 1992.

QUEENSLAND: Due to the tropical heat and humidity, Queensland has a smaller number of OES. Bobtail owners in Queensland and in the coastal areas of central and northern New South Wales have to cope with deadly ticks. They have to learn to notice early signs of ticks and try to overcome the threat with simple precautions like regular bathing and sprays. Pat McLeod of the Tighgum prefix, was a founder member of the Queensland Club, which was founded in 1974. She has been a very successful breeder and is now judging at Working Group level.

NEW SOUTH WALES: The OES Club of New South Wales was formed in 1970. Pat Lansdown, who breeds under the Woolclip affix, has worked as the Welfare Officer for many years and her input has been invaluable. Jim and Meg Hull, who have been breeding under the Southgate affix since 1951, have been involved with the management of the club. Their Southgate dogs can be found behind a number of present-day lines. For many years a separate club existed for OES in the Australian Capital Territory (Canberra). Its affairs have now been taken over by the NSW Club.

WESTERN AUSTRALIA: Western Australia in its northern parts is extremely hot and dry. However, OES are very popular and live in an air-conditioned environment, only coming out early in the morning or late in the evening. The cooler south-west of the State still reaches temperatures of 40 degrees centigrade and more. The heat there is very dry, which makes it more bearable for humans and dogs. The Western Australian Club was formed in 1973. The breeders of the successful Woolliwoof OES, Maureen and Peter Robinson, have been stalwart club members and supporters since Day One. Peter, who is a well-respected judge of the Working Group, is currently the President of the National OES Breed Council. In 1984, Maureen and Peter imported the

*Am. Can. Aust. Ch.
Tarawood's Classic
Impression (imported
Canada): An influential
sire for Australian
bloodlines.*

American Champion OES, Am. Can. Ch. Tarawood's Classic Impression. This dog was bred in Canada, sired by Am. Can. Ch. Briarhalls Tarawood Classic out of Can. Ch. Tarawood's Misty Blue. 'Jimmy' made a great impression in the show ring and also on the breed. He sired eleven litters which resulted in several National Show and State Specialty winners such as Ch. Woolliwoof Meisha (out of Ch. Woolliwoof Sho Classic) BIS at the Tasmania Club Championship Show in 1992, under Lorraine Bond, and Ch. Woolliwoof Allied Spirit (out of Tynycoed Dau Llygad Du) BIS at the South Australian Club Championship Show 1992, under John Tremellen.

Ch. Woolliwoof Allied Invader (also out of Tynycoed Dau Llygad Du) took BIS at the Western Australian OES Club Championship Show in 1992 under Gillian Rowsell. At the seventh National in 1991, under Ivor Thick (England), two of Classic Impression's progeny swept the board. Best in Show went to Ch. Woolliwoof Sho Classic (out of Woolliwoof Snow Biki), with the runner-up going to Ch. Woolliwoof Maccabeus (same breeding). Sho Classic had also been Best in Show at the sixth National in 1989 in Hobart, Tasmania, under Robert Caswell (USA). Runner-up was Ch. Packardia Magnum (Classic Impression – Ch. Jindella Full O'Herbs).

VICTORIA: Victoria Club was founded in 1968 under the influence of Mr and Mrs A. V. Carroll and Mr and Mrs F. English. The affiliation with the Kennel Control Council was granted in 1971, and the first Championship Show was held in 1972, with Mr K. Pierce officiating. Best in Show went to Aust. Ch. Beila Miss Amanda and Best Opposite Sex to Aust. Ch. Beila Master Anthony.

Their second Championship Show was judged by the well-known English judge, Sylvia Talbot. She was the first overseas breed specialist who went over to judge the breed. Since then many well-known breed specialists from abroad have officiated at the Victoria Championship Shows, including Isobel Lawson (Prospectblue), Jean Gould (Rollingsea), Joan Real (Tynycoed), Stuart Mallard (Tuckles), Stan Fisher (Wrightway), Vic Guest (Lamacres), Barry Croft (Malcro), and many more. The club's secretary, Lorraine Walsh, breeds and exhibits successfully under the Packardia affix. Her Ch. Packardia Magnum (Am. Can. Aust. Ch. Tarawood's Classic Impression – Ch. Jindella Full O'Herbs) was runner-up to the BIS winner in 1989 at the sixth National in Hobart, Tasmania, under Robert Caswell (USA), and runner-up to the BIS winner at the eighth National in 1992 at Melbourne, Victoria, under Terry Carter (Canada).

Denise Humphries is very much involved with the Victoria OES Club. Her kennel has made a considerable impact on the breed, especially through her English and American imports. The foundation bitch of her Jindella OES was Aust. Ch. Scruffen Scallywag. Many CC winners at the OESC Victoria Shows descended from her. However, the biggest influence the Jindella kennel has had on the breed was through the English-bred Aust. Ch. Prospectblue Apollo Boy (Prospectblue Andrew – Ch. Prospectblue Twotrees Arabella), bred by Isobel Lawson. He sired thirty-eight Champions, thirteen individual Specialty Show Challenge winners, and seven individual OES Year winners. Apollo Boy was of bigger type with a short body. Bred to different lines, he produced an excellent type of OES, which changed the breed within a short time.

The Jindella kennel was also the home of Aust. Ch. Momarv's All American Boy (Am. Ch. Momarv's That's My Boy – Momarv's Lucky Penny), again a sire of several Champions. Denise Humphries is passed to judge several Groups.

TASMANIA: Tasmania's landscape and climate is very similar to the southern parts of England, providing an ideal environment for the breed. This might be the reason why Tasmania has probably the longest association with the breed in Australia. Despite this involvement with the breed, Tasmania was the last state in Australia to form a club. Jean and Barry McDonald of the Hunson OES prefix were mainly responsible for establishing the club. Their Ch. Movama Manhattan (Aust. Ch. Bluewalder Roly Poly – Jolifoot Tivoli Star), bred by Mrs G. Turnbull, received the Dog Challenge at the First National in 1982 in Sydney, New South Wales, under breed specialist Caj Haakansson, and was also runner-up to the BIS winner at the Second National in 1983 in Hobart, Tasmania, under Jilly Bennett. Pam and Henry Smith, who own the Bescinda Old English Sheepdogs, have also been involved with the club and have been invaluable supporters since its inception.

NATIONAL CO-OPERATION
In 1980 the Australian National Kennel Control (ANKC), an association of Canine controlling bodies across Australia, tried to encourage co-operation between the different states. This was hoped to be beneficial to all canine affairs. Through the work of Judy Chapman and Judy Salt from Victoria, many clubs decided to participate. Taking part were the clubs from South Australia, Tasmania, Western Australia and New South Wales. Unfortunately, this initial National OES Society had to be wound up, as they were unable to conform to the ANKC's formal requirements

for a Breed Council. Replaced in 1988 by the National OES Breed Council, with its strong constitution, it is now recognised by the ANKC as the 'peak body' of OES clubs across Australia. Apart from Queensland, which intends to join as well, all other State clubs are members. The main purposes of the National Council are to promote the breed nationally, to represent the clubs' interests in matters of official opinions, to promote the general welfare of the breed through interstate co-operation, and to oversee the conduct of the annual National Shows.

Since its formation, eight National Specialty Shows have been held, which were judged by a breed specialist from outside Australia. The shows are held in the capital city of the State responsible. Exhibitors from all over Australia come to these shows, providing an extremely high standard of competition. Even during the airline strike in 1989 all the top dogs from Victoria, New South Wales, South Australia and Western Australia somehow managed to get across Bass Strait to Tasmania to the National Show in Hobart. It is interesting that the most isolated States of Tasmania and Western Australia, with almost 2,600 miles (4000 kilometres) to travel from east to west, give the most consistent and the strongest support to the National Shows. Exhibitors from Western Australia usually hire a bus together, which makes the five days travelling across the country less strenuous for dogs and owners.

HENLEY: Owned by Gill Rowsell and Kit Tobias, this kennel started in the seventies with English imports Dalcrest Miss Chellah (Eng. Ch. Barnolby Mr Barrymore – Baroness of Barnolby) and Aust. Ch. Marsh Joyful Fella (Rollingsea Val Ambrose – Marsh Megan). Since the early seventies, Gillian and Kit have bred many Champions and Best in Show winners. They include: Aust. Ch. Henley Lady Juliette (Aust. Ch. Wenallt Cool Boy – Dalcrest Miss Chellah), Aust. Ch. Henley Joyful Lady (Aust. Ch. Marsh Joyful Fella – Aust. Ch. Henley Lady Cassandra), Aust. Ch. Henley The Judge (Aust. Ch. Josias Handsome Fella – Aust. Ch. Henley Lady Cassandra).

REGENCYBLUE: Joanne Sewell's Regencyblue OES are based on the Rollingsea line from England, with her foundation bitch Ch. Rollingsea Suzie Bear (Eng. Ch. Rollingsea Viceroy – Eng. Ch. Rollingsea Venus). Suzie was bred to Aust. Ch. Rollingsea Gladiator, which produced Ch. Regencyblue Balibarba. Her litter to Aust. Ch. Prospectblue Apollo Boy resulted in Ch. Regencyblue Josephine, and a third litter to Prospectblue Tom Jones produced Ch. Regencyblue Miss Eliza. All three daughters of Suzie Bear had great show careers and started a very successful line of OES.

BALUCHISTAN: One of the most successful kennels over many years in Victoria is the Baluchistan kennel, owned by Effie, Sue and Christopher Moore. They have imported several English-bred dogs, notably Aust. Ch. Wenallt Cool Boy (Wenallt Farmers Boy – Wenallt Hot Pants). 'Tripper' was bred by Mrs P. Jones (Wenallt). He gained Best of Breed at both Sydney and Melbourne Royal in 1975 and also became the sire of many Champions.

The Moores most influential import was Aust. Ch. Fernville Gay Future. He was bred in 1976 by Norman Harrison, sired by the famous Eng. Ch. Fernville Lord Digby out of Fernville Gypsy Madonna. Future finished his Champion title at thirteen months of age, winning many Best in Shows in several Australian States. As a sire he was equally impressive, with Champion offspring to several different bitches. Future's two daughters, Ch. Baluchistan Contessa (out of Baluchistan Sapphire) and Ch. Baluchistan Madonna (out of Baluchistan Dream Girl) had a great day at the First National Specialty Show in 1988, in Sydney, under breed specialist Caj Haakansson (Bahlambs), taking Best in Show and runner-up respectively. Sue and Christopher Moore are now breeding and showing with their new affix 'Perfu', while Effie Moore continues with the Baluchistan prefix. Their latest Champion, Perfu Future Folly (Oldoak Ned Kelly – Aust. Ch. Baluchistan Melody), is a fourth generation of Best in Show winners and a fifth generation of Champions exhibited by the Moores. Future Folly's dam is line-bred to Ch. Fernville Gay Future.

HARTWYN: Pauline Hartwell's Hartwyn OES have had a successful time during the early nineties, with Aust. Ch. Hartwyn Royal Pageant CDX (Ch. Talisman Royal Salute – Ch. Penzance Blue Gytha) gaining the top OES award for 1992 in New South Wales. He also achieved Best in Show under breed specialist Barrie Croft (Malcro) at the Victoria Club Show in 1989. At the same show, Barrie awarded the Reserve Bitch CC to Hartwyn Blue Affair, and Best Puppy to Hartwyn Royal Legend. Royal Pageant made history by winning Best in Show at Melbourne Royal from an entry of almost 6,600 dogs. This was the first time an OES achieved this honour at the Melbourne Show. Pauline Hartwell's Aust. Ch. Hartwyn Royal Pageant (Aust Ch. Talisman Royal Salute – Ch. Penzance Blue Gytha CDX) went Best in Show at the Fifth National in 1988, under breed specialist Stan Fisher (Wrightway). The dam of these highly successful Hartwyn OES is Ch. Penzance Blue Gytha, who was bred by Shirley Ritchie. In her time, Gytha was a multiple Group and Best in Show winner. She was also awarded a Silver medal for 'Excellence in Conformation and Obedience' after she won the Sydney Royal 1984 Obedience, with a record score of 196 – a truly great Bobtail behind the Hartwyn's top winners.

GATEVIEW: The Top OES for 1992 in Victoria was bred by Mr and Mrs Shane Armstrong, under the Gateview affix. Aust. Ch. Gateview Everso Portant (Ch. Packardia Magnum – Ch. Hazeman Hey Jude) was Best in Show under Pauline Barnes (Macopa) at the Victorian Club Championship Show in 1990. Under Barrie Croft (Malcro), the year before, he had been Reserve Dog Challenge winner and Reserve Best in Show.

His dam, Ch. Hazeman Hey Jude (Aust. Ch. Olensha Dad's Delight CD – Hazeman Hello Dolly), was bred by Gail Kohlman and Chris Hazell. Their Hazeman Heza Natural was Best Exhibited in Show under Dorothy Malins (Embages) at the South Australian Championship Show in 1983. Best Opposite Sex in Show the same day went to Aust Ch. Hazeman Grecian Girl.

NEW ZEALAND
The first Old English Sheepdog to be registered by the New Zealand Kennel Club was the English import Shepton Starlight, a male born in 1908, bred by the Tilley brothers in the UK, and imported by H. Arkwright. The first OES born in New Zealand which was registered by the Kennel Club, was bred by Mr Arkwright, and this was a male called Watch, born in 1911.

The first three Champions were: NZ Ch. Opihi Rupert (King Robert, imp. UK – Big Gem Robbery, imp. UK), whelped on June 3rd 1931, bred by Dorothy Kerr, NZ Ch. Emma of Opihi (Cardman of Pastorale, imp. UK – Hyacinth of Pastorale, imp. UK), whelped on January 9th 1934, bred by Mr and Mrs Miller, and NZ Ch. Recorder of te Knuite (NZ Ch. Opihi Rupert – Hammerwood Hamadryad, imp. UK), whelped on November 19th 1936, bred by R. M. Ormsby.

THE SEVENTIES
The record for the top sire is held by NZ Ch. Tamandra Blue of Fraeona, with ten Champions to his credit. He was sired by the English import Beckington Bandit out of NZ Ch. Greymist Eureka, bred by Pearl Wansborough. He had a most successful show career, winning Reserve Best in Show at the New Zealand National Dog Show in 1973 under a Mexican judge. The Fraeona kennel was

a top-producing kennel in the late seventies, with many top-winning dogs carrying their affix.

Another prominent and successful breeder around the late seventies was Allan Bradshaw (Bard). Allan no longer breeds OES, but is extremely well-known and respected as a top international all breed judge. He has judged OES all over the world at breed Specialty shows and all breed Championship shows. His Ch. Hannibal Boy of Ushaw was one of New Zealand's top OES in the early seventies, siring many Champions for the Bard affix. Marilyn Russell, with the Blue Saxon prefix, also had a big influence on the breed during the early seventies, producing many Champions. During the late seventies the most important kennels in the North Island were: Rowandale, owned by Kathy and Ian Smith, Biggleswade, owned by Sue and Archie McPherson, and Kerryleigh, owned by Gay and Kevin Barnard. In the South Island, Roosevelt, owned by Tony and Jan Glen, Kadesha, owned by Judy and Les Frater, Harlow, owned by Steve and Liz Hughes, and Kazabari, owned by Annette Buxton, are worthy of mention.

ROOSEVELT: Tony and Jan Glen bred Ch. Franklin D. Roosevelt, who was a Best in Show winner, heading the top-winning list for OES for two years. His litter sister, Ch. Eleanor Roosevelt, was a top-winning female, holding the top New Zealand bitch title for one year in the early eighties. This kennel is also responsible for one other top-winning Specialty in Show winner, NZ Ch. Roosevelt Mary Rose.

INFLUENTIAL IMPORTS
Several OES were imported and they made their mark by siring and producing future Champions. They include: NZ Ch. Mercenden Fair and Square of Tynycoed (sire of three Champions), bred by Joan Real, owned by Annette Buxton (Kazabari), NZ Ch. Pelajilo Virtuoso (sire of one Champion), bred by Jilly Bennett, owned by L. Rowlands, Lamedazottel's Barnum (sire of two Champions), bred by John and Christina Smith and owned by Sue and Paul Bristow. Sue and Paul also own the dual Champion, NZ Aust. Ch. Lamedazottel Good Timing, an all-breed BIS winner in both countries. During the late seventies and the early eighties the breed was totally dominated in the show ring by the Australian import, NZ Ch. Dearborn Sonny Supreme. He was owned by K. & C. Burt and won eighteen Best in Show at all breed level. He also won almost every Breed Specialty Show he attended, and was the top OES in New Zealand for three years. By producing a top-winning son and daughter, he also excelled as a sire.

*NZ Ch. Dearborn
Sonny Supreme:
Winner of eighteen
Best in Show awards
at all breeds level.*

During the early eighties two English imports arrived in New Zealand, Oldoak Enchanting Trouble, and a year later, Oldoak Troublemaker. This litter brother and sister, sired by Ch. Barnolby Troubleshooter from Oldoak, enjoyed tremendous show careers, with Enchanting Trouble winning top bitch from the junior classes and producing four Champions to date, including the all-breed Best in Show winner and record-breaking junior NZ Ch. L'Ausanne Royal Pageant. Troublemaker has dominated the breed since his arrival, being top Group and Best in Show winning OES for six years. He was also top OES in New Zealand until his retirement in 1991. At that time he could look back on 35 Best in Show awards and 217 Challenge Certificates, and he was the sire of eight New Zealand Champions, including the 1991 top OES NZ Ch. L'Ausanne Double Trouble. Due to the amazing success of these two Oldoak dogs, their sire has been top sire in the breed for six years. Both dogs are owned and were expertly shown by Lynn and Barry Espie (L'Ausanne), two extremely dedicated OES fanciers, who have also achieved great success with their own breeding based on these two Oldoaks. They are the current Top Breeders in New Zealand, and to date they have eight NZ Champions, and one Aust. NZ Champion. The current NZ Top OES Trophy is held by NZ Ch. L'Ausanne Double Trouble.

GRAND CHAMPIONS
The breed in New Zealand has six Grand Champions. This status is awarded by the New Zealand Kennel Club to any dog who wins three all breed Best in Show awards under different judges, and

NZ Grand Ch. Oldoak Troublemaker: Winner of twenty-three Best in Show awards at all breeds level.

fifty Challenge Certificates from different judges. The dogs and their achievements are as follows:
NZ Grand Ch. Kadesha Bo Jangles, bred by J. & L. Frater (3 All Breed BIS).
NZ Grand Ch. Crackerjack of Sandiway, bred by J. Parkes (3 All Breed BIS).
NZ Grand Ch. Kadesha Sno Man, bred by J. & L. Frater (3 All Breed BIS).
NZ Grand Ch. Oldoak Troublemaker, bred by D. Oakes, UK (23 All Breed BIS).
NZ Grand Ch. Frenick Futuristic from Oldoak, bred by J. & S. Nicholls (6 All Breed BIS).
NZ Grand Ch. Frenick Silver Cyclone from Oldoak, bred by J. & S. Nicholls (3 All Breed BIS).

Other dogs who would have achieved this status, had this award been in contention during their careers, are: NZ Ch. Dearborn Sonny Supreme, NZ Ch. Burgundy Blue Boy of Kadesha, NZ Ch. Franklin D. Roosevelt, NZ Ch. Hannibal Boy of Ushaw and NZ Ch. Mercenden Fair and Square of Tynycoed.

Chapter Ten

THE STUD DOG

GENERAL CARE

If you own a male OES, your dog will need certain care and attention, which applies equally whether you are using your dog at stud or not. Obviously, the dog should be well fed and will require regular exercise. The Old English Sheepdog must also be kept scrupulously clean so that his coat does not become soiled with urine after lifting his leg.

ASSESSING YOUR DOG

Before you allow anyone to use your dog for stud, you should think carefully about your responsibility to the dog, and to the breed. Your first concern must be whether the dog is sound in temperament *and* body. Many people choose a stud dog after seeing the dog in the show ring – perhaps not even that – and so in most instances they do not have the opportunity to assess temperament. They therefore have to rely on the stud dog owner to make an objective judgement of the dog. Nobody is interested in breeding from an 'ugly' or 'untypey' dog, but, in my opinion, that is less harmful than breeding from a dog of an unstable temperament, be he nasty or nervous. Apart from having a good temperament, he should resemble the breed type as closely as possible. If you are not certain yourself about this, you can contact a local breed club and ask for some help. With most clubs, you do not have to be a member to get help, but the annual membership fee is usually not expensive – and it is well worth it, if you are really interested in the breed.

TRAINING A STUD DOG

Bobtail males are usually not as sexually active as the males of some other breeds. However, they still can be excellent stud dogs if trained properly. Experience has taught me that it is vital to let the young male be used at stud for the first time at around twelve to fourteen months of age, although some breeders prefer their dogs to have a 'try' even younger. This first experience should be with an older bitch – if possible, one who is known to the dog and is easy to mate.

It is very important that the bitch does not tell the male off, when he mounts her, but plays with him, showing him what to do. I do not believe in so-called 'free matings' which take place without help from the owners. From the very beginning, my males have to get used to me holding the bitch, and also helping them to penetrate the bitch. This entails keeping the bitch's vagina steady to help the penis to enter. If the dog is used to this treatment, there will not be a problem of a bitch turning away at the all-important moment. It also makes life easier when the dog has to serve a maiden, who may well be frightened by what is going on.

After this first experience of stud work, I do not allow the dog to be used again for a few months.

Ch. Oakhill Peter Pan: A highly influential sire. His offspring included Ch. Pendlefold Prince Hal, winner of thirty-four CCs.

He still needs to do some growing up in mind and in body. I believe that too much stud work before the age of eighteen months can be harmful, as Old English Sheepdog males are still developing at this age and need all their strength for that. It takes a lot out of a male to mate a bitch, and this should never be under-estimated. After each mating the stud dog should be disinfected. I normally use a 5ml iodine solution, drawn up in a syringe, and squirt it into the skin that covers the penis. This may sound painful, but I can assure you that none of my dogs mind it. This is an important procedure to avoid possible infections. There are other disinfecting solutions that you can use, and your vet will give you advice.

MATINGS WITH OR WITHOUT A TIE

When a bitch is ready for mating she will usually allow the male to mount her after an initial period of foreplay. The penis will protrude and after several forceful thrusts enter the bitch's vagina. Several more thrusting movements push the outer skin which covers the penis, the prepuce, back beyond the bulb of the penis. While this happens the bulb fills up with blood, due to the movements and the pressure on the erect penis. Both bulb and penis swell up to about three to five times their normal size. If all this happens while the penis has already penetrated the bitch's vulva, her vagina muscles will hold the swollen bulb, and consequently the penis, in place. This is called a 'tie'.

Initially then, the tie is caused by the dog, whose bulb has to engorge with blood. Once this has happened it is down to the bitch's vagina muscle to hold or release the dog. Depending on the age of the bitch, the size of her vagina, and the difference in size between dog and bitch, there are occasions when the bitch cannot hold the dog. On the other hand, if the dog is over-excited, his bulb might enlarge before he has entered the vulva entirely. A tie cannot, therefore, take place.

If the stud dog owner is quick enough to hold the dog in place for a few minutes, the mating should still be successful. Only a few seconds after the first ejaculation, which is clear fluid containing no sperm, the thick white ejaculate, which contains the sperm, is pumped into the vagina to swim towards the egg cells and fertilise them. The semen is helped along by the bitch's uterus contractions pushing the sperm forward. A few seconds after the second ejaculation, a third

Eng. Am. Ch. Prospectblue Rodger, bred by Isobel Lawson of the Prospectblue kennel. He was used at stud in the UK and produced Champion offspring before being exported to America.

ejaculation takes place. This fluid looks like clear water and does not contain any semen. In fact, it is a secretion of the prostrate gland.

At this stage most males prefer to dismount the bitch, and to turn one hind leg over the bitch's back. The dog and bitch will now stand side by side. The tie can last a few minutes, for half an hour, or even longer. If no tie takes place, but the stud dog owner is confident that the penis was ejaculating into the bitch's vulva, he must discourage the dog from dismounting the bitch, and try to hold the pair in place, with one hand around the penis and the vulva.

FEEDING
The stud dog needs two good meals a day, one in the morning and one in the evening. These can either be fresh meat and biscuit meals, or a good complete food. Whichever diet you choose, it should be supplemented with some natural yoghurt every day, and a raw egg-yolk twice a week. The meat and biscuit diet will also need some vitamin and mineral supplements. Most complete diets are well-balanced and should never be supplemented with any other vitamins, as this could be harmful. During the periods when my stud dogs are used more often, I feed three meals a day to make sure the dog does not lose any weight. Unfortunately, most bitches come into season at similar times, and so if a male is getting a lot of bookings, he will need a top-quality diet so that he does not lose condition.

STUD FEE
The stud fee is payable after the mating, regardless of whether the bitch goes on to produce a litter. It is important that the bitch's owner understands this before the mating takes place. In most breeds, stud dog owners do not charge for their dog's first mating straightaway, but agree on the amount to be paid once the litter is born.The national Kennel Club issues forms which should be used as a receipt for the stud fee, and this include all the dog's details (name, registration number, owner's name, date of mating etc.). Sometimes both parties agree that the stud dog owner should receive a puppy out of the litter in lieu of the stud fee. I feel that, unless the stud dog owner intends to keep the pup himself, this is not quite fair, as the bitch's owner loses control over where the pup

is going. I like to keep in touch with the owners of my pups, and I would only agree to this if the stud dog owner wanted the pup for himself. You also have to bear in mind the difference between the price of an Old English Sheepdog pup, and a stud fee. Most puppies are sold for a much higher price than the ordinary stud fee. The bitch's owner, who has to spend time and money rearing the litter, most certainly loses out with this arrangement.

FREE SERVICE

A free service should be given if a stud fee was paid, and no pups are born. This is not mandatory as, in fact, the stud fee is for the mating, without any guaranteed outcome. However, most responsible breeders will offer a free service if the bitch misses. The service should be for the same bitch, unless she has become too old or infertile and the stud dog owner agrees that a different bitch can be used.

LACK OF INTEREST IN STUD WORK

Apart from the inherited lack of sexual interest, some dogs, who live in the house as family pets, get so humanised that they lose their natural interest in bitches. I have also found that if the male is not used for stud work from an early age, he may be rather lazy and indifferent.

If you are faced with a lack of interest, the problem can sometimes be solved by giving the homeopathic remedies Damiana D1 and Acidum Phosphoricum D6. Each remedy has to be given three times daily: in the morning on an empty stomach, at midday preferably half-an-hour before feeding, and in the evening, last thing before bedtime.

Many years ago I had an interesting experience in connection with this problem. I had fallen in love with a young male OES, who was owned at the time by the late Mrs F. Backx-Bennink of the famous Reeuwijk's kennel. He was shown very successfully, and when I was offered one of his puppies out of Ch. Reeuwijk's Care For Beauty, I gladly accepted.

When my own bitches came into season, first Ch. High Flyer of Rollingsea, and six months later Ch. Winter Beauty of Rollingsea, we went to Holland to use him for stud. He loved playing with both the girls, but under no circumstances would he have mated them or even mounted them. He was two years old and had sired a litter, but he behaved more like a clown, with no interest in mating. Finally, I ended up using his father, Ch. Ellenglaze Ladies Choice, like several other people who had wanted to use the son.

Then one evening I received a telephone call from Mrs Backx-Bennink asking me if I wanted to buy him. She knew I loved him and felt that he might change his attitude towards canine females once he was out of his father's sight. I will never forget the look on my bank manager's face when I asked him for a loan for a Champion male who refused to mate bitches! Still, after some persuasion he agreed, and Ch. Reeuwijk's Dew Fantasy moved into our house four weeks later.

From that moment, he never looked back, becoming one of the most frequently used and top-producing stud dogs at the time. This experience proved to me that some males might feel dominated by an older dog, and will react accordingly.

KEEPING A RECORD

I always keep records of the bitches my dogs have mated, for future reference. I write down the date of the mating, and the name and breeding of the bitch, and later add the number and sex of the puppies. If any of the pups appear later in the show ring, I keep a written note of my opinion of them. This practice will help you to determine which lines go well with your own breeding, and which are not so successful.

Chapter Eleven

THE BROOD BITCH

Anyone can breed dogs, and you may even be lucky enough to breed good dogs, knowing nothing about breeding and nothing about genetics. However, in order to become a responsible and successful breeder, you should know a few ground rules. No one becomes a good breeder overnight. It takes years of responsible planning and selecting, and sometimes you might even have to start from scratch again if things do not work out the way you expected. For me, the most important lesson came from the late Mrs F. Backx-Bennink, who told me years ago: "Your breeding stock is only as good as the weakest or poorest dog you breed from."

The message is that you should only breed from the best possible dogs. You cannot use a super male on a poor quality bitch, and expect to breed a litter of Champions. If you are lucky, there might be one or two nice puppies in the litter, but even the best pup will still carry the mother's genes, and these will be passed on to the next generation. Therefore, in the long run, it is cheaper to breed only from good sound stock.

ASSESSING BREEDING STOCK
If you are planning to breed from your Old English Sheepdog bitch, she should be a typical specimen of the breed, showing good breed type. She should have a feminine expression, a good harsh coat, good bones, with a sound front and rear, and the desired topline. Above all, she should have an excellent temperament.

Some European countries require breeding stock to be shown at dog shows, and the results must reach a certain standard for the owner to be allowed to use the dog or bitch for breeding. I rather like the idea, as I feel this maintains the quality of the breeding stock.

COUNTING THE COST
Before you mate your bitch you should also be well aware of the cost involved, and you must have enough time and space to rear the pups. I think that litters should be supervised round-the-clock. I do not think it is right for the the bitch to be left alone with her pups: there is always the risk of a puppy being squashed, or the mother might need attention.

To summarise, you should only go ahead if you have:
1. A good, sound bitch.
2. Sufficient time to care for the bitch and her puppies.
3. Sufficient space (your bitch might have a litter of twelve or even more puppies).
4. Sufficient money to cover all expenses (stud fee, whelping box, vet fees, extra food, and so on).
5. Last but not least, you will need a sense of humour, for when the mother stops cleaning up after

her pups – you are left to do all the dirty work! If you can confidently answer 'yes' on all these points, then go ahead and look for the right husband for your bitch.

CHOOSING A STUD DOG

Choosing a stud dog is one of the most difficult decisions you will have to make – and your choice it is always open to argument. In fact, I have been as successful with outcross matings as with line-breeding and in-breeding. During my first few years living in England I could not do much line- or in-breeding as I only brought two males with me which were suitable to breed from. Consequently I had to use non-related dogs for my bitches as well. The thing I always tried to look out for was a similarity in type – something I feel is most important. The distance you have to travel to visit the stud dog should never come into the decision, and it does not matter whether the dog is a Champion or not. It is far more important that the dog, *like your bitch*, resembles a good breed type, is free from major faults and, most of all, has a good temperament.

With related partners, I found the most successful matings were aunt and nephew, grandfather and granddaughter, and half-sister and half-brother. With all these combinations you have to be absolutely certain that there are no known defects in any of the dogs that you could be doubling up on, as they will most certainly be passed on to the pups, quite often in a much more severe form.

THE SEXUAL CYCLE

A bitch usually comes into season every six months, although this may vary considerably. Some bitches have only three months in between their seasons, especially when they are young. There are others who may have as long as nine months between seasons. A normal season lasts for twenty-one days About four weeks before the female starts showing colour, you will notice her urinating more often than normal. Quite often, she will mark a spot after other bitches have urinated – two of mine even lift their legs, like males, during this period. In the first seven days of the season, counted from day one of showing colour, most bitches will not behave differently towards males, although they might be slightly aggressive towards other bitches. The vagina will swell up to double or even three times the normal size, and will become rather hard. The discharge is very dark and is at its heaviest. Some bitches need to wear protecting slips so they do not soil their sleeping quarters, or the carpets etc. – an old pair of underpants will serve the purpose.

During the second part of the season you will notice the swelling of the vagina starts to go down, and the discharge becomes lighter in colour until it is almost clear. Some bitches stop showing colour completely. This is the time when the bitch is ready for mating. She will encourage males, and she will stand for them. At this stage she will not be fussy about her partner, and so you will have to take the greatest care to make sure you do not end up with an unplanned mating and some cross-bred puppies. Ironically, it always seems that unwanted matings are far more successful than the matings you have planned for months, and have driven for hours to get to the chosen stud dog!

The so-called 'fertile' days are usually between the tenth and fifteenth day, counted from the first day of showing colour. In the last four to six days at the end of the season, some bitches will start losing some blood again, others just have a clear discharge. There are some few bitches who do not stop showing colour at all during the twenty-one days. In order to find the right day for a mating, watch for the vagina to become soft and for the swelling to go down.

PREPARATIONS FOR THE MATING

Once you have decided that you want to mate your bitch, the first thing you ought to do – apart from booking your chosen stud dog – is to get the bitch completely checked over by your vet. She

Ch. Zottel's Miss Marple of Lameda with her outstanding litter. Seven of the ten puppies have gained their Champion titles, the other three are CC winners.

should be in a fit and healthy condition: wormed, vaccinated, and exercised, to make sure she is capable of whelping and nursing a litter without major problems for her or the pups.

BACTERIAL INFECTIONS

Most stud dog owners require a swab to be taken from the bitch to ensure she is not suffering from an internal infection. A bacterial infection could possibly infect the male through the mating and prevent the bitch from having pups, so it is an important procedure even if the stud dog owner does not ask for it. This swab is very similar to a cancer smear test for women, and it is sent off to a laboratory for testing. It usually takes between two and four days to get the result so it is advisable to get the swab done either before the bitch is in season, or not later than the second day, in case there is an infection which has to be treated with antibiotics.

The reason for this is two-fold. Firstly, some antibiotics kill the infection, but they also kill bacteria which give the right scent to the male. Secondly, it would be disastrous if the male were to become infected by the bitch. Not only could this cause problems for the stud dog, it could also result in the spread of the infection to numerous other bitches, in the case of a popular stud dog, and this could mean that bitches do not come into whelp, or, even worse, they could suffer from the dangerous condition, pyometra.

THE RIGHT DAY FOR MATING

When your bitch comes into season, you should contact the owners of your chosen stud dog. This should be done as early as possible to avoid the potential disappointment of the dog being booked by someone else. The easiest way to find the correct day for the mating is by getting an ovulation test done by your vet. This can either be done with a blood test, or, even simpler, a vagina swab-test, using Papanicolao solutions. To give an accurate result it is necessary to do more than one test, starting preferably around the ninth day, to see how the cells develop and therefore determining the right day. When your vet gives you the go-ahead and you have made arrangements with the stud dog owner, all that is left to do is to pack some food – and a blanket for your bitch in case it all takes longer than anticipated and you have to stay overnight. I also take some rubber-bands to tie the long leg-coat away from the vagina.

PREGNANT OR NOT?

In the first two weeks after your bitch is mated you will not see a difference in her. Some bitches do not give anything away until about five weeks into pregnancy. I find that the most positive sign of a successful mating is when the bitch has a clear and rather thick discharge, almost like glue. In ninety-nine per cent of cases a pregnant bitch will have this discharge, usually starting from the third week after mating. The best time to look for it is first thing in the morning before the bitch has a chance to clean herself, or when she gets up after a long rest. This discharge, which serves to keep the birth channel moist, increases towards the end of nine weeks.

Another, but not so reliable, sign of pregnancy is the teats changing colour from light pink to red – sometimes bright-red – and this is usually evident around the fifth week. The teats also enlarge, growing to at least double the original size. The reason why these signs are not such a reliable proof of pregnancy is because quite a number of bitches with phantom pregnancies show exactly the same signs, even developing bigger bellies, becoming more quiet, eating more, and changing completely in their temperament. In fact, I have found that bitches with phantom pregnancies change more in their temperament than those who are truly in whelp. However, these bitches with their imagined pups do not have the glue-like discharge, so it is a worthwhile sign to look for.

ULTRASOUND SCAN

A very reliable pregnancy test is the ultrasound scan, and with this you can also determine the size of the litter. I have never used this, because I feel that it is better to leave a bitch in peace. I have also heard from many people that the litter size is not always the same as was predicted. There are sometimes cases where bitches absorb one or two pups which were clearly shown on the scan, and if you were expecting seven puppies, and only four appear, this would be a cause of some alarm, let alone the disappointment. However, balancing the pros and cons, this test has advantages for those who want to know at an early stage if a bitch is in whelp.

PHANTOM PREGNANCY

Unfortunately, there are quite a number of bitches who, as regular as clockwork, come into season and then go through an imagined pregnancy at the time they would be due to whelp. Some bitches get into a very poor state: they stop eating, steal soft toys to look after, and generally feel absolutely miserable. The only solution is to try to discourage your bitch from this sort of behaviour by occupying her mind with other things, like going for walks, playing with other dogs, and so on. If you know that your bitch is affected by this hormone imbalance, you may find that the homeopathic remedy Pulsatilla may help. It has to be given in the recommended strength, three times daily, starting about three weeks after the season. The bitch may still experience a phantom, but the symptoms should be far less severe, and it also helps to prevent the hair-shedding which often happens because of the hormone change. No one is really sure why some bitches develop phantoms. It is usually attributed to a malfunction of certain hormones, but it can also happen if a bitch absorbs very soon after mating, before anyone realises she is in whelp.

Chapter Twelve

PREGNANCY AND WHELPING

During the first three to four weeks of pregnancy I do not change the bitch's routine. I stick to the regime of regular exercise, good healthy food, and regular grooming. Ideally, you should worm your bitch before mating, but if you forgot to do this, it is still safe to worm between the third and the fourth week. After this time, it could cause an early absorption.

EXERCISE
The fertilised eggs take about eighteen to twenty days to settle in the womb. To minimise the risk of absorbing the fertilised eggs, I do not allow a mated bitch to jump about or run excessively during the first three weeks. I do not restrict the bitch from exercise, but I make sure she does not over-do it. Once a bitch is about three to four weeks in whelp she will naturally slow down a little and become more careful. However, there are always exceptions. One of my bitches, seven weeks in whelp, enjoyed her favourite pastime of chasing another dog – and she went at a fair speed! She ignored all my shouts to come back, and when the owner of the other dog assured me that his dog didn't mind, he could hardly believe it when I explained that my bitch was seven weeks in whelp. Later on that day she slept for about two hours, delighted with her morning's exercise!

DIET
Quite a number of bitches stop eating almost completely between the third and fourth week of their pregnancy. Some develop a dislike to certain foods, and some may even experience a kind of morning sickness. This is no reason to worry, as long as you make sure your bitch drinks enough fluid, preferably milk and water. After a couple of weeks most bitches will suddenly start eating normally again, and will make up for any weight loss.

From the fifth week onwards I slowly increase the amount of food for the pregnant bitch, but I divide it into three meals, and in the last weeks of pregnancy I feed four meals a day. As all my dogs get a well-balanced diet all the time, I only need to increase the protein level intake. I do this by feeding more raw meat (beef, lamb or cooked poultry). I also feed more yoghurt during these last few weeks of the pregnancy. Additional drinks of watered down milk are also necessary.

If you usually feed a complete diet, you only have to switch over to one which is designed for bitches in whelp, and feed the additional yoghurt and extra milk drinks. No other vitamin additives are needed, as the high-protein complete food provides everything your bitch needs. If you usually feed meat and biscuits, you will have to supplement vitamins and minerals which you can obtain from the vet or your pet shop.

The best way of knowing if your bitch is getting enough food is by checking her spine. She should get broader behind her ribs, putting on extra weight. However, if you can feel her spine protruding, you will know that most of what she is eating is going into her pups. This could result in her not having the strength to rear her babies, due to the lack of her own body weight. In this case, she should eat more. If she has become a little fussy you will have to tempt her with food she particularly likes.

FINAL PREPARATIONS
In the last week of pregnancy, it is a good idea to give the teats a good clean, and possibly disinfect them with a mild disinfectant. The long belly hair should be cut off as it is very dangerous for the pups – they can easily strangle themselves to death in it. The whelping box should be put up now to allow enough time for the bitch to get used to it. The best place for the box is where you and your bitch usually are, so once she has her pups you will not have to leave her too often.

During the pregnancy I usually save all the newspapers to lay down ready. You will need plenty of old towels. These will be needed for drying the newborn pups, and also for the bitch when you have cleaned her up after whelping. You will also need some small scales to weigh the pups with, some old bed sheets, and some pieces of dog bedding – I always use the fleecy, washable type.

THE WHELPING BOX
The whelping box should be a fair size; it should be big enough for the mother to turn round in and to lie on her side, without touching the walls. The size of my own box is 53 x 39 1/2in. (1m x 1.35m). I can take part of the front wall down, so the bitch can easily go in and out, but when necessary this door can be closed to keep the pups inside. Part of my box is covered with a roof, which is a handy place for keeping the scales and the weight charts etc. The roof-top has a hole on one side for a heat lamp to be fixed, if necessary.

As a safety measure, the whelping box should be fitted with a two-and-a-half wide rail, along all four inside walls, at a height of about six inches. This rail is needed to protect the puppies from being crushed when the mother is lying down. The bottom of the box should be lined with a thick plastic or rubber sheet, that can easily be washed and disinfected. On top of this I put several layers of newspapers, covered by comfortable dry bedding and a bedsheet. All the bedding has to be changed and cleaned regularly.

THE WHELPING
THE FIRST STAGE OF LABOUR
All my bitches whelp in my bedroom so I can sleep in my own bed and still be able to attend to their needs during the night – like changing the bedding, rescuing pups which get caught behind or under their mum, checking that smaller pups get enough to drink, and so on. Unfortunately some bitches are a bit clumsy when they turn round and lie down again. Obviously with the enormous weight difference between the mum and a puppy, if she lies on one and you don't get it out fast, it will suffocate.

Most bitches indicate quite clearly when they are ready to whelp. A normal pregnancy lasts for about sixty-three days, but you should be on the alert from day fifty-seven onwards. Litters born before these days have a slim chance of survival, as the pups are not fully developed. Shortly before giving birth, the bitch's temperature will drop from 38 degrees Centigrade to 37 degrees Centigrade, or even less. Once the temperature is back to normal, whelping is imminent. I take the bitch's temperature three or four times a day from day fifty-seven onwards. I always check the temperature last thing at night to make sure there will not be any surprise pups while I am still half-asleep.

I never leave a bitch to whelp on her own – I feel it is cruel to do so. The bitch depends on the owner for encouragement, and for help with the pups. Apart from that, I am always amazed by the wonder of birth – it is an experience I would not want to miss. It is amazing to see newborn puppies searching for their mother's teat, and then kneading with their little front feet to make the milk flow. The puppies recognise their mother's body smell, and they will wake up when she is just standing near them. One of my bitches, who is very maternal, is always disappointed that none of the other bitches' pups react to her when she goes in the whelping box. She would love to feed any litter, whether it is hers or not!

From the time the temperature starts dropping, labour is under way. You might not be able to see any contractions at this stage, as they are very slight. The bitch will become more and more restless; she will keep asking to go out because of the pressure on her bladder and on her bowel. She will feel uncomfortable, and most bitches will refuse food from now until after the pups are born. With these lighter contractions, the birth channel opens up, gradually becoming wider. The glue-like discharge, which increased in the last week of pregnancy, will become heavier now, sometimes mixed with a little blood.

THE SECOND STAGE

In the second phase of labour the contractions will become stronger, and consequently the bitch will feel more and more uncomfortable. She might even start crying, especially if it is her first litter. The most important thing is for you to stay calm and to reassure the bitch. Every puppy lies in its own fruitbag, and this is surrounded by a waterbag. The space between these two bags is filled with the so-called 'fruitwater', which protects the pup and the navel cord from sounds and from external pressure.

The stronger contractions will bring the pup to the birth channel. The first pup is often a rather heavy one, so the bitch needs quite a few contractions to push it out. The contractions will be regular now, with short intervals between them. Shortly before the pup is born the outer bag bursts, making the birth channel more slippery. The pup usually stays in the inner fruitbag, which keeps it safe until it is born. The time from the fruitbag bursting to the actual birth can be anything from fifteen minutes to an hour, or even more. Some bitches may need help to open the fruitbag, but do encourage the mother to lick her babies. This massage gets the circulation going and is, therefore, very important. Most of my pups have been born head-first, but it is not uncommon for a pup to be born with its back feet first. Normally the afterbirth will come shortly after each pup, looking like a small black and green bag. Most bitches will eat this afterbirth, and it is thought to contain the protein, vitamin, mineral and hormone content which encourages the milk flow. I do not like a bitch to eat more than two or three afterbirths, as they tend to make her rather loose for some days after whelping. However, it is important that you keep count of them, for if the bitch retains an afterbirth it will result in a raised temperature, which will interrupt the milk flow, and it may even cease altogether.

I do not allow the bitch to sever the navel cord, as I have found that most bitches tend to be rather rough with their newborn puppies. They often bite off the cord too short, which results in heavy bleeding. Before you cut the navel cord (about one inch away from the puppy) massage it away from the pup, pushing all the remaining blood from the placenta (afterbirth) towards the pup. As this is the last direct food from the bitch, it would be a pity to lose it. This does not take long, and as soon as the cord looks pale rather than red, you can easily cut it, using sterile scissors.

POST-WHELPING

After the first baby is born, nature usually allows the mother a bit of a rest before the contractions start again. During this time I check the pup for deformities, weigh it, and write the weight down on a separate sheet of paper, together with its sex and markings. After this the pup goes back to the mother, who will lick it all over its body and its belly. Licking the belly and anus helps the pup to urinate and defecate. This first black rubbery discharge out of the anus is called meconium, and this needs to be excreted soon after the pup is born to ensure a normal digestion. If your bitch does not clean and lick her pups immediately, you can help by using a bit of damp cotton-wool (cotton) and gently rubbing the pup's belly. Normally, Old English Sheepdog pups take about two or three days to be able to empty their bladder without help, and at least four to six days to relieve their bowel. Once all the pups are born, the bitch must be let out, and then washed with a mild soap or, preferably, a baby shampoo. After washing the bitch it is important to dry her thoroughly as a damp back-end could make her sore – I always use a hair-dryer for a few minutes. It is helpful if one person can see to the bitch, while another changes all the bedding, carefully placing the pups in a cardboard box, containing a warm hot-water bottle, which is covered with a towel. Once all this is sorted out, the bitch can get back to her babies.

To make sure that there are no more puppies left inside the bitch, most vets recommend a hormone injection. This will bring on some more contractions which will clear and clean out the uterus. Even so, most bitches will have a bloody or even black discharge for quite some time. This is quite normal, and as long as there is no high temperature involved, it is nothing to worry about.

When everyone – bitch and midwives – have got over the initial excitement and exhaustion, there is nothing more time-consuming than watching the mother with her babies. In our house all the dogs live together, and puppies are a family affair, but none of the other dogs are allowed into the room during the whelping. They lie pressed against the door, waiting anxiously to come in and greet the new arrivals. Even the most protective of mums enjoys a feeling of pride when finally her friends sneak in to have a look.

PROBLEMS DURING AND AFTER WHELPING

Most problems during whelping need the attention of a vet or an experienced breeder. However, there are a few things you can do yourself before you call a vet, and this should help to pinpoint whether the problem is serious or not.

THICK GREEN OR BLACK DISCHARGE: If this appears before any sign of contractions, call the vet, as the bitch could be absorbing her litter, and caesarian may be necessary.

POOR CONTRACTIONS: If the contractions are too mild and proper labour is not getting underway, it could indicate puppies that are too small, or a very small litter, or it could be an inherited defect in the bitch. The vet should be contacted and he will decide whether to inject with Oxydocin to get the contractions going. This problem can be avoided by giving a homeopathic whelping aid such as Caullophillium, dosed once daily from the time of mating.

BURST WATERBAG: Sometimes a waterbag bursts without any other signs of the birth beginning. Do not delay longer than two hours before calling the vet – even if it is the middle of the night.

STRONG CONTRACTIONS, NO PUPPY: A bitch can have heavy contractions for more than two hours, and still fail to produce a pup. You might even be able to see the pup, but it keeps going back into the birth channel. An experienced breeder can help, but you must ensure that your fingernails are short, and you must disinfect your hands. The best method is to push one or two fingers up the vagina and get hold of the pup, preferably around its neck, and then gently, working with the contractions, pull the puppy downwards and out. As this procedure always sets up the risk of an infection, it should only be done under special circumstances.

TOO LONG BETWEEN PUPPIES: If your bitch is contracting, but goes from ninety minutes to two hours without producing a puppy, it is probably because she is tired after several hours of whelping. To give her a boost, offer her some coffee mixed with warm milk and lots of glucose.

NEWBORN PUP FAILS TO BREATH REGULARLY: Some puppies take such a long time to be born that they might not have had enough oxygen for a little while, or they may even get fruitwater in their lungs. These pups usually have a good chance of survival, if correctly treated. You will need to shake out the water that may have got into the lungs by holding the pup firmly in your hands. The head has to be supported, and the mouth has to be kept open with one finger. You then shake the pup gently downwards.

When all the fluid has come out, and the pup has been massaged with a warm towel for a few minutes, most will take a big breath of air, scream, and from then onwards all should be well. With all breathing problems, it is important to remember that a room with sticky, used air is not very helpful. Wrap the pup up, and take it to the open window or outside and massage it there.

All the before-mentioned situations will, I am sure, make you realise that one of the most important factors is to have a good relationship with your vet. Make sure you advise him about the mating, and later on give advance warning of when the bitch is due to whelp.

Chapter Thirteen

REARING A LITTER

Rearing a litter of puppies involves a lot of time and commitment – and big litters of ten to twelve pups, or even more, are not rare. You will need space inside the house, and space outside (securely fenced), for the puppies will benefit from playing outside as they get older. Every member of your family should also be aware of the destructive potential of a litter of pups. Wallpaper might have to be replaced and carpets taken up. However, assuming you have taken this all into consideration, you will enjoy every single minute of rearing your puppies, and you will dread the moment when you have to part with them.

DOCKING AND DEWCLAWS
Old English Sheepdogs have docked tails, and this simple operation should be carried out on the first or second day, as long as the pups are born with a normal birthweight. This is also the best time to remove dewclaws. In the past, experienced breeders carried out this simple operation, but now under English law, a vet must be called in. Try to make sure that you use a vet who has docked Old English Sheepdog pups before. If you have any pups that are smaller or weaker, it is better to wait until the third or fourth day.

TRIMMING NAILS
To avoid the bitch getting sore, the pups' front nails should be cut from the time they are a week old. This should be done twice-weekly until the litter is fully weaned. The best method is to hold the pup firmly in one hand, and use a pair of small nail-scissors, just trimming the sharp tips of the nails. Make sure you only cut the white tip of the nail. If you catch the quick (the pink part), the nail will bleed profusely.

WORMING
I start worming my pups at ten to fourteen days of age, using a mild worming paste especially made for young pups. After this, the treatment should be repeated at four weeks, at almost eight weeks (just before the first vaccination) and again at twelve weeks, before the second vaccination. From then onwards, I worm every other month until the pup is fully grown at about twelve months of age. Unless you feel your dog might have picked up worms, it is sufficient to worm adult dogs once every six months, and always remember to worm your dog before a vaccination,

It is advisable to administer worming drops, paste, or tablets, straight into the pup's or adult dog's mouth. If you try and put it into the food, the pups may well refuse to eat it, and you cannot be sure that each puppy is receiving the correct dose. With all worming drugs it is absolutely essential to read the instructions carefully. You need to know the exact weight of each pup, to make absolutely sure that you do not overdose. Giving too much of a worming drug to a young pup could be fatal – so be safe rather than sorry, and double-check the weight of each puppy before you administer the drug.

This might sound rather complicated, but worming is an essential part of rearing a healthy litter of pups. Over-dosing can be fatal, but, believe me, a major worm-infestation can also be a killer. Following treatment, the worms are usually passed out within twenty-four hours. It is important to take extra care in cleaning and disinfecting the whelping box at this time – especially the areas where you pick up the excreta – to prevent reinfestation.

VACCINATIONS
Opinions vary as to the best age to vaccinate puppies for the first time. Some believe that the course should start as early as eight weeks, other advise starting as late as twelve weeks. I feel it is best to ask your vet and be advised by what he recommends. I do not let my pups leave for their new homes until they have at least their first vaccination for distemper, hepatitis, leptospirosis and parvovirus – and nowadays, parainfluenza is included as well.

All five vaccines are now available in a single shot and will protect the pup against these awful diseases once the booster has been given, four weeks after the first vaccination. A week after the booster, your pup is ready to face the world and go out and meet strange dogs for the first time.

EARLY GROWING STAGES
Puppies are born blind and deaf. They are absolutely helpless and could not survive without their mum, or some other means of outside help. In Old English Sheepdogs, a puppy's ears lie backwards on to the head at birth, and they take about two or three weeks to go into the correct position. At this time you will notice that the puppy can hear. The eyes open when the pup is about two weeks of age, but it will still take at least seven to fourteen days weeks before the pup is able to see anything but light and dark shadow. Newly-opened eyes are a dark-blue colour due to a protecting film over the lens.

Never try to force the eyes to open. If you feel that a puppy's eyes are not opening properly, just gently wash them with cotton-wool and lukewarm water from the inside towards the outside. When the pup is about four weeks of age you can detect the eventual eye colour. With Bobtails, you can have two brown eyes, two blue eyes, or one of each, depending on the eye-colour of the parents or ancestors.

When the litter is seven to ten days old, the pups will try to get up on their feet – they are still quite wobbly, but very determined to start walking. Even though they cannot see or hear at this stage, they find their way around the whelping box pretty well. They can smell their mother from quite a distance, and will react immediately when she walks past the box.

By the time the puppies are about three weeks of age they will start exploring their surroundings. A whelping box with low walls is not a safe place any more, as the pups will try to climb out. Not long ago, one of my pups climbed out of the box, aged just four weeks, and I discovered him with the five adult dogs, as proud as could be! The adults were a little bewildered, but fortunately they were careful not to tread on the youngster.

At about three weeks of age, the first milk teeth are pushing through. Unfortunately for the bitch, these first teeth are rather sharp, although they are much softer than the second teeth. They appear first in the upper jaw, usually starting with the big side canine teeth, followed by the middle teeth, and then the bottom jaw and the back teeth. If you were picking a show puppy, it would be very

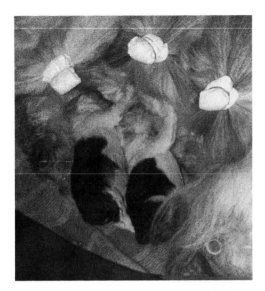

Five-day-old OES puppies feeding from their mother. In most cases the bitch's belly-coat is trimmed, as it can be very dangerous for the puppies. Alternatively the coat can be left untrimmed, but it should be put in 'crackers', so that there is no danger of the puppies getting caught up in the long hairs.

A large litter, but they are fairly evenly matched in size. Note how dark the body-coat appears at this stage.

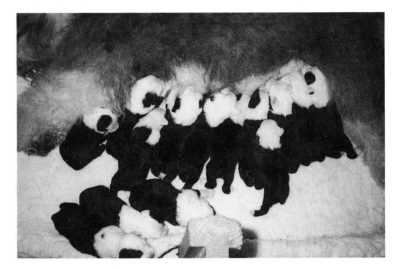

helpful if you could judge adult dentition on the placement of the milk teeth. Unfortunately, a scissor bite in milk teeth does not give a guarantee of the same bite in the adult jaw.

I have seen crooked milk teeth ending up in a perfect scissor bite, and I have also seen perfectly placed milk teeth ending up as an incorrect adult bite. One of the reasons for this, apart from inherited mouth problems, is the fact that the upper and lower jaw do not grow at the same time. In fact, the right side does not grow at the same time as the left side. So it is understandable that outside influences, such as a knock, can result in incorrect bites.

From as early as three to four weeks you can feel the testicles coming down in males. Obviously, you have to be very careful when feeling for them as puppies can quite easily be put off and pull one or even both testicles up again, which could result in future problems.

It is a good idea to weigh puppies at regular intervals in order to monitor their growth.

HANDLING PUPPIES

Newborn pups should not be picked up too often, and then only by people who are known to the bitch. Some bitches do not like their babies to be picked up at all during the first week. If this is the case, it is advisable to weigh and check the pups while mum is outside for her toilet, as you do not want the bitch to become upset. None of my bitches mind me picking up their babies, but they strongly object to other people doing so.

Make sure you never frighten a pup while picking it up, and never try to grab hold of a retreating puppy. It is far better to kneel on the floor and talk calmly until the pup decides to come to you, then pick it up gently. When you pick up a puppy, make sure you do not place your hand or arm under the elbow, as this could weaken the ligaments and the pup could become loose at the elbows. Children should not be allowed to pick up puppies of any age, without supervision. The pups are very agile from an early age, and a sudden fall could do serious damage.

Once the bitch has settled with her babies, I try to handle the pups frequently. I hold them in my hands, stroke them, talk to them, and try to make them feel comfortable lying on their backs. As the long adult coat needs so much attention, I feel it is vital for the puppies to get used to human hands as soon as possible. I start using a soft brush on the pups from about five weeks. This is only for a few minutes every day; if this is done regularly the pup will get used to the feel of it and will not object later on in life.

At about eight weeks, Old English Sheepdog pups start becoming very boisterous and may nip or even bite more often than you would like. Do not hit your puppies, but say "No" in a firm voice – while rescuing your ankle or trousers! Obviously the puppies are only playing and trying to find out rights and wrongs, so it is advisable to wear boots when you go in your kennel or playpen, rather than frightening the pups by shouting at them.

WEANING

The average size of an Old English Sheepdog litter is about six to nine pups. A mature Bobtail bitch, in healthy condition, will have no trouble feeding this number of pups on her own for the first ten days or even two weeks. All you will have to do is make sure is that she gets plenty of fluids, such as milk and water, and she must have at least three good meals a day. There are many brands of top-quality complete diets on the market, especially designed for the lactating bitch. This diet will provide her with all the nutrition she needs during this time. Being a bit of a health freak myself, I give all my dogs natural set yoghurt every day – and I also give this to my nursing bitches. It helps the digestion, and the build-up of necessary bacteria in the intestines.

Puppies must be weighed regularly to check they are putting on enough weight. This should be done at the same time every day, either before the pups have been feeding or afterwards – but make sure you stick to the same routine. Old English Sheepdog pups usually lose about 20 grams (1oz) of their birthweight during the first two days, but they should then regain this weight loss and start putting on weight. The weight gain can vary from 10-15 grams to 30-50 grams (1/2oz to 2oz), or even more, according to the initial birthweight of the individual pup.

If everything goes well and the mother has enough milk, I start weaning when the puppies are two weeks old. To start with I give the pups some steak mince rolled into small balls, putting one ball of mince into each puppy's mouth, twice daily. For the first two days the pups get very small amounts so they will not react with upset tummies. Obviously, it is impossible to determine an exact time to start supplement feeding. Some mothers have so much milk that they can easily feed their litters until three weeks or even longer, while other bitches struggle to feed their puppies for as long as two weeks. Apart from regular weight control, the most reliable sign of growing pups is a contented litter, either sound asleep after feeding or playing with each other. Hungry pups cry, showing you that they are not getting enough to eat.

As the puppies get used to solid food you can give three or four small balls of steak mince a day. You can also introduce a little rice pudding or baby porridge. You will be surprised how quickly the puppies learn to eat from a bowl, and once they are feeding themselves you can gradually increase the amount of food, and also the number of meals. Between the fourth and fifth week I feed my pups four or five times daily, with the last meal late at night. I prefer to feed a complete diet developed especially for growing puppies, as the vitamin and mineral content is just right, and nothing needs to be added. If you are feeding meat and cereal or meat and biscuits, you will need to add the correct amount of vitamins.

I have never had poor eaters in my litters – in fact, rather the opposite. If I am not careful, the pups would eat so much they would scarcely be able to stand! However, over-eating has to be avoided as it can damage a puppy's health and also its bone structure. Puppies that are too heavy might end up being cow-hocked or even dysplastic. Most manufacturers provide a feeding guide, but remember this is only a guide. Some pups need more than advised to look healthy, some are perfectly happy with less food. A young pup should look sturdy without having a big belly; the body should be well-muscled and have strong bones, and the coat should look thick and shiny.

When I am weaning puppies, I do not leave water available at all times, as I think puppies often drink more than they need, filling up their stomachs, which puts them off their food. Depending on the time of the year and the temperature, I put water down for them several times a day, and once the puppies have had a drink, I pick the bowl up again. This also has the advantage of stopping the puppies from playing in the water, or tipping the bowl over.

PLAYTIME
It is very important to spend enough time with young pups, playing with them and also brushing their coats. The pups should spend time with their mother, even after she has stopped feeding them. She will teach them how to behave and will give them confidence.

From the fourth week onwards you should make sure your puppies have plenty of human contact – with males and females. This is the time when the pups start to develop their own little personalities, and the more you socialise them now with your own dogs, with friends, and, if possible, with children, the better it will be for their developing temperament. At this stage, you should also start standing your potential show pups, holding their heads up; you will be surprised how quickly they learn, and how much they enjoy the attention.

The favourite puppy toys in our house are empty cartons and boxes, plastic bottles, and tennis balls. Soft toys are hardly ever suitable as most Old English Sheepdog pups specialise in pulling them to pieces, and then they try to eat the inside material. Old leather shoes and house slippers are also favourite 'toys'. It is very important to keep pups occupied with different things to play with. They can get a whole day's fun out of a empty box from the local supermarket – it can be used to play hide-and-seek, and when the the pups tire of this, they can shred it into little bits! I never give my puppies towels or rags to tear apart. Jaws are very soft at this stage, and can be damaged by too much pulling and tearing.

If the weather is dry, I like my puppies to play in the garden – chasing each other, pulling out precious flowers, digging up soil and playing with falling leaves. This not only keeps them occupied, it also also gives them the opportunity to experience different smells and tastes, which is important for a developing puppy.

HAND-REARING
Every breeder's nightmare is a litter without a mother. This could happen if the bitch has not got any milk, or she may have an infection in the teats, which means she cannot feed her litter. Occasionally you may have to cope with the tragedy of losing your bitch, due to a caesarian or a heart attack, and the pups survive.

Some eight years ago I had to hand-rear the litter which produced my Champion bitch, Miss Marple. When the puppies were seven days old, I noticed that the mother's milk was starting to look rather thick and yellow. However, by this time one male puppy had already had too much of the infected milk, and despite great efforts by myself and my vet, the pup could not be saved. Since then, I always check all the teats daily. This is important, as there might only be one infected teat. The milk should be off-white in colour and flow out easily, without any thickness to it.

When I had to hand-rear my litter of pups, I had not learned how to tube-feed pups. So I had to bottle-feed eight puppies every two hours, day and night, as well as having to pump out the mother's infected milk. Anyone who has raised a litter like this will understand how you feel after two weeks. You are constantly tired, worried about losing your puppies, and to add to this, the bitch would not tolerate the protective suit we tried to put around her nipples. If she had accepted this, she could at least have gone in with her puppies and kept them clean, but as she was determined not to wear clothes, we had to separate her completely. The risk of the pups feeding from her was just too great.

It was a very trying time, but the litter resulted in some super dogs, with Eng. Ch. Zottel's Miss Marple of Lameda, the most famous and most successful OES bitch of all times in England, and Eng. Ch. Zottel's Moonlight Serenade of Lameda, another Group winner, and, in Europe, Int. Ch. Zottel's Mosche and Int. Ch. Zottel's Magic Touch. Three of the four Champions have already produced Champion stock. So looking back, all the effort was well worth it, and it proves that you should always do your best to keep sound and healthy pups alive.

If anything like this happened again, at least I now know how to tube-feed a puppy. It really is so much easier and much less time-consuming. Once you overcome your initial apprehension, it is actually less dangerous than bottle feeding. The risk of getting milk into the lungs is much less, and a pup that is fed by this method does not get so tired. All you need is a thin tube and a syringe, which can be obtained from your vet. You then measure the length from mouth to the stomach of each pup by holding the tube along one side of the pup, and finally mark the tube with a pen. Fill the syringe with your puppy milk, possibly with some camomile tea added. Hold the pup's head with one hand, and open the mouth with the fingers of the same hand, then use your other hand to push the tube down until you reach the mark. There are only two places for the tube to go: the lung and the stomach. The lung is obviously much higher up in the pup's body, and therefore you would not be able to get the tube down as far as going down into the stomach – and this will be evident by the pen-mark on the tube.

   If you reach the lung, just gently pull the tube out and start again. Once the end of the tube is in the stomach, empty the syringe into it. A newborn pup needs about 10-15 ml of fluid every two hours. With a little bit of practice you can easily feed a normal size litter within twenty minutes. This method of feeding a pup is also very helpful with smaller and weaker pups. A smaller pup might get pushed away by bigger brothers and sisters, and even if you try to ensure that this pup gets its fair share, it will usually wear itself out, working on the teat, before the milk even flows. Many good pups have been lost this way, but two or three days of regular tube-feeding could make a vital difference.

   I do not agree with people saying that nature should take its course. To me, this is the same as saying that babies should not be put into incubators or tube-fed. One method is as artificial as the other, and I regard both creatures as having the same right to live. Depending on the initial birthweight I would administer about 15 ml every two hours to a newborn pup. This amount can be increased daily. Keep an eye on the pup's belly; it should be round and solid, but not sticking out like a ball.

   Obviously there is still no alternative for the bitch's first milk. The colostrum milk is very important to the puppy. It contains a mild laxative, which helps the pup to get rid of a rubbery black discharge which builds up in the pup's bowels prior to birth, and until this has been passed out, normal digestion is not possible. The colostrum is also very rich in protein, mineral and fat. Therefore, you should always try to let every pup have the chance to get some of it, whichever method of feeding has to be pursued afterwards.

PICK OF THE LITTER

The 'pick of the litter' is the name for the best puppy in the litter. Although this sounds perfectly straightforward, it is very hard to select a pup unless you are extremely familiar with the breed, and you have a detailed knowledge of the breeding lines of the litter. Many pups have been sold into pet homes because they have not been rated as show potential, only to turn up in the show ring a few years later – much to the surprise of the the breeder!

   I can remember many occasions where my own pups looked like ugly ducklings at the age of seven weeks, and they have not started to blossom until six months or even eight months, suddenly developing into beautiful swans. Quite often it is the head which is least appealing, although the rest of the body looks quite balanced. Ch. Zottel's Miss Marple Of Lameda (UK joint CC recordholder) had a litter brother called Mosche who was like this. He was almost identically marked to one very glamorous-looking litter-brother, with the name Mr X. They were similar in body shape, only Mosche appeared to have almost too much bone for a puppy and he had enormous feet. The main difference, though, between the two brothers was the head. Mr X looked absolutely gorgeous with plenty of head coat, while Mosche's head looked like a big square box

It takes years of experience to assess puppies for show potential – and even then it is all too easy to make mistakes!

with no head coat at all. His ears were far too big, hanging down almost like a Spaniel's ears. Mosche was to go into a pet home, and Mr X was to go to a young family, who wanted to show. However, on the day they were due to be collected, I was unable to be at home. The inevitable mistake was made – they got mixed up: Mosche went to the show home and the gorgeous Mr X went to the pet home. I used all my powers of persuasion, but the pet people refused to give up their puppy – and I could not really blame them. The show people decided to keep their 'ugly duckling' because they loved his temperament, and they had been waiting for a long time to get a puppy from me. The rest really is history. Aided by a very good upbringing in the form of feeding, exercise and grooming, Mosche changed into a most beautiful swan. He gained the Swiss, German, International, and the VDH Champion title, on his way also winning Groups and Best in Shows. As I moved to England, I have never seen Mr X again, but he could not have grown into a much better specimen than Mosche.

So be warned – the 'pick of the litter' is only a matter of opinion. I feel that only after years of breeding with the same lines, and to the same type, is it possible to judge a litter with any degree of confidence. Extremely small pups can grow into the biggest of the litter, and the other way round. However, there is one rule of thumb: if a young puppy is a good moving animal, I have never seen it grow into a poor mover.

When I pick a pup for myself, I want to see the litter when they have just been born, then again at six weeks and at eight weeks, making my choice at twelve weeks. Obviously it is always easier to assess your own pups, because you can watch them every day, and monitor their development. For me, the most important features are overall balance and personality. A pup has to have the 'little extra'. This is difficult to explain, as it may be different for each person who assesses the litter, but I want to feel certain vibes coming over from the pup to me. This may sound funny – but it is the best explanation I can give.

LITTER REGISTRATION
The litter must be registered with the national Kennel Club, and the regulations vary slightly from country to country. Make sure you fill in all the appropriate forms at the correct time, and apply for transfer of ownership papers when you sell the puppies.

APPLICATION FOR AN AFFIX
Anyone who wants to become a serious breeder should apply for a kennel name or affix. This means that your chosen kennel name will be put in front of every pup's individual name. The appropriate forms can be obtained from the national Kennel Club.

The chosen word should be a made-up word. No specific words or names are allowed to be used as an affix. All the applications are published in the Kennel Gazette (the official Kennel Club magazine) in order to allow other affix holders to object to names too similar to their own. If there are no objections received within a month of publication, the applicant will normally be granted his first choice of affix, or otherwise, in order of preference.

EXPORTING A PUP
Most breeders will be asked at some time for a puppy to be sent abroad. I feel that only experienced breeders should accept enquiries from foreign countries. It is very rare that the future owners will be able to come and see the litter themselves, and so they have to trust the breeder to pick out the best possible puppy. Preferably, the breeder should select a puppy which is strong in the qualities which are lacking in the average dog in the importing country. For example, if you are aware that the country in question is known to have mostly incorrectly coated dogs, your puppy should come from parents with absolutely excellent coats, and so on.

Most countries require a valid health certificate, and the puppy should also be fully vaccinated to avoid any infection. If the puppy is going by plane to its new home, the booking should be made at least five days prior to departure, to avoid the disappointment of a fully booked plane. If not accompanied, dogs have to fly as cargo, which means most airlines want the dog to be at the point of collection at least two and a half hours before the flight.

Most airlines have got a wide range of travel containers, and so you can choose the correct size. The dog should have enough space to stand up, turn round, sit and lie down, with a minimum of two inches to spare on either side. Do not choose a box which is much bigger than needed. It not only increases the flight price, but a dog could be injured if there is turbulence en route. It is better not to give a dog any food before a flight in case of vomiting or even diarrhoea. I just give some water with glucose on the day of the flight, but no solid food. A well-reared pup can easily cope with a day without food, and it will travel much more safely.

One important point must not be forgotten when you are applying for the health certificate. All male puppies require a signature on the back of their export pedigree forms to confirm that both their testicles are fully descended. Dogs being exported to Scandinavia, Australia or New Zealand require special vaccinations and blood tests. Information packs can be obtained from the embassies in question.

Chapter Fourteen

HEALTH CARE

INFECTIOUS DISEASES

Any of the following infectious diseases can be avoided for the most part by regular vaccinations. I therefore strongly recommend that every puppy should be vaccinated at the appropriate ages (usually eight and twelve weeks) and thereafter once every year. As yet, there is no proof to substantiate the theory that older dogs build up immunity to infectious diseases, and so it is irresponsible to take risks by not giving regular boosters.

DISTEMPER: This disease was first discovered in 1905 by the Frenchman, Carre. The distemper virus usually enters the body through the respiratory tracts, where it multiplies rapidly in the cells around these organs. In less serious cases it acts as a single organism; in complicated cases there will be several other organisms which cause secondary illnesses, such as lung infections.

The first signs, which become evident six to nine days after contracting the virus, are heightened temperature which may be scarcely noticeable, followed by runny eyes and nose, sometimes accompanied by diarrhoea. The disease spreads rapidly in all body tissues and nerve cells. It also affects the brain cells, and so nervous cramps or fits may result, which may continue even if the dog survives. Another sign often seen in a dog that has suffered from distemper is badly discoloured 'distemper teeth'.

HEPATITIS: The hepatitis virus was only recognised as a separate virus infection in 1947. Until then it was believed that the inflammation of the liver was caused by the distemper virus, especially as the first signs of hepatitis are very similar to those of distemper. In fact, the hepatitis virus is identical to the virus which is responsible for the fox disease called Enceptalitis, even though the reaction in the two species differs. The disease is transmitted through urine and saliva, and considering the natural habit of dogs is to sniff and to lick, it is easy to see why the disease is so highly contagious and spreads swiftly among unvaccinated dogs. The individual susceptibility depends on several circumstances, such as age at the time of contraction, general health, and the amount of immunity given by the mother's colostrum.

To start with, the saliva and other discharges contain the live and active virus. Later on it is only found in the kidneys, but here it can survive and stay active for a year. This explains why a dog who has completely recovered from the disease can still infect other dogs through urine.

LEPTOSPIROSIS: There are several leptospirosis bacteria, but only two are commonly found in dogs, leptospira icteron haemorrhagial and leptospira canicola. The first was also found to affect humans (Weil's disease), causing fever and shivering fits. In contrast to most other bacteria, leptospirosis reacts well to several antibiotics, especially if it is diagnosed early. Dogs which recover after the infection are usually immune to it for life.

CANINE PARVOVIRUS: Cases of canine parvovirus were first reported in 1978 from America, where whole litters and many adult dogs died from this highly contagious disease. Since then it has spread all over the world, and some unlucky breeders lost half of their breeding stock before a vaccine was found.

The first vaccine used was the same which protects cats from the feline enteritis virus. Some breeders believe that the high amount of infertility in all breeds, which occurred for a few years after the first outbreaks of parvo, was caused by these inoculations with the live feline vaccine. This is difficult to substantiate, but nevertheless, these first vaccinations were reasonably effective, and fewer cases of parvo were reported.

Subsequently, when the virus was identified, a special canine parvovirus inoculation was developed. The virus is believed to be able to stay alive and active for up to six months; it can survive in the atmosphere, on shoes, on hair – virtually everywhere in the environment

The most common signs of parvo are high fever combined with vomiting, plus severe diarrhoea which contains blood and has a particularly strong smell. Without treatment, the constant diarrhoea causes the dog to dehydrate and eventually to die. Apart from treating with a wide spectrum antibiotic, the most important treatment is therefore to give enough fluid. In serious cases, which are accompanied by persistent vomiting, this usually necessitates the use of intravenous drips. If you can tube-feed, the most soothing fluid is sage tea.

If a kennel has an outbreak of parvo it is necessary to enforce stringent hygiene, and to prevent visitors coming into the house or kennels if there are unvaccinated puppies around.

GENERAL AILMENTS
BAD BREATH: The reasons for bad breath are usually dirty teeth, or teeth that have gone bad. This can be avoided by regular cleaning. If all the teeth are OK, bad breath could be the result of an upset stomach or kidney problems. If it persists, the vet should be consulted.

BLOAT – GASTRIC TORSION: This is one of the most unpredictable serious conditions which can occur in large dogs. Explained in layman's language, it is a condition where the stomach twists on its ends and then fills up with gas. The gas is produced through the fermentation of food in the stomach, and because of the twisted position of the stomach, the gas cannot escape naturally.

There is no guarantee that a dog will survive this extremely painful condition, even if taken to the vet immediately. The first signs are usually restlessness, and the dog may try to vomit. Within a relatively short time, you can see the stomach swelling up, eventually looking and feeling as big as a ball. The individual treatment depends on the experience of the vet, and also on how quickly the dog is taken to the surgery. It is imperative that the stomach is relieved from the build-up of gas. This can be done by passing a special tube down into the stomach, or if the pressure is too great, needle puncture may be effective. So far, the best advice to prevent this killer is to feed large dogs their food spread over at least two meals. Never let your dog drink too much at once, never exercise after feeding, and never feed immediately after exercise.

COUGH: A persistent cough can have several serious causes and should therefore not be overlooked, or taken lightly. If there is any indication that it could be highly contagious kennel cough (a dry cough similar to children's whooping cough), do not take your dog into the vet's waiting room, as other dogs or puppies could become infected. The best course of action is to describe the symptoms to your vet, and ask for an appointment after surgery hours. Nowadays there are fairly reliable vaccinations available for kennel cough. Other reasons for coughing could be dust, or infection. Your vet will advise the appropriate treatment.

DIARRHOEA: The most common causes of diarrhoea are a sudden change of food, feeding too much protein, or infestation with worms. Unless there are other signs which indicate that the dog is really ill, the best way to stop diarrhoea is to starve the animal for 24 hours. Fresh water should be made available, but no solid food. After the twenty-four hours is up, start by giving small quantities of boiled fish or cooked chicken and boiled rice. Cottage cheese and natural yoghurt also help to rebuild the natural bacteria in the intestine. Persistent diarrhoea or loose stools, in combination with any other unusual signs of discomfort, needs to be treated by your vet.

EAR INFECTION: Most ear infections can be avoided by regular cleaning of the ears and also by plucking the excess hair out of the ear. Some OES are known to have rather small ear canals where it is more difficult to remove wax, and so extra care should be taken to avoid discomfort. There are many different products on the market for cleaning ears, and you can ask your vet for advice.

The first signs of an ear infection is a continuous shaking of the head and scratching behind the ears. Any ear infection is not only very irritating but also painful for the dog and should be treated properly. Persistent discomfort sometimes indicates the presence of mites or yeast.

ECZEMA: There are two different types of eczema – dry, and wet eczema –and there are many reasons for a dog suffering from either type. These include the presence of parasites, flea and food allergies, hormone imbalance, inherited proneness to eczema, or unkempt and dirty coats.

Apart from regular grooming, which prevents a dirty coat, you will need to enlist the help of a vet or even a skin specialist to establish the reason for the eczema and to prescribe the correct treatment.

FLEAS: In some years fleas seem to reach epidemic proportions, and only regular spraying with flea-spray will keep your dog free of them. It is always important to treat bedding and sleeping quarters as well as the dog. The dog flea can also live on humans, and the most obvious sign is a multitude of red and very itchy spots. Fleas can also transmit tapeworms to your dog, so the greatest care should therefore be taken to keep your dog free of fleas.

For the OES I do not recommend using a flea shampoo, as it would remove the natural oil out of the coat. The regular use of powder, a flea spay, or a flea collar are as effective, and more practical for an OES.

GRASS SEEDS: During the summer months the danger of a dry grass seed working its way into your dog's pads, ears, or sometimes even under the skin, cannot be underestimated. Long-coated Bobtails should be carefully checked for this nuisance after every walk through fields or grass areas in order to avoid skin infections.

LAMENESS: Any persistent lameness, front or rear, should always warrant examination by your vet. It could be only a pulled muscle which needs rest for a couple of weeks, but in a more serious case there might be a torn ligament which needs treatment. Or even worse, it might be hip dysplasia or elbow dysplasia, where special treatment is required.

MASTITIS: Mastitis is the term for hard and swollen mammary glands in a nursing bitch. This usually happens if there is more milk produced than the puppies can drink. In serious cases, the condition brings about a high temperature. Mastitis is very painful and needs immediate attention by a vet.

PYOMETRA: This is the term used when a bitch's uterus becomes filled with pus. This bacterial infection usually occurs soon after a season, and it is quite often caused by a hormone imbalance.

    There are two kinds of pyometra – closed and open. Open pyometra can be easily detected by a heavy discharge either yellow, brown, green or even black in colour. Closed pyometra does not show any discharge. Both infections are accompanied by extreme toxaemia, thirst, and very often a high temperature. In most cases, the only way to save the bitch is to remove the uterus.

WORMS: Any dog, however well looked after, can get worms. Eggs and larvae remain contagious for several months, and they can be transmitted in so many ways that it is almost impossible to avoid them. Regular worming is therefore essential, and this means treating your dog every six months, even if there are no obvious signs of a worm infestation. If you suspect your dog has worms, you should give immediate treatment.

    In addition, bitches should be wormed before mating, and puppies should be wormed at the age of two weeks, four weeks, eight weeks, twelve weeks, and thereafter once a month until fully grown. It is recommended to worm nursing bitches at the same time as their pups.

    It is most important to read all the instructions carefully, and to give the exact amount according to the individual bodyweight. There are many different kinds of worms, but these days most vets have tablets which can be safely used to get rid of all types in one dose.

HEREDITARY CONDITIONS
BLINDNESS: Recently there have been quite a few reports of blindness in the OES as a result of hereditary cataracts (HC) and central progressive retinal atrophy (CPRA). It can be argued that a dog suffering from an hereditary condition such as hip dysplasia is still able to lead a nearly normal life, in most cases. However, a dog that is blind from birth is deprived of everything, and I do not think this constitutes a reasonable quality of life. It is essential that all breeding stock is regularly eye-tested, and only the animals which are found to be clear should be used for breeding.

DEAFNESS: Deafness occurring in the older dog is not an hereditary condition, but as in humans it is a sign of old age. However, deafness occurring in a puppy is a serious cause of concern. Luckily, the OES has not had many recorded cases of deaf puppies.

    For an inexperienced breeder, it might not be easy to notice a deaf puppy, because it will react by copying the litter brothers and sisters. The puppy will run towards you together with the other pups, and will play quite normally. However, if you isolate an affected puppy you can soon detect the difference, as the puppy will only react to things it can see, and not to noises.

    Obviously, it would be very difficult to train a deaf puppy. Commands would have to be visual, and this means that a recall when the pup is out of sight, off-lead, would be impossible. In fact, the only way to train a deaf puppy would be if it grew up with another puppy or an adult, and was able to learn just by copying the other dog. Still I would expect it to be rather hard work, and it is debatable whether it is worth prolonging the life of a deaf puppy.

ENTROPION: This is when either the upper, the lower, or both eyelids turn inwards, and the eyelashes constantly rub on the cornea. The eyes get irritated and they water all the time. This condition can be corrected by surgery, which is usually successful. However, a dog which has had entropion is obviously still carrying the genes for this inherited disease, and it should be kept as a pet only.

HIP DYSPLASIA: The most common multifactorial hereditary disease in dogs is probably hip dysplasia. It affects all kinds of dog breeds, small and large, to different degrees.

Hip Dysplasia is the term used for any abnormality found concerning the hips. This might be the result of malformed bones, or the femoral head may not fit correctly in the hip socket. There are many different schemes to diagnose HD, in fact virtually every country has its own programme. This makes it more difficult for breeders to assess a score from another country, and I think a universal scoring system would be a great step forward.

In the UK dogs must be at least twelve months old to be X-rayed and scored under the BVA scheme (the official Kennel Club scheme). This is the required age for official X-raying in most other countries. The exception is America, where dogs have to be two years old before their X-ray plate can be taken for the official OFA scoring (the official scheme of the American Kennel Club). In Germany, Switzerland, Denmark, and the Scandinavian countries, it is compulsory to have breeding stock X-rayed with a clear to normal result, before the permission for breeding is given.

Most countries agree that the problem of hip dysplasia must be tackled, but opinions as to how to go about it differ greatly. It would be easy enough if you could say with confidence that if you only bred from clear stock, you would not get dysplastic offspring. Unfortunately this is not the case, and quite often breeders who have had generations of clear stock are suddenly faced with the problem. Breeding from one hundred per cent clear stock could also eliminate dogs which might have slight signs of dysplasia due to bad management. It is also true that in countries where breeding stock must be certified clear, many dogs with valuable breed characteristics have been lost to the breed, in favour of less good specimens who have clear hips.

However, breeding from dogs who are not certified clear or normal should only be left to experienced breeders who know the lines and are prepared to face possible consequences. It would be far too much to expect a novice breeder to run on a whole litter of puppies until five or six months of age in order to be able to do a preliminary X-ray. But by keeping the whole litter for this length of time, you can ensure that all the pups are raised and fed in the same way. This is very important when assessing hips, as a lot of damage can be done by too much exercise and over-feeding. Incorrectly raised puppies would therefore not give a true picture of inherited hip dysplasia, but they might well show bad results due to poor management.

Several years ago tests were carried out in the USA where pups from dysplastic parentage were raised in small pens – too small for the pups to be able to jump up or play. It was found that when a puppy had to sit down most of the time, the femoral head was permanently pushed into the socket. The pups were also put on a special diet, which guaranteed enough, but not too many vitamins, proteins and minerals, in accordance with their restricted life.

These puppies were found to be clear of any clinical signs of hip dysplasia at the age of nine months. These results made quite a few scientists rethink their attitude towards hip dysplasia. Obviously, the pups could not be declared clear of genetical hip dysplasia, but it is also obvious that the environment has got a great influence on any hip development.

I would certainly prefer my puppies to grow up in a normal environment, which includes a reasonable amount of freedom. This 'normal' environment includes walks of up to fifteen minutes at a time until about five months of age. I also believe that playing with pups of the same age, or supervised playing with adult dogs is important for a young puppy to develop a normal temperament. From the age of about five months, the bones of an OES are stronger and the joints are tighter. You can therefore slowly start to give the dog more exercise, even though special care should be taken if pups and adults are kept together.

AUTOIMMUNE THYROIDITIS AND HYPOTHYROIDISM: A great deal has been said and written about thyroid diseases and related conditions in OES. Most available literature comes from America and is hardly ever published in Europe.

It seems unlikely that these diseases should only affect dogs in America. I believe that many illnesses and sudden deaths, which are certainly not uncommon in the OES in England or in Europe, are not tested properly, and might have been avoided.

Thryoid problems can be the reason for many other discomforts, such as hypothyroidism, autoimmune thyroiditis, chronic skin disorders, reproductive disorders, temperament problems, chronic infections, joint/bone disorders and blood diseases. If you are in any doubt, ask your vet to do a thyroid test on your dog.

THE VETERAN OES

Depending on the general state of health in body and mind, some Bobtails can be considered to be old by the time they are nine or ten years of age; others I have owned, or met, still behave like youngsters at twelve years old. This depends on the overall condition of the OES: how the dog was fed through his life, how often he was ill, and probably most of all, on how regularly the dog was and still is exercised. Plenty of exercise and a healthy diet is what every doctor recommends for his patients, and it is what all responsible breeders recommend for their dogs. I would also recommend taking your dog to the vet for a check-up every six months from the age of about ten years onwards. A regular check-up cannot do any harm, and it may help to detect an illness right at the beginning when there is still a chance to cure it.

GROOMING: I, personally, do not like an Old English Sheepdog to be completely clipped, but, on the other hand, I do not expect my old dogs to keep still for several hours in order to be groomed. When I feel that the dog is no longer enjoying the grooming sessions, I cut the coat down to

Some Bobtails age better than others. Ch. Reeuwijk's Fabulous Lady, still enjoying life to the full at twelve years of age.

about five or six inches. This leaves enough coat so that your OES still looks good and resembles a sheepdog, but it is much easier to keep clean and free of knots. Extra care has now to be taken with cutting the nails, cleaning ears, and most of all, with cleaning the teeth. Like humans, older dogs are more likely to suffer from decayed teeth. Depending on how bad they are, your vet may have to extract some teeth. However, it is important to keep the teeth as clean as possible. In Germany, there is a saying that the teeth are the policemen of the body. By paying extra attention to the teeth, you can avoid a lot of other trouble, like kidney problems, which are quite often connected to bad teeth. A regular weekly session, lasting two hours, should be sufficient time to spend on grooming and overall cleaning. I use a Mason Pearson bristle and nylon brush, and a very wide comb. The brush takes out enough undercoat to avoid knotting, and the comb is used for the coat behind the ears and under the elbows.

EXERCISE: Some older dogs lose interest in their walks, especially if they have not been used to regular exercise. My oldest Old English Sheepdog, 'Estee Lauder', is nearly twelve years old, and even though she sleeps a lot, she would be most upset if we did not take her out for her daily walks. In fact, once she is outside in the park she still bosses all the other dogs, barking like crazy and

Ch. Cinderwood By Jupiter of Craigsea, winning a CC at nine years of age.

rounding them up. At times we really can call her the most boisterous dog in the house – and she is definitely the noisiest!

If your OES is not quite so active in old age, a daily walk is still important. You do not have to take the dog for a long walk, but I feel that half an hour every day is essential to keep older dogs fit and interested in life – provided the dog has no major health problems, such as bad hip dysplasia or rheumatism.

In wet weather, the elderly OES has to be dried properly after coming home. Damp and muddy feet have to be washed, and preferably blow-dried. Remember, the more care you take of your old companion, the more enjoyment your dog will get from its latter years.

FEEDING: Feeding the older dog is quite similar to feeding a young dog. Like a youngster, the veteran OES needs more vitamins and minerals, and in autumn and winter, the dog will benefit from two cod-liver oil capsules given daily. There are specially designed complete diets for the old dog. They contain less protein and have a different fat level to the normal maintenance diet. The reason for this is that kidneys and digestive systems do not work as well as they used to, and the lower protein and fat level takes this into account. For people who do not like to feed a complete diet, I would recommend feeding the older dog on chicken or fish and rice or pasta. Vitamins and minerals have to be added to this kind of diet. There are many good vitamin products on the market especially developed for the needs of an older dog, and these are available in most pet shops.

DEATH: This is the hardest part of owning any animal because, under normal circumstances, our dogs pass away before us. Our duty is therefore to make it as easy as possible for our dog when the time has come. To me, this means allowing a dog to die gracefully if there is an incurable illness which deprives the dog of a normal and happy life. I would always do everything possible to keep a dog alive for as long as there is a chance of recovery. Once that is not the case, I feel you have to be strong and let the dog die with dignity – even if that means an injection by the vet.

This is one of the hardest decisions the dog owner is faced with, and having gone through this myself, I know the agony you can feel. One voice tells you that there could be a miracle, and another voice tells you to be kind and sensible, which, at the time, is the last thing you want to hear. You can only think of all the good times you have had together, and that makes it even harder to make a decision. I do not think that anyone is capable of rational thinking at a time like this. I, therefore, put all my trust in my vet to advise me whether there is a chance of recovery or not. No responsible vet likes to put a dog down if it is not necessary, especially if he has known the dog from being a puppy. Once a joint decision has been made to save the dog from any more suffering, I feel it is important for the vet to do a house call. If you can possibly avoid going to the surgery, it will be less traumatic for your OES. Even though your dog might be very ill, he might still know what is going on, and great care should be taken to ensure this final procedure is carried out with sensitivity and dignity. If all this has put you off owning an Old English Sheepdog, I can assure you that the fun, the laughter, and the love you get from owning one of the most adorable creatures on this earth, is well worth all the heartache at the end of your dog's life.